THE MORALITY OF THE SCHOOL

Also available in the Cassell education series:

P. Ainley and M. Corney: *Training for the Future*
G. Antonouris and J. Wilson: *Equal Opportunities in Schools*
N. Bennett and A. Cass: *From Special to Ordinary Schools*
C. Christofi: *Assessment and Profiling in Science*
G. Claxton: *Being a Teacher: a Positive Approach to Change and Stress*
C. Cullingford (ed.): *The Primary Teacher*
B. Goacher *et al.*: *Policy and Provision for Special Educational Needs*
H. Gray (ed.): *Management Consultancy in Schools*
L. Hall: *Poetry for Life*
J. Nias, G. Southworth and R. Yeomans: *Staff Relationships in the Primary School*
J. Sayer and V. Williams (eds): *Schools and External Relations: Managing the New Partnerships*
R. Straughan: *Beliefs, Behaviour and Education*
S. Wolfendale (ed.): *Parental Involvement*

The Morality of the School

The Theory and Practice of Values in Education

Mike Bottery

CASSELL

To Jill and Derek, without whose help this book would not have been possible.

Cassell Educational Limited
Artillery House
Artillery Row
London SW1P 1RT

First published 1990

British Library Cataloguing in Publication Data
Bottery, Mike.
 The morality of the school: the theory and practice
 of values in education. – (Cassell education).
 1. Education. Ethical aspects
 I. Title
 370'.1

ISBN 0–304–31832–9 (hardback)
  0–304–31830–2 (paperback)

Phototypeset by Input Typesetting Ltd, London

Printed and bound in Great Britain by
Mackays of Chatham Ltd, Kent

Contents

To every complex problem there exists a solution which is neat, simple, and wrong.

Introduction

Well you find us having a free activity period this morning, and in our free activity
period each little individual chooses his or her own form of occupation. Get out from
under the table there please Sydney. Yes, some of us paint and some of us do plasticine
work or go to the sandtable over there. We feel that each little individual has got to
get to the bottom of himself and learn what he wants of life. Who is making that
buzzing noise? Well stop it please, Neville. Hazel dear, come away from the door
and get something to do. I do love to see them all so happily occupied, each little one
expressing his own personality . . . George, *don't* do that.

Joyce Grenfell's wonderfully observed picture of a very English infant school teacher
has caused a gentle smile to cross many a face over the years. It is painted with love
and affection and is just the slightest bit tongue in cheek. What is sometimes missed
on listening to the monologue is the very clear philosophy of education behind it, a
philosophy laden with values. From the very first line it is implicit that free activity
is a 'good thing' and that finding out what one is and what one wishes to be are also
'good things'. Many people may agree with such values, but they are at the very
least debatable. Over 2,000 years ago Plato argued that the purpose of education is
not to let children 'do their own thing', nor to let them find out what they want from
life, but to fit them for the role in society to which they are most suited. The two
values of individual choice and social utility may coincide, but they need not. A child
may well wish to do something and be totally unsuited to it. The idea of free activity
periods, then, under a socially oriented educational philosophy, would be at best a
waste of time, at worst an opportunity for the child to unlearn the role society is
giving him or her.

  In similar vein, when Sydney is told to get out from under the table, or Neville to
stop making his buzzing noise, or George to stop doing whatever it is he is doing,
the message is clear: certain behaviours are valued, others are discouraged. Education, then, is radically, unavoidably, impregnated with values. Every educationalist
is inevitably involved, just like Joyce Grenfell, in choosing what is worthwhile for a
generation to know and how a future generation might think and behave.

  Are these, though, *moral* values? Why talk of 'the morality of the school'? Are
educational activities such as choosing what people might know and how they might
think and behave essentially moral in nature? It depends, of course, on what you
mean by 'moral'. The meaning of terms like this and hence their application have
been argued about since the beginnings of western philosophy, and a brief introduc-

tion to a book is not the place to get embroiled in this debate. However, a working definition of morality might be: 'that area concerned with the ways in which people treat and affect other people'. The reader may have already begun to formulate objections to this definition. Since amendments to it will be made as the book progresses, it can suffice as a beginning.

If, then, this definition is adopted for the time being, it becomes clear why the subtitle of the book is 'The Theory and Practice of Values in Education'. The subject of values must be of major concern for the morality of the school in two ways. Firstly, values must be of concern if the holding of them affects other people. This book will therefore include the discussion of social, political, individual and religious values, for holding and living according to them will almost certainly affect others. To take the cases given above, how a future generation might behave is clearly a case for moral concern, because in normal circumstances one person's behaviour will affect others. Even what may be regarded as purely personal behaviour – deciding whether or not to wear a seat belt – may have knock-on effects for others. The person not wearing a seat belt may be killed and leave a spouse and children without financial support. Similarly, what a person thinks will be a case for moral concern in any situation where this thought is translated into action. So, finally, the choice of a curriculum – how a person will think, and what he or she will think about – will almost certainly have consequences of a moral nature, because such experience will affect thought processes which will probably then be reflected in behaviour.

Secondly, the manner of translation of *any* values in the school will be a matter for moral concern, for how they are taught will affect the way that a future generation thinks. Thus, even if one is capable of producing cases of values which do not appear to involve others, there is still one overarching moral problem with education, and that is the problem of who *decides* upon what goes on in the school. The values behind any choice concerning curriculum, management strategies or discipline procedures will necessarily affect the way other people think and behave. They are meant to. Education is precisely about the choice of future thought and behaviour. Moral concerns are, therefore, central to the school. And this is why the problem of morality is not a simple curricular subject but permeates all levels of the institution. *The Morality of the School*, then, is a book about what educational institutions should be doing to increase an understanding of their involvement in this area, about whether they should be concerned with the promotion and discouragement of certain moral values and about how they might promote certain actions and discourage others.

This book will be advocating involvement by the school in this area. This is for two reasons. The first is the unavoidable impregnation of values in education. What cannot be avoided, and what affects practice so fundamentally, must be attended to. If not, values continue to have their effect but in unexpected and unintended ways. It is much better to be aware of and to manage the unavoidable than to let it have its effect uncontrolled.

The second reason stems from what is taken to be an essential part of the task of an educational institution. This is to allow young people the opportunity, in the company of trained professionals, to deal with value issues in an environment which facilitates reasoned, balanced, tolerant discussion. The school, even more than the family, can be the institution best equipped to help young people in this process. The school, then, can be the best place for dealing with moral values.

This being the case, this book has three main functions. One is to examine the kinds of justification given for holding moral values, and in so doing allow the teacher to enter into this argument. Decisions in this area cannot and need not be left to the 'experts'. Teachers can and should take part in this dialogue, for it is only by doing so that informed practice is ensured.

The second function of the book is to locate the values with which the school is involved and at what levels, and to promote an understanding of these. As values permeate all levels of an institution, so one would expect a similarly multi-layered understanding. In tackling this, the book provides a structural model by which teachers may approach and deal with the subject.

The third function is to provide a start in the classroom. Throughout the book and in the seven appendices a variety of approaches and strategies are described which the teacher may adopt in the classroom. These are not meant to be exhaustive. They are intended to provide a start for the practitioner, who can then add to them from other sources, aided by the kind of framework suggested.

An initial step in this overall process is to allow practitioners to become more aware of their own value stances within education. The first chapter does this by asking the reader to complete questions in a simple (and hopefully enjoyable) exercise. This is intended not only to sensitize readers to their own value orientation, but also to highlight the possible positions of other interested parties. This chapter is an introduction to the kinds of viewpoints and arguments which have seen active service throughout the history of ethical and educational thought. It allows readers to become acquainted with the arguments at a personal level without expecting them to master a history of western philosophy at the same time.

However, if moral issues are to be dealt with in an educational context, then it is very clear that they must be dealt with in terms other than just at the level of individual response. Another perspective is to recognize that individuals are participants in the fabric of the larger community, and that their reactions will to some extent reflect, be affected by and change the fabric of the larger whole. Thus the presence and effects of different values at the level of society must be recognized and acknowledged as well. Chapter 2, then, is an historical review of the treatment of values teaching, examining how dominant social and political values have affected the way in which schools have treated this subject. Societal attitudes to the possibilities of an objective moral code are seen as being of central concern, for they help to bring out some of the more fundamental ethical questions which have occupied thinkers for the last two millennia.

This historical review ends with an examination of present social and political values, and argues that there is a need for a focusing of effort by teachers on four areas of concern: the need for greater rationality; empathy; self-esteem; and co-operation among pupils. Strategies for these are then suggested throughout the book.

One cannot leave the matter here, though. There is a further perspective which must be attended to if one is to understand the full impact of values on the school. We must go further than looking at either personal or societal reactions to these problems. We must also examine the philosophical theories which have generated and been generated by them. The influence of these theories is immense, and yet they too have their orthodoxies and heresies. They too need to be questioned. This being the case, Chapters 3, 4 and 5 take a closer look at the fundamental problems of ethical objectivism, subjectivism and relativism, and ask the question: is it possible to have an objective moral code which can be taught to all? The implications of this question for educational institutions and society as a whole are vast. If it is possible, then schools can be transmitters of such values with few problems of justification. If this is the case, and we know some things to be good and some to be bad, our concern centres on what is the most effective way of getting this across. Educational problems will lie much more in applying than justifying. If on the other hand there are no such objective values, then the problem returns to the justification of the exercise: what right do I have to teach one set of values rather than another? These chapters suggest that there is a middle way between the two viewpoints, which has large implications for other areas of the curriculum as well.

But if there are problems at the philosophical level, there are undoubtedly problems at the psychological level as well. It is sometimes thought that because psychological theories report factual material they are value free. One of the functions of Chapters 6 and 7 is to indicate that psychological theories are as value laden as any philosophical theory, and to show that they all prescribe particular views of how people should be looked at and treated. The examination of such theories, then, is of a moral nature. A related function is to point out that such theories are also tentative: their findings are open to revision. These two chapters, then, hope to sound two warning notes for teachers and to advocate a guarded approach to the application of psychological theories.

Thus far discussion has centred on factors impinging on school practice without dealing with it directly. It has looked at personal value systems, at the influence of society and at the status of philosophical and psychological theories and their effects upon the school. It is time to look at practice. Chapters 8, 9, 10 and 11 look specifically at problems of translation, both in classroom and school-wide terms. Chapter 8 examines the thorny issue of content, and suggests a way of approaching and classifying content without being over-prescriptive by proposing the division of morality into five areas of concern. This not only makes the subject more approachable and easier to handle, but also suggests a number of teaching strategies stemming directly from the subject's formulation and application. Chapter 9 looks at one major focus of concern mentioned earlier in the book, that of co-operation, and provides a variety of strategies suggesting how it might be implemented. Chapter 10 concentrates specifically on the problem of implementation at an organizational level, and gives a number of devices and structures to help carry out this implementation. Like the rest of the book, it suggests that as moral values permeate all levels of educational establishments, so approaches to dealing with them must be similarly diverse.

One final and vital aspect of implementation is that of the stance which a teacher should adopt in dealing with difficult and controversial topics in the classroom. Whilst the book generally advocates an attitude of tolerance of other opinions and acceptance of diversity, there are undoubtedly some controversial issues which present clear, even urgent reasons for adopting one particular attitude, so that many might feel it too much of a luxury to allow children to make up their own minds. Chapter 11, therefore, tackles this question.

It is one of the core concerns of this book to show that there is a constant interaction between the practice of values education inside schools and interests and pressures beyond the school walls, and Chapter 12 begins to establish links between implementation in the classroom, school-wide policies and such pressures from outside the school by means of a review of possible approaches to the evaluation of this area.

Evaluation and assessment are seen as being intimately related with moral concerns in two ways. Not only are they essential to good teaching in this area of the curriculum, but the very style of evaluation says something about the way in which subjects, practitioners and students are viewed. As many evaluative strategies at the present time are affected by external pressures for accountability, it is argued that one must look again outside the school to examine the nature and purpose of these pressures.

This movement out of the classroom to look at the values and practice of school-wide policies is continued in Chapter 13 when management strategies and the values that they may be transmitting to teachers and pupils are examined. Management is seen as the linchpin of the school; it is the interface between classroom practice and demands from outside the school. How it is conceptualized and implemented, then, has crucial effects upon this classroom practice, and also indicates the kind of treatment being suggested for practitioners and pupils. Its influence upon the morality of the school cannot be exaggerated.

Once again, the pressures urging for particular approaches may be seen in many cases as emanating from beyond the school. And once again, therefore, the school is being seen as part of a greater societal fabric. This picture is completed in the final chapter, when an attempt is made to answer the fundamental question: granted that schools are but one institution in a complex society, what role can and should they have in the nurturing and propagation of values? This question is tackled through an examination of the concept of civic responsibility and the place that schools might have in the fostering of this. By so doing, this chapter argues once again that the business of helping young people to arrive at a satisfactory answer involving the treatment of other living beings is a central concern of the school and society as a whole. Schools cannot abnegate their responsibility in this area, it is suggested, but neither can the wider community.

Chapter 1

Values Behind the Practice

Travelling can be a pleasant and profitable occupation for its own sake. One can enjoy and benefit from the experience without being too much concerned with the final destination. Indeed, for some people, the travelling may be the only thing that really matters. The means become the end or purpose of the journey.

Having said that, the travelling may become much more pleasant and profitable if the traveller knows where to depart from and has learned something about the places to be visited on the way, and if this travel is placed within an overall framework which sees it as going somewhere – a final destination. The journey would then be enjoyed and the reasons for it understood. An extra dimension would have been added.

Attempting to decide upon the correct relationship between morality and schooling can be rather like this. To make as correct a decision as possible one needs to be aware of how present attitudes within society came to be held. One also needs to know about the values, sets of beliefs and ideologies which motivate people at the present time – and so where they want to go. Added to this, it is very important to be aware of present constraints acting upon society – what forces outside people's control are pushing them in one direction rather than another. Unless such factors are taken into account, the travelling – the day-to-day running of the school – will not be understood, and in the long run may well be damaging to its recipients.

It is doubtful if any school or teacher is in the worst-case position just painted. But it is uncomfortably true that the sheer pressure of the school's day-to-day running can prevent the taking of a measured look at issues like those raised above. Some teachers may even be surprised to find that their practices do not coincide with their avowed aims, or that they are repeating the mistakes of the past through not being aware that these mistakes have been made before.

This and the next chapter, then, will ask the question: where are you going? The present chapter will look at the kinds of educational values and ideologies it is possible to hold, and the kinds of relationship between morality and the school that are likely to follow. The next chapter will place such beliefs in an historical perspective and show that the problems teachers face today are both the same as and different from those of the past. They are the same because the same questions recur. But they are different because social, economic and political conditions alter, and so the problems may present other faces.

However, before taking an historical perspective on the relationship between

Table 1.1 *Four codes of education and their effects*

View	Type of knowledge valued	Role of the child	Role of the teacher	Status of society and type aimed for	Linkage between morality and schooling
Cultural transmission	Cultural heritage	Passive imbiber, one of many to be graded	Guardian, transmitter of appropriate values	Main determinant of knowledge content, teaching style. Elitist, static	Objectivist. Permanent values to be transmitted, internalized, practised
Child centred	Based on child's experience and interests	Active, involved, unique constructor of his or her own reality	Facilitator, constructor of beneficial situations for child	*Individual strain* At best irrelevant, at worst intrusive and damaging *Communitarian strain* Democracy aimed for	*Individual* Imprecise blend of individual development and expression of pre-existing tendency to care for others *Communitarian* Development of community values as preparation for criticism and reform of society. Both subjectivist, probably relativist
Social reconstruction	Topic/problem centred, based on present pressing social issues needing to be resolved	Active, critical identity gained through interaction in social groups, each seen as contributor	Facilitator, constructor, selector of relevant materials/problems/issues; critical guide, guardian of value from the past	The focus of rational criticism and change. Democratic	Critical analysis of society's values to be undertaken in terms of validity and social utility
GNP code	That which is conducive to the furtherance of the nation's economic well-being, generally technological/scientific/practical bias	A being to be trained to fit into economic machine. Initiative and activity encouraged only as far as this dovetails with ultimate occupational destination	Trainer, constructor, transmitter, low-order member of hierarchy	Source of content, teaching style. Hierarchical model for schools to copy	Values conducive with future role in society's economic hierarchy – respect, hard work, obedience to be transmitted and internalized by some: creativity and discovery fostered in others

morality and schooling, we begin by describing and analysing the major educational ideologies which have generated such relationships in the past, and continue to do so now.

Everyone, in some form or another, has certain basic beliefs about education – about the type of knowledge to be valued, the role of the child, the teacher and society in the process, the type of society to be aimed for and ultimately the preferred relationship between morality and schooling. These normally cohere into particular philosophies of education. It is important, then, to realize and to reflect upon one's own beliefs.

This can be achieved by means of the following simple exercise. Below are three groups of statements. Read the eight statements in group A, and assign fifteen marks between the eight statements in the group. You may give approximately equal weights to each statement, or assign the entire fifteen marks to just one statement, or give the bulk to just one or two about which you feel particularly strongly. Once this is completed, do the same for groups B and C.

Group A

1. All aspects of individual development are important.
2. Children must be given an understanding of the timeless depths and mysteries of knowledge.
3. Learning should be an active social process which is guided but not dominated by teachers.
4. Children should make their own choice of topic to study.
5. Schools must produce a well-trained motivated workforce which can compete in international markets with other industrialized countries.
6. Teachers should help pupils in the process of understanding, appreciating, criticizing and, when older, changing society's norms and institutions.
7. Schools must be involved in the selection of elites, for different levels of ability require different provision.
8. Pupils must be given the kinds of practical skills which will equip them to earn a living once they leave school.

Group B

1. A school should be democratically run, with rules and punishments negotiated and agreed by all its members.
2. Certain kinds of knowledge have more value and are more important than other kinds.
3. In a rapidly changing world, it makes little sense to transmit bodies of knowledge established in a previous era.
4. The school should be seen as one part of a machine furthering the economic prosperity of this country.
5. Only a minority of people are capable of contributing to the pool of worthwhile knowledge.

6. The school should organize itself upon the principle that the interests and needs of the child are paramount.
7. The curriculum should be organized in a rational and democratic way so that current institutions and norms may be analysed, criticized, and, if necessary, alternatives suggested.
8. The curriculum should be centrally concerned with those areas of knowledge which contribute to the wealth-producing aspects of society.

Group C

1. Maturity can only come about through the exercise of responsibility and freedom.
2. Public examinations should be used to assess the acquisition of knowledge.
3. Pupils should be seen as active in making sense of their learning, rather than as passive recipients of transmitted knowledge and values.
4. Discussion, criticism and creativity must be linked with the promotion of economic goals.
5. The school should be an institution which fosters constructive criticism of society.
6. Schools should be seen as a means of changing society.
7. Disciplinary techniques should be chosen and imposed by those in authority.
8. Schools should be accountable to society for what they produce; the quality of their output can be assessed by objective criteria.

Marking

Now assign the marks from the statements to these views of education:

Cultural transmission	Child-centred	Social reconstruction	GNP Code
A2	A1	A3	A5
A7	A4	A6	A8
B2	B1	B3	B4
B5	B6	B7	B8
C2	C1	C3	C4
C7	C5	C6	C8

The higher the mark, the more inclined one is to a particular ideology. The four categorizations are developments of an initial typology by Malcolm Skilbeck (1976), and a brief summary of the main points of each can be seen in Table 1.1 on p. 7. It is important, however, to show in more detail how the adoption of any one of these ideologies will influence the way in which the relationship between morality and schooling is perceived. Each of the educational ideologies, therefore, will be examined in some detail.

The *cultural transmission* model tends in practice to have two central tenets to its belief system: (a) concentration on a society's cultural heritage; and (b) the association of such a heritage with a small minority, its elite, who will be educated in such culture, whilst the majority of the populace receives a different type of education suited to its lesser intellectual capability. In many cases this less intellectual education is calculated to 'gentle' the majority into acceptance of its (inferior) position in society.

Clearly, notions of manners, hard work and obedience to authority will come near the top of any list of values and morals to be transmitted to such a majority. However, the two tenets – of a cultural heritage, and of an elite – are not necessary to one another. It is quite possible to believe that a cultural heritage should be passed on to all of the population rather than to a select few, just as the existence of an elite does not have to be linked to the transmission of a cultural heritage.

It would seem, however, that the cultural transmission model in its fully developed form – the transmission of a cultural heritage to an elite – is antithetical to the ideals of a democratic society. A more restricted version, concentrating purely upon the transmission of a cultural heritage, is not so. The implementation of a National Curriculum in Great Britain can be seen in this light. Such a core of subjects common to all pupils assumes that there are certain areas of knowledge which should be passed on to all citizens if they are to benefit from a full range of educational insights. It is not, therefore, a code which need be held exclusively by conservative or liberal. It can be seen as the natural conclusion to a process of the comprehensivization of schools, in that it provides all with fair access to society's past and present wisdom.

In like manner, the part of the cultural transmission model in the relationship between morality and education deserves very serious consideration, for it could be argued very plausibly that human beings would not be fully human without the benefit of the accumulated moral and social wisdom and practice of previous generations.

The cultural transmission model, however, has three major weaknesses. Firstly, by stressing the existence of solid and eternal facts and values which can be transmitted from one age to another, it says little or nothing about the temporality of knowledge and the impermanence of certain beliefs and values. Further, it gives no yardstick by which to decide between the two, about what should be kept and what should be discarded. In terms of values, it may end up at the popular level by saying little more than 'this is what we did in the past, so we should do it now'. At the very least, its proponents need to be critical of their own heritage.

Secondly, the cultural heritage transmitted to the present generation was not consciously selected by previous generations as that which they would like to pass on. Cultural or value transmission is not the clean-cut affair sometimes simplistically painted. What has come down is not just the carefully selected gems of insight into the human condition necessary for the furtherance and development of civilization, but to some extent the product of accident, vested interests, fashion and what fitted in with the prevailing beliefs of the next generation on. Ignoring this dialectical element distorts the truth of the genesis of cultural and moral beliefs, and thereby presents a false model for schools to adopt.

Lastly, each creative act in this cultural transmission was the product of a critical analysis of what had gone before. The creators took what was on offer, saw things from a slightly different angle and produced something related to but distinctly different from that which had gone before. If they had not done so, culture would have remained stagnant at Stone Age cave paintings or belief in evil spirits. The cultural transmission model makes little or no mention of this. And yet such creativity is not the preserve solely of the Tolstoys, Newtons or Mozarts of this world. It applies in less distinguished form to the 'normal' adult and child as well. Those who adopt a transmission model generally picture the child as a receptor, passively accepting those values taught. But even a cursory glance at the findings of work of psychologists like Piaget (1932) and Kohlberg (1981a) in the field of moral development suggest that the process is much more two-way. On these accounts, the individual is active and interactive with the values transmitted, each person's understanding of them being subtly different. This difference depends upon what each person selects as important and relevant features of a situation. Such interaction must be recognized in any adequate account of a viable educational – and moral educational – viewpoint.

The second ideological standpoint described is the *child-centred* model. This ideology is strongly at odds with a conception of humanity as being bad by nature. Rather, this badness is seen as the product of being a member of society. Humans, therefore, are seen as basically good, society as corrupting that nature. So one can see two major strands of the child-centred ideology here, an anti-society, individualist stance and a belief in the inherent goodness of humans.

Unlike the cultural transmission model, with its stress on objective knowledge to be transmitted, the emphasis and attention here is upon children, on their unfolding natures and their subjective interests. This being the case, the material for children's education must come from within their own experience. As this will vary from child to child, so the impressive edifice of a cultural heritage erected by the cultural transmission model is shown to play but a very small part in children's education. Children, moreover, are perceived very differently. Rather than being the passive imbibers of predetermined materials, children are now seen as active and involved, constructing from their own vivid and authentic experiences personal and individual realities, very different from the objectivist picture painted by cultural transmission theorists. Each child will have different interests and different experiences, each interpreting them differently. This being the case, each construction of reality must of necessity be unique. The picture of education has moved from one painted at the level of society to one painted at the level of the individual child.

It is sometimes thought that the role of the teacher then becomes fairly peripheral to the educative process, being little more than its facilitator. This, however, need not be the case, for he or she may instead be seen as planner, constructor and developer. The teacher must be aware of each child's developmental possibilities, interests and capabilities. The teacher must then so structure conditions surrounding the child that the best possible use is made of the environment. In this way, the pupil's interest and spontaneity will be channelled into areas which will be of most benefit to him or her.

As with the cultural transmission model, so the child-centred one need not be the doctrine of the liberal. David Cooper (1987), for example, has attacked the notion of multicultural education from a child-centred standpoint. He argues that one needs to begin the child's education from where the child is, what he or she understands, and that multicultural education can be nothing more than a 'Cook's tour' which leaves the child bewildered and confused simply because education is not located within the child's own cultural experience. Whilst there is an enormous amount to quarrel with in such a view – the assumed lack of understanding by the child, lack of teaching ability by the educator and unbridgeable divisions between materials from different cultures – the point is simply that one must not assume that child centredness is an essentially liberal doctrine. It can be used by either end of the spectrum, and attacked by either end as well!

The relationship which the child-centred educator sees between morality and schools is to some extent problematic, taking at least two different possible courses. Firstly, there is the individualist strain, an imprecise blend of individual value development through experience, and the expression of inborn sympathy for other people's needs and difficulties. And secondly, there is also the more twentieth-century communitarian approach seeing a development of community values as preparation for the criticism and reform of society.

There are at least four major difficulties with the child-centred approach.

Firstly, implicit in a lot of child-centred literature is the assumption that children are 'naturally' good. This stems largely from the writings of Rousseau. Such a view is a welcome antidote to the belief that children are inherently bad, but it describes the true situation no more accurately. There is now much psychological evidence to suggest that at the earliest ages children are capable of producing both altruistic and egocentric behaviours (see Chapter 7). If this is the case, then leaving children to 'do their own thing' does not make much sense either educationally or morally. Much more sensible is to decide on what one wishes the child to grow into, and then favour behaviours which lead in that direction. Leaving the child to develop 'naturally' is no more than an abnegation of responsibility.

Secondly, it is surely a very limiting education which focuses only upon the child's interests. Whilst it makes good sense to begin from where the child begins and move out from there, the real danger with such a set of beliefs is that it could prevent the child from appreciating others' thoughts, feelings and beliefs. One of the key concepts in Kohlberg's (Kohlberg *et al.*, 1983) model of the moral development of the child is the notion of individuals being faced by 'optimum cognitive conflict' – being put in a position where they are challenged to make better sense of moral beliefs than they do at present. Limiting children to their own interests could leave many without this opportunity.

Thirdly, it is not at all clear how child-centred educators are to answer the charges of relativism in their approach to morality. How do they arrive at a standpoint where they can evaluate what the child should do, or indeed what society should do? To say that society is inherently bad is no more than invective and helps us not at all. Similarly, to state that the child is inherently good seems to say little more than that whatever the child does of its own accord is good, and there are few who could agree with that, in terms of either the child's own best interests or the rights of others. A thoroughgoing child-centred educator would have to accept that each child is a law unto itself, and essentially there is no way of choosing between the values of one and the values of another. In which case, how does one choose between the child who helps others and the child who kills them? Some of the child-centred insights are undoubtedly valuable, most notably in steering attention back to the rights and needs of the individual, but on its own this approach does not seem to be able to provide a complete answer.

Lastly, it is not at all clear that the educational focus should be upon the individual as such. If the cultural transmission model neglects the importance of the individual in the linkage between morality and education, it could be argued that the child-centred model exaggerates it. Too much emphasis upon the individual can lead one to neglect the needs of the society in which that person lives. No one is an island, and the linkage between morality and schooling, it might be argued, should focus upon the relationships within society which go to improve that society. This leads us directly into the third perspective.

The *social reconstruction* model is an ideological perspective which does not seek to impose society's values upon the individual, nor does the individual have to tread a lonely and solitary path towards self-discovery. The individual and society are seen as being mutually beneficial. Society benefits through the focus on, appreciation of and, where needed, change of values *by* its members for the betterment *of* its members. By involving all its members in this cultural renewal, the model encourages both stability and growth. The individual benefits through being exposed to and critically appreciating the inherited values of the society, and through being accepted and recognized as having an important contribution to make to the process of renewal. The process and the product of education come together in a way which does violence to neither concept.

Social reconstructionism, then, shares some of the properties of both the cultural transmission and the child-centred models, but is different from both in a number of ways. Firstly, it is an ideology which, much more than the previous two, is seen as a vehicle for the change of society. Whilst the cultural transmission model is essentially concerned with preserving the past, and the child-centred model is little concerned with change in society *per se*, social reconstructionism sees the major task of education as precisely this – the reform of society through education. Its subject matter, therefore, differs markedly from the other two models. Whereas the cultural transmission model will view the transmission of the society's cultural heritage as education's main function, and the child-centred model look to a curriculum developed from the child's capabilities and interests, the social reconstructionist will see the curriculum as being composed of pressing social issues which need to be resolved, and therefore will probably organize it on a topic-based approach. Like the child-centred educator, the social reconstructionist will view the child as being active and critical in his or her learning, but in a much more social and interactive manner. The social reconstruction teacher will share values of both the child-centred and the cultural transmission teachers – critical of existing society in many ways, but also aware of the fact that there are many things within society worth preserving, and acting as both selector of that which is to be criticized and changed and guardian of that which is to be valued and retained.

There are a number of possible criticisms of the social reconstruction model.

Firstly, there is the problem of the enormous responsibilities that are given to teachers. Not only are they the selectors of social issues to be discussed (and the definers of them as 'problems') and guardians of that which is to be preserved, but they are also seen as possessing the critical acumen to perform these tasks, as well as facilitators and constructors of relevant teaching materials. There are many – including the teachers themselves – who would question whether teachers have the abilities or the resources to perform such tasks. There is also the moral question of whether teachers, or any one particular group, should be given this immensely important, influential and potentially subversive role.

Secondly, there is the fundamental question of whether there is a need for change to quite the degree normally envisaged in the proposals of the social reconstruction model. There is a radicalism here which might seem inappropriate to many in the stable western democracies, and which might also neglect the virtues of both the cultural transmission and the child-centred models. Valuable aspects of the cultural heritage of a country may be neglected in the passion for social reconstruction and renewal, just as the needs and interests of the individual child may be neglected in the movement to social reform. There is a need for balance between all three elements.

Finally, there appears to be an unresolved tension within the ideology itself over the issue of teachers as cultural guardians. Whilst the movement is profoundly democratic in its aspirations, there is a large element of elitist philosophy encapsulated within it, for the teacher is to be cast as the expert, the guardian, the selector, the transmitter. It would seem that this ideology could slip all too easily from democracy into elitism.

Where does the individual school or teacher fit into all this? It will be apparent that if there is an implicit justification for a particular kind of relationship between morality and the school within these three educational ideologies, then it is vitally important for the teacher and school to realize where they stand and where they want to go.

Moreover, an awareness of the preferred ideological stand will make the teacher and school that much more sensitized to attempts at imposing other ideological definitions upon them. In this context, there is a fourth ideology which has become increasingly important in its influence over the last 10 to 15 years in this country, which had strong repercussions in the linkage between morality and schooling.

For want of a better term, this ideology will be called the *GNP (gross national product) code*. Its main features will be described here; its influence upon morality and the school is reserved for the next chapter. Its ideology focuses upon producers and consumers, upon technological sophistication and economic viability, and sees the school essentially as being the training ground for the roles which pupils will take up in the market-place once they leave school. In so doing, the school benefits society by providing a well-trained, motivated workforce, which can compete in international markets with other industrialized countries such as the United States, West Germany and Japan, but it also benefits pupils by providing them with the skills to fit in to such a society, for they will be equipped for work and so able to earn a living and live contented lives. The curriculum consists of all that is conducive to the furtherance of the nation's economic well-being, and tends to be technological/scientific/practical in orientation. The pupil is seen as a person to be trained to fit in to the economic machine, and so initiative and active involvement are encouraged as far as these attributes dovetail with ultimate occupational destinations. The teacher is a trainer and transmitter, a constructor of appropriate (effective) teaching techniques for this training and transmitting, but essentially a fairly low-order member of the economic hierarchy. The values seen as worth transmitting are those conducive to fitting the child for his or her future role in society's hierarchy, and vary with what is required of that particular individual at that time. Such values as respect, hard work, punctuality and obedience may be prized, but so also may creativity and discovery. It is very likely, though, that values like social criticism and self-expression are seen as either undesirable or irrelevant.

The GNP code, then, is essentially technological/industrial in orientation. It has, however, certain features of the other ideologies which confuse it with them. For example, and as just noted, the values it transmits may be much like those of the cultural transmission model – emphasizing hierarchy, obedience, respect, punctuality and good manners. On the other hand, it tends to divert the curriculum away from notions of cultural heritage to skills, issues and materials which are seen as more 'relevant'. Relevance, creativity and discovery are values also seen in the child-centred ideology, though located with the child as ends in themselves, whilst with the GNP code they are seen as a useful tool to the end of economic productivity.

It is possible yet again to see apparent contradictions in political orientations. Thus O'Hear (1987) has criticized the GCSE in Britain precisely because of its relevance – its failure to orient itself to the initiation of children into independent, non-relevant (not *ir*relevant) bodies of knowledge – essentially the cultural transmission point of view. Here, then, the GNP code can clearly be seen to be distinct from the cultural transmission model, in many ways its political partner. The GNP code has an orientation very much its own.

Now whilst it is recognized that parts of the educative process must concentrate upon providing an industrial society with individuals equipped with the requisite skills, this cannot be its whole or even its main function. There are then a number of criticisms which must be made of this ideology.

Firstly, in failing to critically transmit the cultural heritage of the past, the GNP code appears to fail to distinguish between means and ends in ideology, for it fails to answer the question 'where are we going?'. We are certainly going somewhere by means of a healthy industrial base, but it is a culturally impoverished society which sees a healthy economic position as being the principal end to aim for. By failing to ask vital questions about ends, the GNP code does not begin to answer questions about the basis of its own validity.

Moreover, it does not only fail to satisfy the requirements of the cultural transmission model in terms of the denigration of transmitting the society's cultural heritage. It also fails the child-centred and social reconstructionist educators. It fails them by almost completely omitting from discussion the interests and insights of the individual. Both child and teacher as active contributors are ignored, to be included only minimally as functionaries within an overall grand design. Such a course, it would seem, is fertile ground for apathy, alienation and possible violence.

And finally, the GNP code is in total opposition in certain crucial respects to the aspirations of the social reconstructionist, for it assumes that a particular form of economic structure is the desirable state for a society, and thereby leaves no room for the role of teacher or child in social reconstruction as there is essentially to be no criticism, no reconstruction. Not only has the ideal society been defined, but it is in existence – devoted to the pursuit of national wealth as its prime objective. It is an ideology then which, if adopted in a thoroughgoing manner, contradicts the major tenets of the other three ideologies.

Now it must repeated that there is room for all four models within a complete and balanced ideology, and consequently in any theory of a proposed relationship between morality and schooling. Cultural heritage needs to be retained and transmitted. The interests and capabilities of the child need to be taken into account. The school must initiate the pupil into rational criticism for the improvement of society as a whole. Pupils must be given an education which enables them to gain a job once they leave school, and which helps them contribute to the society's economic health. Danger arises when one ideology gains too much support, and stifles the insights of the others. A large part of the argument of this book will be that the GNP code has gained too preponderant a place in this country, and that its concepts and values are being transmitted into schools in a manner which will ultimately cause great damage. This has not happened overnight, but has been a gradual infiltration which because of its gradualism has gone undetected and unchallenged for too long.

It is part of the argument of this book, then, that there are a number of things which can be done to defend a more balanced relationship between morality and the school. Initial considerations must centre upon an understanding of the various ideologies contending within the school and society. Any person interested in education must be aware of their own ideological stand, as well as the stands of those they may wish to criticize. This chapter has attempted to facilitate this awareness. The kinds of linkages between morality and schooling which have been made in the past, how these previous attempts have affected the present and what might be wished for in the future should also be studied. This is the subject of the next chapter.

Chapter 2

Past, Present and Future Perspectives

A proper understanding of the term 'morality', and the function of the school in the transmission, criticism or reformulation of that morality, can only be fully understood by looking at how society as a whole views these matters.

Probably the best way of appreciating this is to look at the issue from an historical perspective, and see how different times have viewed 'morality' and 'schooling' and the relationship between them. This chapter, then, will begin with such an historical survey, and then move on to look at ways in which society tends to view this at the present time, before finally making prescriptions for focuses needed in the future.

Now it is not unusual for people to fail to link particular events with the changes in society that surround these events. The more complex and pervasive the change, the less likely it is, paradoxically, that this link will be made. In terms of education, this can be seen in a failure to associate problems in the relationship between morality and schools with the cultural arena of the society in which schools participate. Yet there can be little doubt that any area of understanding or belief is informed and interpenetrated by other current areas of theoretical and ideological understanding or belief.

In the case of the moral dimension of schooling, it is possible to see the shape of the moral curriculum, in its widest sense, as in part the educational manifestation of the 'desirable' social and political attitudes for society as a whole. If this is accepted, then it becomes crucial to understand the ethos of the society in which schooling has taken place, for this will not only facilitate an understanding of the previous manifestations of the moral curriculum in this country, but also to some extent predict its future orientation.

Perhaps the central problem in the relationship between morality and schooling is the validation of a curricular approach. In this country, this has been closely bound up with philosophical questions of ethical objectivism and relativism. Where the sources of authority have been seen as unproblematical (because of the status of the Bible and/or the ruling class) then moral education in the school has tended to take on an objectivist character. In such circumstances, it has generally been believed that there are certain moral principles which can and should be taught, and moral education has then essentially consisted in teaching children to be good in certain very specific ways. Method, content and intention have all gone neatly together.

However, where the sources of authority have been more problematical (because of the increased self-confidence of the lower classes, and/or the influx of non-Christian religious and cultural ideas), and charges of indoctrination are seen more as a rebuke than as a mere comment on the effectiveness of the system, then writers have felt less inclined to teach content as objective. In such cases they have done one of two things. Either they have opted for something close to relativism, suggesting that one's moral stance is essentially a matter of personal choice, and there is no way of ultimately deciding between stances, or they have to some extent tried to opt out of the problem by arguing that content can be left to one side and that there should be a concentration upon methods and procedures of working out how moral education should be conducted, the form of enquiry it should take. The logic behind this latter approach seems to have been that if one gets the educational method correct, problems of content, objectivism and indoctrination will take care of themselves because one is equipping the pupils with the intellectual tools to tackle these problems. These issues will be dealt with shortly.

The present chapter, then, begins with an examination of the historical background to the moral curriculum in Great Britain, by means of which the central problems of objectivism and relativism can be examined and understood. It will examine three major approaches to the teaching of morality in the school. They may be described as:

(a)   the ruler and ruled code (1820–1960)
(b)   the self-chosen code (1960–74)
(c)   the GNP code (1974-?).

If the previous 150 years of English educational provision are examined, it is possible to discern the three codes of morality described above. Whilst the dates given are only approximate, and elements of one period's morality are to be seen in another's, there can be little doubt that these shifts have resulted in three very different conceptions of the need for a moral education curriculum and of its implementation. A fourth code, a suggestion for the future which attempts to answer the major questions and problems raised by the three previous ones, will form the endpiece of this chapter.

On the basis of the examination of the first three codes, four focuses of attention for the teacher will also be suggested. The 'bedding' of these focuses will, however, be left to the next two chapters.

Before beginning, though, it is perhaps worth stressing again that by 'moral curriculum' is meant far more than the contents within a school's written curriculum. The hidden curriculum of both school and society will be examined, for a morality is sometimes far more effectively implemented through other institutions and practices than it is through classroom lessons and materials.

THE RULER AND RULED CODE

This code was essentially the product of two main forces: a dominant aristocratic upper class and the needs of an industrial revolution. Whilst the upper classes educated their children into a morality of the right and a duty to rule, the lower classes were socialized into an acceptance of their lowly position in society and of routines making them pliable to the needs of the factory. Robert Lowe spelt out the precise aims of popular education in 1867 when he said:

The lower classes ought to be educated to discharge the duties cast upon them. They should also be educated that they may appreciate and defer to a higher cultivation when they meet it, and the higher classes ought to be educated in a very different manner in order that they may exhibit to the lower classes, that higher education to which, if it were shown to them, they would bow down and defer.
(Quoted in *Times Educational Supplement* 21 June 1985: 4)

He was not by any means alone in this belief. In 1872, the editor of the *School Board Chronicle* wrote that the working class were the 'barbarian class . . . the uncivilised' and the School Board:

have to instil into the minds of the children Knowledge . . . not to undertake the Quixotic task of indoctrinating the rising generation of the working and labouring classes with the dogma of equality . . . but . . . knowledge of their places in society.
(9 November 1872: 399, quoted in Marsden 1977)

Different kinds of schools promoted different moralities which together produced a unified hierarchical code. There was little need for discussion or disagreement, for each person was educated in a kind of perverted Platonic way to know his or her place and to be suited to it. Even the potential trouble of an aspiring middle class could be accommodated: the upper classes had their public schools and their right and duty to rule, the lower classes had their elementary schools and their submission and duty to obey and the middle classes had the ability to buy their way into 'respectability' by way of the grammar and lesser public schools, which led to a morality of hard work, thrift and self-help. Coleridge (1862: 41) described the purpose of education as the preservation of this unified code by means of the subversion of the underprivileged classes when he said:

Its real tendency is to preserve the existing map of society while it softens its demarcations.

How similar is this to the comment made by Marx (1959: 587) that:

the more a ruling class is able to assimilate the foremost minds of a ruled class, the more stable and dangerous it becomes.

This process was helped, as MacDonald (1976) has shown, by nineteenth-century textbooks being pervasively religious and exhortatory in character, not only encouraging the working class to work hard and behave soberly, but also attempting to inculcate an acceptance of and resignation to the social conditions of the time.

Well into this century, the attitude still prevailed. In 1924 the popular hymn 'All Things Bright and Beautiful' was still exhorting people to believe that:

The rich man in his castle, the poor man at his gate,
GOD made them, high or lowly, and order'd their estate.
(*Hymns Ancient and Modern* 1924: 469)

Moral attitudes were to be instilled through other avenues as well as religion. Physical education was seen in these terms in 1913–14:

The principal needs for children of this age are the inculcation of habits of discipline and obedience on the one hand, and the promotion of all round physical development on the other. [The official syllabus] provides all that is necessary or desirable.
(Board of Education Report 1913–14, quoted in Musgrave 1978: 101)

Similarly, the Report of the Chief Medical Officer in 1919 to the Board of Education saw his remit as being rather more than the physical health of children:

> For our business is not only to instruct the child or the adolescent and provide him with information on Hygiene, a body of knowledge, but to teach him actually *how to live*, at the top of his capacity, avoiding the evil and choosing the good.
> (p. 171, quoted in Musgrave 1978: 101, emphasis original)

Such statements are unashamedly objectivist in character: there is an unambiguous good and bad, so 'moral principles' can and must be taught. All this was to change. The first real cracks in this monolith came about with the First World War. The need for fit manpower in the trenches brought home to the ruling classes the poor physical condition of its workers, and led both classes to question the conditions in which the other half lived. Moreover, the trenches were a great leveller – the machine gun bullet killed lord and labourer indiscriminately – and both had to endure the same kinds of hardship. The lord saw that the labourer was more than sub-human; the labourer saw that the lord was less than super-human. And the manner in which so many from the lower classes volunteered and were killed led to a sense of the injustice of social institutions in general. As H. A. L. Fisher said of the 1918 Education Act:

> every just mind begins to realise that the boundaries of citizenship are not determined by wealth, and that the same logic which leads us to desire an extension of the franchise points also to an extension of education.
> (Quoted in Wardle 1976: 35)

It seems no mere coincidence that the next major Education Act came with the closing of the Second World War.

However, extending the franchise and education led inevitably to the greater voice of the underclasses: no longer would they accept the role in society assigned to them by those with power and money. The growing Labour Party represented a dissent from prevailing social, political and moral consensus. The middle classes, given a taste of power in the late nineteenth century, liked it and were not quite so acquiescent in support of the aristocracy. And after the Second World War, when the influx of Caribbean and Asian workers to this country to satisfy labour shortages also brought distinctively different cultural and religious patterns, moral consensus began to break down. In 1964 it was still possible for the Commonwealth Immigrants Advisory Council to declare that:

> If their parents were brought up in another culture or another tradition, children should be encouraged to respect it, but a national system cannot be expected to perpetuate the different values of immigrant groups.
> (p. 7)

Such an assimilationist policy, however, was already rapidly becoming outdated.

THE SELF-CHOSEN CODE

It is very difficult to promote an objectivist code of morality in education when substantial portions of the population no longer accept this objectivist version. For a start, morality had looked in the past to the Christian religion as the natural foundation for its arguments, but increasingly found it could no longer do so. Religious thought was having as much difficulty with objectivity as was morality. As early as 1912, Leuba had included in an appendix 48 definitions by different writers as to the meaning of a religious attitude. This was well ahead of its time in recognizing the fragmentation of religious attitudes. Campbell (1957: 248) could still speak of religious experience as:

> a state of mind comprising belief in the reality of a supernatural being or beings endued with transcendent power and worth, together with the complex emotive attitude of worship intrinsically appropriate thereto.

However, the seminal *Honest to God* by John Robinson (1963), drawing its inspiration from the work of Tillich and Bonhoeffer, produced an earthquake in theological circles in this country. Objectivism was seriously called into question by a leading Church figure for the first time when he stated that:

> we are reaching the point at which the whole conception of a God 'out there' . . . is becoming more of a hindrance than a help.
> (pp. 15–16)

Robinson questioned the traditional conception of religion, and consequently threw doubt upon the objectivist moral stand as well. The approach he took was not objectivism, not relativism, but an agonized questioning in which each person was encouraged to come to his or her own understanding of the religious urge through an *inductive* process of question, reflection and tentative answer. As he wrote in 1964, comparing it with the traditional *instructive* approach:

> The inductive approach is more dangerous. The ends are not prescribed, the answers are not settled beforehand. But this is only to say that a real *decision* is involved in any responsible moral choice.
> (p. 41, emphasis original)

Two things are noteworthy in this. The first is the danger that in laying aside the objectivist approach, for whatever reasons, one leaves oneself open to the dangers of relativism. One has only to look at the recent thought of a theologian like Don Cupitt (1984) to see how far down the road such thoughts can lead one:

> God (and this is a definition) is the sum of our values, representing to us their ideal unity, their claims upon us and their creative power. Mythologically, he has been portrayed as an objective being, because ancient thought tended to personify values in the belief that important words must stand for things. . . . Values do not have to be independently and objectively existent beings in order to claim our allegiance . . . thinking of values as objective beings out there does not help us in any way to progress towards a clearer understanding of the special part they play in our lives. We can do without that mythological idea.
> (p. 269)

So there is a danger of running into relativism. But the other thing to notice is the notion of 'moral choice'. Formerly the only moral choice had been between good and bad, and moral education had consisted in teaching the difference between them. Now there was perceived to be a plurality of moralities, so that what was important for one person was not necessarily so for another. This displayed itself both in terms of curriculum materials explicitly designed for 'moral education', and also in the kind of approach taken by theorists to the problem of objectivism and relativism in this area. Let us look at four examples in particular.

    A. *McPhail, Ungoed-Thomas and Chapman* (1972) based their research and findings on what adolescents saw as their most pressing personal, social and moral problems. The results highlighted some very important areas – for instance, that others' feelings, needs and interests should be taken into account in school much more than they are – and formed the basis of the subsequent Schools Council Project materials for developing in young people a more considerate way of life.

This is indeed a radical shift from a morality imposed upon the pupil. Instead of content being seen as 'objective', 'true' or 'given', this is a programme which looks for its content in those who are about to receive it. In so doing, such an approach avoids the kinds of objectivist difficulties mentioned above. But it does so at a price.

Firstly, the type of questions one asks tends to limit the kind of replies received. So if the questions are generally concerned with interpersonal relationships, as this research was, then that is the subject which will be returned. The areas highlighted are very important. But, crucially, the research could not by this method determine what other areas not mentioned by the children should also be included in a comprehensive curricular provision. As a procedure for defining the full extent of the linkage between morality and schooling, it will not do.

Secondly, the research seems to be a clear case of a commission of what philosophers call the naturalistic fallacy – that one cannot decide what should be taught from factual material alone. If the children had suggested in their replies that much more time should be given to persuading black people to leave this country, would that be included in curricular materials? People's social and cultural situations provide a particular viewpoint which may not adequately reflect the full or correct content for concern. The research, then, fails to provide a genuine philosophical or epistemological justification for the materials which followed. Whilst much of the material was and still is intensely interesting and usable, it still needs an underpinning which it cannot provide by asking its recipients.

B. *John Wilson's* work (see his section in Wilson, Williams and Sugarman, 1967) took another approach. Rather than locate justification with the recipients, Wilson used philosophical analysis to identify four elements which make up the constituent parts of moral education. Thus, PHIL is concerned with understanding the concept of a person; EMP with conceptualizing and being able to identify with various emotions; GIG with the mastery of factual knowledge relevant to moral decisions; and KRAT with an alertness to moral situations and an ability to make moral decisions and implement them.

Essentially Wilson is interested in enabling children to think in moral terms without prescribing any one value position. He is concerned with the structure of moral reasoning rather than with the content. Again this avoids the problem of objectivism by refusing to prescribe one position; but it is open to a number of problems.

Firstly, it is at least questionable whether teaching form rather than content *will* make children more moral. They may become expert moral reasoners without acting or thinking morally. If Wilson then were to say that this is where his EMP factor is involved, then one has to ask what material he will use to improve this capability – and we come immediately to the problem of objectivism and content, for the selection of any content must necessarily be a personal and less than objective choice.

The second question, then, must be whether it is *possible* to teach form without content. It is difficult to understand what this can mean, for it would seem that all form must be embedded in some kind of content for it to have any meaning at all.

And lastly, linguistic analysis is a problematic area of philosophy, for as a number of writers have pointed out (see, for example, Adelstein, 1972), there is a strong suspicion that much of it is little more than the analysis of concepts into what each philosopher would like them to be – it is a matter of prescription rather than analysis.

Wilson's analysis of the concept of moral education might seem intuitively plausible to some, but what if Nietzsche were to rise from his grave and say that the concept should be analysed differently – that at least one of its constituents is the fact that people should spend less time caring about the mass of humanity, dispense with common social rules and strive to reach their own pinnacle of perfection? What can Wilson say to this? At face value at least, Nietzsche's analysis has as much right to our attention as has Wilson because they both seem essentially to be prescriptions rather than descriptions. We may intuitively warm to Wilson's more than Nietzsche's, but that is no basis for justification.

C. *The values clarification approach* (Raths, Harmin and Simon, 1966), whilst it espouses the use of rationality and logic in reaching moral choices, can give no guide as to why one choice is ultimately better than another. This approach slips almost completely into the relativist camp. The approach, widely used in North America, prescribes a seven-step valuing process by which children come to choose and create their own values. These steps are:

(a)   choosing freely
(b)   choosing from alternatives
(c)   choosing after thoughtful consideration of the consequences of each alternative
(d)   cherishing, being happy with the choice
(e)   prizing enough to be willing to confirm the choice to others
(f)   acting or doing something with the choice
(g)   acting repeatedly in some pattern of life.

However, to quote the authors (p. 227):

> It is not impossible to conceive of someone going through the seven value criteria and deciding that he values intolerance or thievery. What is to be done? Our position is that we respect his right to decide upon that value.

'Intolerance' and 'thievery' sound strange bedfellows with a respecting of rights. Something has gone very badly wrong. Lockwood (1975: 46) nails the difficulties of the position very clearly when he says:

> The advocates of values clarification do not seriously entertain such fundamental questions: assuming Adolf Hitler, Charles Manson, Martin Luther King, and Albert Schweitzer held values which met the seven criteria, are their values equally valid, praiseworthy, and/or good?

The values clarification authors do not of course want to allow a generation of rapists, murderers and fanatics to inherit and run society, and yet on their approach they can do nothing about it. Whilst acknowledging the problems of objectivism, they have failed to provide an alternative which prevents the excesses of relativism.

D. *Lawrence Kohlberg's* (1981a) immensely influential work on movement by the individual through stages of ethical reasoning, facilitated by the cognitive conflict induced by the discussion of moral dilemmas, has been particularly appealing precisely because it represents a well-argued attempt at resolving the objectivist/relativist problem. It seems to give objectivism a cloak of scientific respectability. The title of one of Kohlberg's earlier and most famous papers (1971) – 'From Is to Ought: how to commit the naturalistic fallacy and get away with it' – attempts to do precisely this. Kohlberg describes six developmental stages of moral reasoning (Table 2.1) which are invariant in sequence, progressively more integrative and culturally universalizable in form if not in content. Here in the scientific proof of the existence of these six psychological stages is one's objectivity, and here is the 'is' by means of which one moves to the 'ought' – what one must do to produce a 'good' person by moving the individual through these stages from the lowest to the highest. Kohlberg strenuously denies that this is a way of marking off one person as 'better' in the ethical sense than another. All that these stages do, he argues, is to present more adequate ways of resolving moral conflicts and of taking action in ethical areas. Kohlberg is playing to the anti-objectivist camp here and attempting to show that he is not prescribing so much as describing. As with Wilson, he is claiming that he is concerned with form and not with content, for he is dealing with the style of reasoning rather than the content which goes into a particular problem.

However, this surely does not solve the problem. If we ask Kohlberg what he means by the sixth stage being more 'adequate' than the fifth, then he must reply that it is in some sense 'better'. But 'better' must mean better for somebody, and inevitably Kohlberg is drawn into making an ethical judgement, claiming that this stage is better than that stage in some absolute sense. He cannot avoid the issue. His 1983 publication does attempt to retract this 'is' to 'ought' assertion, but does so only at the expense of producing a less interesting account which in effect says that there are stages of ethical reasoning but that he is not going to make any comments as to their implications for morality and moral education. The thesis becomes safer but far less interesting. The problem of ethical objectivity and relativity cannot be avoided.

In his later work, Kohlberg became increasingly interested in the creation of a school 'ethos' – the 'just-community approach' – which would provide the kind of working atmosphere within which people could relate in a caring and responsive manner to others. To this end, two 'schools-within-schools', one at Cambridge High, Massachusetts, and the other at Roosevelt High in the Bronx, New York, have been initiated by Kohlberg and his colleagues, in which staff and pupils meet to democratically discuss issues of the running and management of the school. The attempts have been interesting and thought provoking (see, for example, Hersh *et al.*, 1979 and Woodhouse, 1986), and suggest a variety of ways in which the school can more directly face and discuss its central values. However, there is no further movement on the validation of an approach. This being the case, the situation seems to be rather like that with the material of Peter McPhail – very interesting and almost certainly of use to the teacher and the school, but needing a theoretical underpinning.

These four approaches, then, are symptomatic of a fundamental problem which is posed whenever a monolithic objectivist morality is overturned. The problem is essentially putting something else in its place which is not another covert form of objectivism, and which does not become embroiled in the difficulties of relativism. Whilst these approaches have had their successes, the present author believes that there is still a fundamental disquiet amongst teachers, parents and politicians who are unhappy with objectivist attempts at moral teaching, whilst equally unhappy with attempts to avoid objectivism which fail to present a satisfactory rationale for their practices. In essence, what is still needed is a reasonable solution to this problem. It is partly because of the lack of such a solution, though probably much more substantially because of perceived economic problems in society, that a third form of morality has presented itself in very recent years.

Table 2.1 *Kohlbergian stages of justice reasoning*

A woman is dying because she is suffering from a very dangerous disease. So far there has been no medicine which can cure it. But now a scientist invents a drug which can cure the disease. However, the scientist wants a great deal of money for the drug. The sick woman's husband, Heinz, tries to raise the money for the drug but can't find enough to pay the scientist. What ought Heinz to do? Why?

Content		Reasoning which focuses on the life issue (Heinz should steal the drug)	Reasoning which focuses on the law issue (Heinz should not steal the drug)	Form
Pre-conventional	Stage 1	because if you kill someone you'll be in jail for a long time and for stealing you aren't punished much.	because if he does he will be caught, locked up, etc.	People see rules as dependent on power and external compulsion.
	Stage 2	if he thinks his wife would help if he were dying	because if you commit a crime you have to go to jail long enough to make up for it; because if you steal you only have to pay back the person.	People see rules as instrumental to reward and satisfaction of needs.
Conventional	Stage 3	because he tried to be decent but now feels he has no choice; or because he would have the best of intentions.	in order to leave a good impression on the community; or so that others won't get the wrong impression.	Rules are seen as ways of obtaining social approval.
	Stage 4	because he is obligated by his marital responsibility, wedding vows, covenant of marriage, etc.	because respect for the law will be destroyed if citizens feel they may break the law any time they disagree with it.	People hold the views that authority knows best, that 'doing one's duty' is most praiseworthy.
Post-conventional	Stage 5	because that is part of the implicit social contract which all human beings have with one another; because responsibility to others is one of the basic principles that life is founded upon, etc.	because if individuals are to live together in society, there must be some common agreement; or because laws represent a necessary structure of social agreement.	Moral rules are seen as there to maintain a social order but on a kind of 'social contract' basis.
	Stage 6			Behaviour is defined by ethical principles chosen in terms of universality, consistency and comprehensiveness – justice being the overriding consideration.

THE GNP CODE

The GNP code has become an increasingly powerful factor in the social and political ethos of both the United Kingdom and the United States. To the extent that examples of the 'self-chosen' code of moral education have not gained a place in the National Curriculum in Great Britain, one can assume that such proposals have not found favour with the DES. This dislike has no doubt been enhanced by the APU's failure to produce any viable means of assessment in this area as it stands at the present time. There are few things more galling to the educational bureaucrat than an area of schooling which is not amenable to simple 'objective' testing. It makes the job of prescribing aims, laying down precise objectives and testing for the correct implementation and attainment of such objectives that much harder.

It must therefore be a distinct possibility that the area will die off in the taught curriculum through (planned?) neglect, and a GNP code of morality will enter schools through the back door of school management techniques, assessment of value-for-money practices and official approval of what is regarded as 'important' – in other words, a linkage between morality and schooling via the hidden curriculum. What, then, are the essential features of this GNP code?

Perhaps the most important is that it is a politico-economic code in a much more strident way than either of the previous two. The ruler and ruled code is undoubtedly politico-economic in nature, but also has within it elements of monopoly by one ruling group with a certain amount of consensus by those ruled, undergirded by a particular version of the Christian religion. The self-chosen code is essentially social in nature with political leanings: it verges at times towards the anarchistic in its belief in people 'doing their own thing'. The GNP code, then, is much closer to the former, but has some extra features as well.

One is that in many respects it is non-party and non-class based in character. It was, after all, the Labour party which first urged such a code upon schools by setting up the APU in 1974, and with Callaghan's Ruskin College speech in 1976. Shirley Williams' Green Paper of the following year hinted at changes which are now much more tangible: a national curriculum, national performance testing and teacher appraisal were Labour proposals which were continued by the Conservative party when they returned to office. As in the United States, both parties wanted an increase in centralism and the politicization of education. And underlying this general move have been a number of ideas which explain the widespread acceptance of these policies in political circles, in the media, and in the public's mind as well. These can be asserted in five separate propositions:

The schools' responsibility for economic decline

Britain has been in a state of relative economic decline, which is largely the fault of schools and particularly teachers for not providing pupils with the kinds of skills which will make Britain a world leader once again. This being the case, it is high time that central government became actively involved in what is going on in schools and had a considerable say in it. A hierarchy of control is needed, with teachers being at the bottom of this hierarchy. As Lawton (1980: 12) has pointed out, the dominant metaphor has changed from 'partnership' to 'accountability'. A basic premise, then, is that schools are there to adopt, or adapt to, policies formulated else-where. (It is also worth noting that commonplace pronouncements like 'teachers will adapt this to their own circumstances' pass the most difficult part of making it work in practice to teachers, whilst not allowing them any say in the formulation. Also, any failure in the plan can be firmly located with the practitioners – 'they didn't put it into practice properly'.)

The need for a return to the 'basics'

There is a need for a return in schools to the 'basics' of education, for these have been neglected by teachers. These basics must be assessed in clear, objective ways, so that everyone can see what is going on. Methods or subjects which claim not to be amenable to clear objective testing, such as those to do with creativity, conceptual development or values appreciation, are to be treated with suspicion and be down-graded in an educational priority list. As has been noted above, this could well be the interpretation given to events following the APU's failure to produce means of assessment in the areas of personal, social and moral development. The bureaucratic syllogism seems to go like this: 'If it's not a basic it's not worth teaching. Basics are assessable. So anything not assessable is not a basic. Therefore anything not assess-able is not worth teaching.'

Education's role in the economic good of society

The education services of this country are designed primarily for the good of the society, rather than the whims and desires of the individual. Individual choice is fine, as long as it contributes to the good of the country, and by 'good' is meant the economic good. This good is determined by working out the needs of industry and fitting the schools' provision to its requirements. Thus the well-being of the country is essentially measured in terms of its GNP, for an expanding GNP is the foundation of all society's other activities. Much more space can be devoted to means, much less need be devoted to ends. It is then possible to talk more of 'effectiveness' than of 'acceptability'. Inevitably, with a definition derived from economic requirements, there is a restriction on what education means, on the notion of the teacher, and on the concept of the pupil. This will be dealt with in much greater detail in later chapters.

The need for a monolithic morality

There is a need for a simple and understandable morality for society as a whole, one on which all can agree. Individual morality, like individual choice, is fine, but not when it conflicts with the 'good' of society. Too much freedom is not healthy, and there has been too much freedom. Of course, it might be argued here that part of the present shift in political thinking is precisely *away* from monolithic bureaucracy to individual enterprise and choice. After all, are not initiatives like LMS (local management of schools) and greater powers for governing bodies examples of greater individual freedom? However, this is not necessarily in direct contradiction with the overall tone of the GNP code because such individual choice as is favoured is to be exercised within this overall social morality. The 1988 Act, for instance, still leaves room for ultimate DES intervention if LMS is mishandled or governing bodies do not perform up to par. This being the case, there is room for criticism of existing institutions within society, but only where this criticism is 'appropriate' – and appropriateness is determined by what is 'good' for society, which is determined by its economic needs.

The example of the United States

GNP policies owe much to the American experience. Callahan (1962: 246) traces its origin as far back as 1900 in the USA, where:

> educational questions were subordinated to business considerations; administrators were produced who were not, in any true sense, educators; . . . a scientific label was put on some very unscientific and dubious methods and practices; and . . . an anti-intellectual climate . . . was strengthened.

In his examination of the educational reports in the 1980s in the USA, Passow (1984) sees the same concerns as in Great Britain: achievement, raising standards, getting value for money, locating economic problems in educational provision, getting back to the basics and dispensing with the frills, making education more accountable.

THE EFFECTS OF THE GNP CODE

This GNP code, then, has been strengthened over the past fifteen years by Government policies. Whilst the preceding morality had been one essentially of freedom of moral expression, restriction on economic manoeuvre and concern for those seen as underprivileged, the GNP morality has instead stressed conformity of moral expression, freedom of economic manoeuvre and concern for the opportunity to profit from one's endeavours. This change in public morality has had both beneficial and deleterious effects. These may be summarized as follows.

Firstly, there tends to be an attitude – in those who have succeeded either economically or politically – of 'if I can do it, so can you'. On the benefit side, there may well have been in the past an overprotection of the individual, possibly leading some to lose self-respect and to lack the effort to better themselves, and a growing attitude of 'learned helplessness' which allowed the state to look after people's welfare. The growth of current attitudes and legislation has helped to dispel this. The trend in recent years has undoubtedly been a belief in the morality of standing on one's own feet, but this has at times been accompanied by a lack of appreciation that some are more able to stand on their own feet than others. This philosophy has to some extent informed attitudes to ethical issues which then locate the problem as being the fault of the sufferer. Examples might be: drugs – it's their own fault for getting hooked; AIDS – it's their own fault for being promiscuous; poverty – it's their own fault for letting themselves get into that condition. By a concentration on individual success and fulfilment in a competitive environment, there is the possible downgrading of co-operative efforts, and a consequent lack of empathic understanding of others' difficulties.

Secondly, the concern to improve the ability to profit from one's endeavours has the beneficial effect of making people more involved and more satisfied in their jobs. But it can also have a deleterious effect in that this profit is normally made at the expense of others, both at an individual level and at the level of the community. Indeed, this philosophy, if taken to its extreme, makes it unfashionable to think in terms of 'is this good for the community as a whole?' or even to accept that the notion of 'community' is a valid one. The sole criterion for action becomes 'do I profit from it?'. This may produce greater productivity in the short run, but is likely to have divisive consequences for society in the long run.

Thirdly, if 'official' attitudes are seen as supporting the growth of competition and the respectability of winning at the expense of somebody else losing, then this will undoubtedly be transferred (is being transferred) into the school situation, by means of more overt means of assessment of pupils and schools. A 'good' school in Britain is then defined in terms of how many children pass the tests at 7, 11 and 14 and how many GCSEs it gains each year, regardless of the social ethos within the school. Such competition is fine for the successes, but is disastrous for those schools which are more clearly labelled as failures, and for the pupils within them. (For a classic description of the corrosive effect of failure on self-esteem, identity and academic achievement, see Hargreaves, 1967.)

Lastly, and relatedly, where the concepts of education, teacher and child are limited to models based on economic productivity, this can do little for the teacher's or the child's self-concept. Inevitably they must feel themselves being reduced in terms of how others – politically more powerful others – value them. The worth of the teacher or the child is assessed in terms of effectiveness once again – how effective is the teacher at turning out the required product, how effective is the child at becoming what society wants him or her to become. And this effectiveness is inseparable from the manipulation of human beings into compliant forms of behaviour.

FOCUSES OF CONCERN

The conclusions are far reaching and disturbing. History is unlikely to repeat itself. An objectivist, monolithic morality like the ruler and ruled code is unlikely to take hold in this country again in quite the manner it did before, nor would this be desirable. It is also unlikely that a self-chosen morality will be given its head in schools again, because of the failure to provide an adequate rationale for it. Recent legislation – particularly the 1988 Education Reform Act – suggests that teachers will never again have the same degree of autonomy and control over what goes into the school curriculum. Finally, the effects and implications of a GNP code are clearly working their way into schools. With this kind of background, it is undoubtedly the case that a consensual morality is needed, but one which focuses on specific strategies for remediation of problems within society, and which promotes the moral and social health of its participants.

This survey of previous approaches to the teaching of morality in schools suggests to the present writer that there are four major areas which need the school's, and society's, urgent attention. These are described in the following sections.

The fostering of the child's self-esteem

It is being suggested that an essential prerequisite of the moral development of the pupil is that he or she should feel sufficiently secure, loved and trusted to be able to reach out and help others. One of the most worrying consequences of the GNP code is that because of the competitive ethos of this code, there will be many losers, both in terms of academic results and on the job market. Self-esteem is an essential quality which affects how individuals see and treat not only themselves, but also each other. In terms of self-perception, if individuals perceive that society does not care about them or their future prospects, they are unlikely to view themselves or that society with any great regard. In terms of treatment of other people, there is now a substantial body of psychological evidence (see for example, Murphy, 1937, Staub and Sherk, 1970 and Hoffman, 1976) which suggests that the child who feels insecure, who is not loved, is usually the last to help someone else. It is precisely those who are secure, who do feel loved and trusted, who make the prosocial moves. If this is the case, then it is vital that right from the beginning of the school career and throughout it as they go through successive crises of growth, identity and adjustment, the school gives children support, comfort and security. The teacher's and school's act of producing a caring and supportive environment is part of their moral duty to their charges; to enable children to develop socially and morally towards others. The fostering of children's self-esteem is a crucial element in the development of the moral being.

The heightening of the child's empathy

If one of the less pleasant effects of the GNP code is a concentration upon one's personal advancement, an almost egocentric preoccupation with self, then it is important that the school should seek to reduce this effect by providing children with opportunities for understanding that others may not have their point of view, may not have their abilities, may not have had their start in life. There is an American Indian saying which states that until one has had the chance to walk in another's moccasins, one should never judge that person. Cognitively understanding an action is sufficient neither to fully comprehend why it is performed nor to want to understand why it was performed. Empathy is the vital ingredient which not only provides for reflective understanding and tolerance, but also acts as the mainspring to action. When one knows and feels a situation, then both the cognitive understanding and the motivation to do something about it are present. It is, therefore, only by providing children with such opportunities that qualities like tolerance and the appreciation of others' difficulties and suffering can be gained, and incorporated into a total perception of the world. Without them, society is that much less humane and caring.

The furthering of co-operation between children

If the GNP code promotes competition between students, then the school must be extremely wary of its effects. For instance, students must view others as fellow competitors, and so probably with a certain amount of suspicion and hostility. The chance of viewing fellow students as others to befriend, or as people who might contribute and improve their own learning opportunities, is severely curtailed. The result is likely to be one which runs counter to the aims of a society based on trust, understanding and helpfulness.

Yet this does not have to be the case. Higher academic results do not need to be pursued to the detriment of finer social feeling within the classroom situation. Co-operation between pupils can not only lead to generally better than average academic performance, but it has significant beneficial effects on the ways in which pupils see each other, how they get on in class, and how they perceive themselves (see Aronson *et al.*, 1978). Beyond the school, a strong case can and has been made for believing that the nature of sport – whether competitive or non-competitive – has causal connections with the aggressiveness of society. Specifically, the more competitive a society's sports, the more violence and aggression one is likely to see within that society (see Orlick, 1978). Far from aggression through competition acting as a cathartic release for members of that society, it instead appears to act as a model of desirable behaviour. One might ask oneself, if the primary mechanisms of learning are through reward, punishment and modelling, what kinds of behaviour are rewarded, punished and modelled in competitive situations? Will bettering others not be rewarded, co-operation punished and actions whose principal aim is to win modelled? Team games may to some extent alleviate this condition and encourage co-operation between individuals within a group, but the ultimate aim is the same. Co-operation is only a second-order virtue; competition is the first-order virtue. In such circumstances, the furtherance of co-operation between children as a first-order virtue appears to be an urgent task of teacher and school.

The promotion of rationality

Rationality is needed in at least three related ways. Firstly, it is vital in complex areas of judgement where one must, for example, balance the effects of actions in the short term against their long-term consequences. Further, it is needed in the imaginative understanding of the distress not only of individuals, but also of groups and races. In both cases the limitations of empathy are most apparent, and the necessary blending of the two is very important. Israely (1985) reports examples of educationally subnormal children who try to help other children. Their feelings for the distress of other children are at least on a par with the feelings of 'normal' children, but, significantly, their execution of such help begins to falter with more cognitively complex situations, particularly those where they need to understand the feelings of others. In such situations, the spirit may be willing, but the understanding is weak. A high degree of sophisticated rationality is essential.

Secondly, rationality is needed not only where comprehension of factual materials relevant to ethical situations is demanded, and where the ability to follow and retain complex argument is essential. It is also needed where the ability to comprehend and deal with issues that are not easily resolvable is called for. This may include issues of principle which on their own might have our support, but which placed in proximity to another within a specific situation may lead us to the conclusion that both are worthy principles, though we cannot hold both at the same time. In Kohlberg's classic 'Heinz' dilemma (see Table 2.1), does one support the chemist's right to make a profit from his own endeavours and his own property or Heinz's desire to preserve his wife's life? When a man is contemplating suicide, does one respect his right to take his own life or argue that his wife and children have a greater claim to his continuing his life, both emotionally and economically? Where one sees a friend stealing company property, does one adhere to the principle of friendship and not report her or to the principle of honesty, report her, and get her the sack? In such dilemmas, the correct course of action may not be immediately apparent, but one thing is clear: they will be better resolved where the individual is capable of taking all the relevant factors into account and weighing them in the balance. The use of rationality does not guarantee a solution, but it provides a much better chance than tossing a coin or taking someone else's advice simply because they say so.

This chapter, then, has presented an overview of previous attempts at linkage between morality and the school, and has made its own suggestions as to what should constitute focuses of attention for the foreseeable future. To repeat, these have been:

(a) the fostering of the child's self-esteem
(b) the heightening of the child's empathy
(c) the furthering of co-operation between children
(d) the promotion of rationality.

However, the prescription of these four focuses needs firmer backing. The previous theories were criticized in the light of objectivist/relativist problems of justification. Briefly put, the ruler and ruled code suffered from the problems of justification of an absolutist objectivist standpoint; the self-chosen code exhibited attempts to avoid this problem; whilst the GNP code appears to fail to recognize the problems at all. Any code, it is being argued, must deal with this most important of ethical questions – on what basis can one assert that a particular code should be adopted by all within a particular society? The four focuses have not, so far, been justified in this kind of context. What is needed, then, is a rationale for a fully fledged approach which does not make the kinds of objectivist claims of the past, but which does not fall into a relativist position either, and which rises above the GNP code just described. The task of the next chapter, then, is twofold. Firstly, the problems posed by relativist arguments must be faced once more and shown to be not only dangerous in terms of their practical implementation – essentially what was said in criticism of the values clarification approach – but also ill-founded at the philosophical level. Secondly, a proposal will be made for a relationship between morality and schooling which avoids the problems of both objectivism and relativism.

Chapter 3

Towards a Trans-Social Code

Chapter 2 ended with the question of whether it is possible to arrive at a position between objectivism and relativism with regard to ethics and morality. It is necessary to arrive at such a position because the type of relationship between morality and schooling ultimately adopted needs justification. As was seen in Chapter 2, objectivism in its more absolute forms has generally been discredited in this country. But the other horn of the dilemma, relativism, has its own problems. Adoption of relativism is, I would argue, as unpalatable as the kinds of objectivism previously adopted. It does *not* necessarily lead to an attitude of tolerance to others by those following different ethical codes. If ethical relativism is defined as the doctrine that there is no rational way of deciding between different moral judgements, then it is more than likely that holders of such a doctrine will not even try to understand other beliefs, for they have already accepted that they have no rational means of doing so.

Relativism, it is being suggested, is no more helpful than objectivism in finding a viable role for morality in the school. But there are many who, disliking the idea of it, feel compelled to adopt it because of the evident moral diversity. It is undoubtedly the case that throughout history, and within different societies at the present time, there are numerous moral codes, all claiming to be the correct way for people within society to behave towards one another, the natural world and themselves. Is it possible to counter this evidence?

Before doing so, it is necessary to attend to meanings again. As has just been argued relativism can be taken to mean:

(a) that there is no rational way of deciding between different moral judgements. It is argued, for example, that there are no criteria outside the society in which one lives by which one may judge the rights or wrongs of infanticide. We may think it wrong, but to an Eskimo it might have been quite allowable 50 years ago.

However, it can also be taken to mean something very different, namely:

(b) that in estimating the quality of an act, one must take the circumstances surrounding the act into consideration. On this argument, the Eskimo might agree that infanticide *per se* is wrong, but that it is condonable because of specific circumstances within the Eskimo community, such as lack of food: by allowing the weakest to live and consume food, all may die.

The first of these two meanings is undoubtedly the stronger. Indeed the second may be taken and used *against* the first. Thus the fact that there is a diversity of moral practices around the world is not seen as implying that there is no way of deciding between them. Circumstances alter cases, and were circumstances in all cases equal, then a judgement of the relevant acts *would* be possible.

It is important to note the distinction in meanings because an acceptance of the second meaning – which many people would agree to – does not entail acceptance of the first. Indeed acceptance of the second could be used to suggest that there *are* certain fundamental human values common to all societies. So it is essentially against the acceptance of the first definition of relativism – that there are no criteria by which one may judge different moral practices – that we are concerned to argue here.

To decide between these definitions, we can ask what the variations in moral practices are due to. Can they be explained purely in terms of circumstances, or is there something deeper? Ginsberg (1968) suggests six reasons for variations in moral practices between societies.

(a)   There are variations in moral practice because there are cultural and historical variations in what is known about a particular area of knowledge, which then have implications for our moral judgment. For example, new scientific knowledge can drastically alter our understanding of the nature of an action, and in so doing change our view as to the morality of that action. An example might be the way in which an understanding of personality disorders has prevented the classification of some women as witches and having them burnt alive.

This clearly belongs to the weaker of the two definitions; it is possible to conceive of different societies having different moral rules and standards because of their differing degrees of understanding of the factual area surrounding the issues, these two societies essentially having the same moral outlook. If their understanding of such issues was comparable, it is quite legitimate to believe that their moral outlook would be essentially the same as well.

(b)   There are variations in moral practice because different environments necessitate different emphases on rules and customs. An example might be the killing of old people – necessary in some American Indian cultures, but increasingly dispensed with as material circumstances changed.

Again, this undoubtedly belongs to the weaker of the two definitions – it is quite possible to hold that different societies because of different pressures hold different standards, yet were those pressures similar, the standards would be similar as well.

(c)   There are variations in moral practice because societies differ in their belief in which second-order virtues are necessary for the achievement of primary needs. For example, one society may believe that monogamy (a second-order virtue in this case) is necessary for the protection and care of the young (a primary virtue).

Two things can be said here. Firstly, whilst one society may believe in monogamy and another in polygamy, this does not prevent each seeing the other work in practice and changing its beliefs if so desired. But more importantly, both societies share the same primary value – more important than the secondary – the protection of the young. This is, then, not a good argument for the strong version of relativism.

(d)   There are variations in the range of persons to whom moral rules are held to be applicable. Aristotle, for instance, could not conceive that free men and slaves might have a common nature, just as western society is only just coming to grips with the belief that black people or white women might have a political and economic equality with white men.

At first glance, this seems a better argument for the hard form of relativism, for it cannot be denied that a person may not understand why a principle is being applied to a particular class of people. This, then, is difficult to square with the notion of universality. And yet it may still be possible. The factors and circumstances surrounding a person's value stance may so affect his or her perception of reality that, given a different set of circumstances, he or she may come to hold very different views. Hard relativism, then, is not proven.

(e)   There are variations in moral practice due to differences in emphasis or balance of the different elements in moral life – one person or society can hold a virtue to be paramount, whilst to another it is considered virtually worthless.

Ginsberg (1968: 247) gives the example: '*Above all things*, my brethren, swear not' (emphasis original). Ginsberg points out that some differences in emphasis are easily explained – circumstances may change so that what was necessary at one time becomes not so. But how is one to explain the injunction to swear not *above all things*? It is difficult to imagine a set of circumstances where this is regarded as a matter of life and death. Perhaps, though, this is not an argument for hard relativism, but an inability on our part to appreciate just how situations and circumstances can change one's view and perspective of reality. If that perspective consisted of a central belief in one's ancestors living in another world with an ability to come back and punish, and a further belief that the taking of their name in vain was rather like robbing them of their identity, then we may begin to understand how the injunction 'swear not' could attain such primacy.

(f)   Variations in moral practice are due to differences of insight and general level of development, intellectual and moral.

This does not seem to be too strong an argument. New knowledge or circumstance can generate at least two different changes. Firstly, it may well force one to look at old problems anew – that of personality disorder quoted above may be a good example of a situation where new knowledge changes one's conception of 'madness', 'witchcraft', etc. Or, secondly, it may force one to deal with entirely new ethical problems – the ethical problems generated by *in vitro* fertilization, for instance. Should a daughter be allowed to donate ova to her mother, so that the mother becomes both mother and grandmother at the same time, the daughter both mother and sister at the same time? These issues could not even have been raised 30 years ago, but this does not indicate ethical relativism in the hard sense, for it is again quite legitimate to argue that those societies who have not encountered these problems yet may, given that circumstances are similar, come to similar ethical conclusions and actions.

   The conclusion must be rather similar to that arrived by Ginsberg himself (1968: 249):

amidst variations moral codes everywhere exhibit striking similarities in essentials. There are no societies without rules of conduct backed by the general approval of the members. There are none which do not regard that which contributes to the needs and survival of the group as good, none which do not condemn conduct interfering with the satisfaction of common needs and threatening the stability of social relations.

If this is the case, and the hard version of relativism does not have to be accepted, then there is some reason for believing that there may be certain core values to which all societies would assent. At the same time, one can ask whether one needs to accept an absolutist objectivist stance to argue that there are certain basic features of human social life which are the *sine qua non* of people continuing to live together in a fair, stable, happy and strong society, where people do not resort to violence to get their own way and settle their differences. Are there, in other words, certain basic moral principles to which all might agree to submit? This might sound at first very much like objectivism, but the following discussion should show that this does not have to be the case.

Consider the following list of eight principles, which are extracted from C. S. Lewis' (1947) examination of the ethical systems of the major historical and current civilizations. Could these, or variations upon them, be counted as universal?

(a)   Treat others as you would wish to be treated yourself.
(b)   Have special concern for those close to you.
(c)   Respect your elders.
(d)   Be responsible for the youth of society.
(e)   Do not take from another what is his.
(f)   Do not lie.
(g)   Help those weaker or less fortunate than yourself.
(h)   Be prepared to stand up and fight for your rights and beliefs.

Some immediate objections may be raised. They might be:

(a)   What if they don't like the same things as me?
(b)   What is moral about this injunction?
(c)   What if they're unpleasant, and not worthy of respect?
(d)   How can you care for a whole section of society?
(e)   Can't you take a loaf of bread if your child is starving to death?
(f)   Do you tell the Nazi where the Jew is when he asks?
(g)   What good does it do me?
(h)   Isn't life more important than a set of beliefs?

The present writer would argue that answers can be given to these objections, and this is where the four focuses of attention described in Chapter 2 may be of great help. Consider them again. They were:

the fostering of the child's self-esteem
the heightening of the child's empathy
the furthering of co-operation between children
the promotion of rationality.

If one looks at the eight principles described by C. S. Lewis, it could be argued that it is precisely *through* the implementation of these four focuses of attention that the attainment of these eight principles is likely to be achieved. The fostering of self-esteem is a central feature of any principle which prescribes care as a virtue. The heightening of empathy is a central feature of any principle which desires an accurate translation of the feeling of care into the practice of care. The furthering of co-operation is a central feature of any principle which has as its ultimate aim the creation of a civilization in which human beings are to live together without tearing out each other's throats. The promotion of rationality is a central feature of any principle which believes in solving problems by talking about them rather than fighting, which subscribes to notions of justice and truth, which accepts that the practicalities of situations demand common sense.

Specifically, let us look at the criticisms of these principles, and see where these four focuses of attention play a part.

(a)   'Treat others as you would like to be treated' is a sub-clause of the general principle 'try to be fair and just' – and the best rule of thumb is to start from how you personally would feel. It does not limit, but rather provides a starting point for working out what is best for other people. It suggests that rationality should be used, but should be broadened by empathy.

(b)   'Have special concern for those around you' is a practical injunction rather than a moral principle *per se*. It is suggesting that by practice one comes to understand, and from this practice and understanding one can then extend concern to strangers and non-humans. Again one has a rational principle, which suggests that empathy is learned through personal experience, and can then be used to widen the circle of concern.

(c)   'Respect your elders' is many-faceted rather than simply prescriptive. It does *not* have to mean unthinking obedience which is dependent on age. It assumes that elders have already performed their responsibilities towards the youth of society. It urges care of those less strong, compassion for those with failing powers, but also patience with those who may be wise with age, but have difficulty expressing the wisdom of experience. It urges the young to be patient. It might also suggest that one day they will be old too. It is therefore a rational principle which prescribes co-operation between members of a society. It suggests empathy for those who have a different life situation from oneself, and it prescribes the boosting of the self-esteem of one's elders.

(d)   'Be responsible for those younger' does not urge one to go out and care for all the youth of society. But it points out that society is an interdependent organism where, for one to be truly happy, the other members must be as well. If the youth of society are not brought up to understand and respect its rules and regulations, what will happen to society and its other members? All must have a responsibility in this. It is therefore a rational principle, again prescribing the co-operative society and the boosting of self-esteem.

(e)   'Do not take from another what is his' is not a blanket prescription, which must be followed blindly. It can allow that there may be debate over whether something actually belongs to another; it can allow that another principle may take precedence in certain circumstances. The right to life is an obvious one. This is where education towards judgement of a situation comes into play, where the child must be educated to autonomy. But it can still stand as a central principle, for in effect it says that if there are no special circumstances, then it will stand. This is very different from saying, as values clarification would, that one can choose whether to steal or not. Stealing is wrong as a moral principle, but there may be circumstances where the principle must be waived. This principle then bases itself upon the concept of rationality, and suggests elements in society of co-operation and empathy.

(e) 'Do not lie' may be dealt with in the same way. There may be situations where lying is an acceptable form of behaviour – to save someone's life, perhaps. But this is not to say that lying is a matter of choice. It can be intrinsically wrong, but still be condoned if circumstances necessitate its use. The judgement of the necessity of the circumstances can be viewed as part of the educative process, and part of the rational process.

(f) 'Help those weaker or less fortunate than yourself' is a practical injunction in that it reminds one that weakness and good fortune are relative to person, time and circumstance, and that theirs may be one's own fate soon. It is also a practical injunction in that it foresees the envy, jealousy and divisiveness of a society that does not have this as a central principle. It is a logical and moral point in the sense that, like Rawls' 'original position' (1971: 17–22), it argues that a just society is one based on the status of the member in the worst position. This principle therefore contains all four focuses of attention. It is a rational practical injunction. It urges understanding through empathic awareness. It prescribes the boosting of the self-esteem of those weaker or less fortunate. It sees society as a co-operative venture between both weak and strong.

(g) 'Be prepared to stand up and fight for your rights and beliefs' is, again, a practical injunction. It recognizes that human beings are not angels, and not all members of society will be persuaded by the logic or the morality of principles. Similarly, it recognizes that not all other societies need have adopted these principles, and others may utilize principles of force, terror or aggrandizement as their motivating principles. In these cases, it is imperative for the 'moral society' to be prepared to fight for its existence, for its principles. Ultimately, it benefits all the members within that society. It therefore can be considered a rational principle which urges a co-operative view of society from its members.

One further and general criticism of these eight injunctions, or any injunctions drawn from other societies' practices, is that this is nothing more than a rather blatant commission of the naturalistic fallacy – that one cannot move from the description of what has happened or is happening to be the case to the assertion that this *ought* to be the case. It provides no moral argument as such. The answer to this must be that only an inductive and conditional argument is being offered. It is only being suggested that *if* one wishes for the kind of society which promotes stability, happiness, fairness, justice and strength, then past history suggests that these injunctions should be adopted. If however one wishes for an unstable, unhappy, unfair, unjust or weak society, then one may certainly adopt other injunctions. And if it is further argued that the eight principles proposed are *not* the ones to produce the kind of society desired, then anybody is perfectly at liberty to suggest another list. This chapter certainly proposes this list, but perhaps more importantly gives a procedure for determining the kinds of principles which are to be claimed as fundamental. They at the very least get one started.

The list does, however, have one major drawback. The principles are expressed at such a level of generality that they have the good fortune to be strongly supportable but also, and because of this generality, they are very limited as practical injunctions.

In like manner, it might be argued that even the four focuses of attention are hampered in this respect – that there may be occasions when they come into conflict with one another, and that there is no clear resolution of their priority. The translation into practice involves circumstances and situations, and when this happens, principles become entangled with people and their subjectivities.

What is needed then is the joint recognition of fundamental moral principles and the necessity of their subjective implementation. This, it would seem, has to be at the core of an adequate understanding of the nature of moral theory and practice in school. We have looked at objective absolutism, and decided that whilst such a stand is untenable, there is some truth in the idea that there are fundamental principles which a consensual society can adopt. Now it is time to look at the other side of the equation. We have looked at hard relativism, and seen that whilst that stand is equally untenable, there is truth in the idea that credence must be given to the individual situation and circumstance. This being the case, it is time to describe the translation from the fundamental to the subjective.

If such a position can be reached, three major benefits will be derived. Firstly, an adequate philosophical underpinning will be provided for teachers which will allow them to define and defend a practical approach to morality in the school. Secondly, and following directly from this, there is much less chance of teachers being bulldozed into accepting standards of evaluation and assessment which are antithetical to their own approach. The politician and bureaucrat tend to prefer the more 'objective' forms of evaluation. If the viability of limited objectivity can be sustained, teachers are in a much better position either to argue for more appropriate models of evaluation or to devise their own. And lastly, it will be seen that these problems – of objectivity, evaluation and accountability – have direct bearing on all other areas of the curriculum, and can be justifiably taken on board by areas of the school other than the moral. This, then, is the subject of Chapter 4.

Chapter 4

Objectivity and Tolerance

So far it has been argued that there are objective moral principles but that these are only objective in the sense that they can be adopted if one desires a particular kind of society. The problem remains, however, that the level of generality of these principles prevents their use in any real setting. One must take into account the particular circumstances surrounding an event, as well as the subjective element in human dealings, if one is to arrive at a correct understanding of their application. Indeed, it will be argued, it is precisely this understanding of individual circumstances and human subjectivity which will help the formulation of a viable relationship between morality and schooling, for it is the appreciation of individual circumstances and subjectivity which children need to understand and deal with.

This being the case, it is necessary to do two things. The first is to go back to first principles, and ask what is meant by the terms 'objectivity' and 'subjectivity'. If it can be shown that there are several levels of meaning in these terms; this will add considerably to an understanding of the complexity of the process of arriving at moral decisions. The second is to trace in some detail the kinds of circumstances which affect moral judgements, particularly interrelationships between facts and values, and show how these complexities must produce a degree of subjectivity in value judgements. Both of these actions should, then, suggest a need for care and tolerance in dealing with moral matters.

Now it seems possible to discern at least six different levels at which the term 'objectivity' is normally used, and therefore corresponding uses of 'subjectivity'. They are:

(a) 'ideal' objectivity
(b) 'logical' objectivity
(c) 'categorial' objectivity
(d) 'trans-social' objectivity
(e) 'social' objectivity
(f) 'personal' objectivity.

A little time must be spent in describing them.

'Ideal' objectivity

This is the objectivity accessible to an omniscient being alone; the total perception, knowledge and understanding of all things past, present and future. This is a level of objectivity above that of morality as defined in this book, for the definition has been essentially practical, as conducive to the good of society and those living within it. Thus, with ideal objectivity, *all* human experience is necessarily less than objective. However, the aspiration to this level is part of human nature in a broadly religious sense, and thus has a worthwhile place on the curriculum. It will be apparent that here I am separating the moral from the religious, though in a later chapter I shall attempt to show that there is a close connection between them.

'Logical' objectivity

This is the objectivity derived from the use of concepts as indispensable to intelligibility as the law of identity, of non-contradiction and of deduction; their contradiction would leave communication and understanding an impossibility. As Pring (1972: 27) points out, where basic canons of rationality are treated as 'problematic' and 'open to enquiry', it is not possible to understand of what such an enquiry might consist. Therefore the teacher, or any thinking individual for that matter, cannot remain neutral about its application. Where individuals or cultures suggest that their approach can be both non-rational and as tolerable as any other, then one must argue that this is not permissible. Neutrality by the teacher, as shall be seen, is both possible and desirable at lower levels of objectivity, but at this level it is not open to negotiation if intelligibility is to be retained. The teacher simply cannot let his or her pupils choose to be rational or non-rational. Rationality is the key part of the structure in which any recognizable form of teaching must be grounded.

'Categorial' objectivity

This is the level of objectivity founded upon those categories which structure and sustain human experience. In asserting that there is this level, one is saying that it transcends the level of culture, that certain features of human experience are embodied within all cultures and ways of life which could not be different because of their uniquely human way of doing things. At least four different sorts of categories have been asserted. These may be described as:

(a) mental categories – those concepts seemingly essential to any human being's conception of what it means to function as a human being, such as motives, thoughts and intentions
(b) perceptual categories – those concepts created by having the senses with which human beings are endowed – sight, hearing, touch, smell, and taste
(c) moral categories – those concepts created by the manner in which human beings in any society must treat one another. They may include such things as non-infliction of pain, telling the truth, equality, fairness and keeping promises
(d) knowledge categories – there are certain forms of knowing which are fundamen-

tal ways of describing human experiences, and all school curricula must therefore be divided into such categories. Hirst's (1974) 'Forms of Knowledge' is a
recent and powerful example.

Clearly, all four of these are structures of human experience. They are almost
certainly not mirror images of the 'ideal' objectivity mentioned above, nor even
adumbrations, but extractions suited to the human purpose.

Further, they do not appear to produce quite the kind of unintelligibility which
would occur were one to try and deny the law of identity or non-contradiction. One
may find it hard to imagine a person who lacks motives, or one who lacks the notion
of certain perceptual categories, or one to whom notions of equality and fairness are
simply not applicable, or one who divides his or her knowledge forms differently,
but there does not seem to be any *logical* reason why such people should not exist.
What would happen if this did occur is that we would have to radically alter our
concept of what a person was in order to accommodate this change.

For instance, the mental categories may at first look unassailable, until one realizes
that very young children may make some sort of sense of the world without their
use. There is evidence to support the idea that the concept of purposes and intentions
is foreign to many three-year-olds (see Lickona, 1976). There seems no logical reason
why a tribe of people should not be discovered tomorrow who make much more
limited use of them than we do. At the same time, our present conception of what
makes up the mental workings of human beings would have to be radically revised.
This, however, would be an empirical, not a logical revision.

Similarly, the perceptual categories are not all-inclusive, but rather a selection
tailor-made for a creature called a human being. To the extent that we cannot bounce
sound like a bat, sense dampness like a woodlouse, detect ultraviolet light like a bee
and have no heat-seeking sensors like a rattlesnake, we are deficient in our perceptual
categories. It is possible, admittedly, to develop instruments to compensate for these
deficiencies, but having only come to know of these deficiencies in the last couple of
hundred years, there is no reason to believe that all forms have been detected in this
scientific epoch. It follows that there must be much of the external world which we
cannot detect, and of which we cannot be aware.

The status of the moral categories has been the concern of much of Chapter 3. It
has been argued that there are virtually no moral qualities which could be described
as being essential to the definition of humanity. They function as vehicles for the
kind of society in which one wants to live. In this sense, moral criteria are relative
to cultures, but the adoption of some are necessary for certain kinds of cultures. In
this sense only can they be described as universal. Having said this, it would be hard
to imagine a society functioning in which the concept of truth-telling was totally
absent, but this category in some ways lies nearer to logical objectivity than to
anything else. After all, the concept of truth embodies the principles of identity and
non-contradiction rolled into one. It might also be argued that keeping promises is
an essential feature of humanity. Could a society function in which promise-keeping
was absent? Probably not, but it does not have to be adopted as a central moral
principle. It is possible to conceive of a society in which its members existed by
pursuing a course of cheating and breaking promises, in which to break a promise
and get away with it was seen as a mark of distinction. This being the case, whilst
the concept might be universal, the practice of it need not. In the same vein, other

candidates to this list might be the treating of all as equals, or the treating of people as ends in themselves, or the principles of fairness and justice, but Nazi Germany, Stalinist Russia and apartheid South Africa all testify to lack of need in practice.

Finally, this is not the place to go into a detailed criticism of Hirst's forms of knowledge. Suffice it to say that there is a voluminous literature on the subject which denies the inclusion of the forms of knowledge at the categorial level (see, for example, Adelstein, 1972, Pring, 1976 and Brent, 1978).

'Trans-social' objectivity

Apart from the concept of truth, then, there do not appear to be any moral concepts which are essential to a conception of humanity. Having said that, it has already been argued at some length that there are a number which are 'trans-social', in the sense that if one wishes for a particular form of society, then these particular values must be adopted and made central. They therefore transcend particular societies and cultures.

How does one differentiate between the trans-social and the purely cultural? The answer must be in terms of the consequences for that society. To take an example, were all members of a particular society to cease to exchange rings as part of a marriage ceremony, the consequences for that society would be nothing more than a little inconvenience whilst alternative forms of ceremony were used. If, however, a trans-social principle, like one of the eight listed on p. 36, were no longer practised, the consequences for that society would be nothing short of disastrous for its overall health.

It has to be admitted that there may be occasions when it is not clear where the demarcation line lies between the trans-social and the social. Where this demarcation line is unclear, so will be the teacher's recognition of his or her duty to present issues in a neutral manner, whilst undergirding the discussion with reference to the non-neutrality of a trans-social framework. Where, however, the concept is likely to be culture bound, or 'socially' objective, as it will be shortly termed, then the teacher must be much more careful, for one is out of the universalizable as such and into that area where the universalizable and social entwine. The trick comes in knowing which is which. 'Objective' moral principles in the sense listed above may be easily identified but their translation into social practice is made more difficult by the possible conflict with other principles, and also by the conjoining of these principles with purely relative social customs. The separation into different categories, for many practical examples of beliefs, can be extremely problematical.

One further and very important point must be mentioned. If even trans-social moral principles are chosen, why cannot they be presented as choice to children in schools? The answer is that, logically, they must, but with two caveats. The first is that choice can only be presented when a choice is understood. It would be meaningless to present choice on these matters to a toddler. So the time for presentation of this choice must be a matter of professional judgement. Secondly, and when this time is reached, the child's developing autonomy must be respected, but this does *not* mean that the teacher has to present these principles in a neutral manner. The argument must be that if the child desires to live in a society which is unjust, uncaring and unstable, then he or she does not have to adopt such principles. And he or she will be treated in an unjust and uncaring manner. The argument, I would suggest, is an open and shut one. Clear trans-social principles can act as criteria for the judgement of practices and beliefs of lower levels.

'Social' objectivity

This is the objectivity derived from a group consensus on what counts as real or important. It is more objective than individual opinion, as it attempts to arrive at a standard to which more than one person can agree. However, it is obviously consider-ably more subjective than 'ideal', 'logical', 'categorial' or 'trans-social' objectivity. In the moral sphere, it means purely relative cultural practices. In dealing with purely cultural matters, assuming that one of the aims of the teacher is to eventually enable children to form their own judgements, then the entry of a neutral position on such matters becomes a moral necessity. With the involvement of higher levels, however, neutrality can be seen as a positive evil. To repeat, the difficulty is to know in a particular instance with which level one is dealing. This issue will be seen to be of crucial importance in Chapter 5 when the status of scientific knowledge is examined.

'Personal' objectivity

When a person is described as being 'objective', something much more limited than one of the five groupings above is meant. It is more along the lines of an open-mindedness by an individual to take note of other points of view which may contradict the one held, and for that person to adjust their own point of view accordingly. It is hardly ever meant that the said individual is capable of approaching an objectivity in any of the other senses mentioned above, for there are all sorts of factors – genetic, sexual, age related, racial, psychological, previous experience – which prevent a more 'objective' point of view.

No doubt some of these factors will also apply at the level of 'social' objectivity, but even within the most homogeneous of groups, because of other personal factors mentioned, they will have their peculiarly personal effects. When it comes down to it, the individual's perception of morality is heavily veiled. To the extent that each of the lower levels is a restructuring of the higher levels, then the individual is permanently faced with looking through layer upon layer of distorting prisms. Figure 4.1 gives an idea of these distorting layers through which one must pass.

But having said this, it must be repeated that this is *not* the same as saying that each individual's moral point of view is equally valid. There *is* categorial objectivity, as there is the realm of trans-social objectivity. Each is a stage up from the subjectivity of the others, and it is possible to use them as criteria by which to evaluate the relative worth of particular moral viewpoints – even if it is not always clear to which particular level of 'objectivity' a particular moral concept or idea belongs.

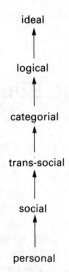

Figure 4.1 Levels of objectivity

So far then, it has been suggested that there are 'objective' moral principles, but that this objectivity is possible at only a certain level: that of trans-social objectivity. There is no principle (except perhaps the principle of truth) which is essentially part of what it is to be human. One could imagine human beings adopting practices totally counter to accepted moral principles without ceasing to be human. However, these moral principles are objective in the sense that they must be adopted if one desires a particular kind of society. At the same time, this 'objectivity' has its reverse side, its subjectivity, and just as important as the realization that there is a criterion by which one can judge practices and beliefs is the appreciation of the fact that one may never be quite sure when such 'objectivity' is reached.

This is the case, not only with the question of values, but also in all other areas of human knowledge. And this subjectivity of human knowledge is not only caused by the kind of 'veiling' factors mentioned above, but also by the interdependence of facts and values. If such interdependency can be shown to be the case, then the involvement of the values dimension in all other areas of the curriculum can be shown to be something more than an interesting sideshow. Rather it must be one of the central aspects and problems of human understanding. The next chapter explores this idea.

Chapter 5

Facts, Values and the Educational Enterprise

In this chapter the dependency of values upon facts and the dependency of facts upon values will be examined. Whilst the former is undoubtedly of great importance for the teacher, it could be argued that the latter is of even greater significance for education, as it suggests that the value dimension is a hitherto neglected but vital part of a full comprehension of the nature of human knowledge.

Thus, the values people practise are derived either from a revelationist approach, usually within a particular religious tradition, or from the adoption of principles which it is believed enable people to live together within a certain kind of society. In the first case it is a belief in the truths of a particular religious tradition which generally determines the principles to be adopted, whilst in the second it is an understanding of the world. However, in both cases, the application of moral values depends to some extent upon the facts of this world, for each individual's perception of the application of these principles will be heavily veiled by the input of the social and personal levels of objectivity. If, as has been argued, an individual's understanding of the world is selective and limited, it follows that the perception of the correct application of these values must be also; in other words, to some extent, their practice will incorporate these varying levels of 'objectivity'.

Now so far all that have been described are conditions affecting the perception of 'facts', which in turn must affect the perception of values. This is gentle, one-way travel between facts and values, about which many may feel uncomfortable, but will probably acknowledge. 'Facts' may not decide the issue alone but a decision without them is nonsensical. One cannot seriously make a reasoned judgement about foetal research, hallal meat or nuclear deterrence without knowing the factual background.

How much more disconcerting though is the proposal that facts may depend upon values, if only because this challenges a popular myth – that there are 'facts' which are solid, permanent and unchangeable. Upon them, it is believed, one can rely. However, it is important to nail this myth if the important part that values education can and must play within education as a whole is to be understood. The world is a considerably more complex and fascinating place than the dogma of solid, reliable facts would have us believe. A dependence upon factual data is not as warranted as many would believe; human society is engaged in a constant modification of its understanding of the relationship between facts and values. In order to justify these claims the relationship will be examined in two main areas of human knowledge: history and science.

HISTORY

To begin with, consider the notion of an historical fact. What, after all, *is* an historical fact? At the level of ideal objectivity or logical objectivity, there is little problem. History could not proceed without the law of identity, the law of non-contradiction and the use of deduction. In terms of categorial objectivity, history must embody those aspects of human existence which define humanity – their mental, perceptual, moral and knowledge categories – but this in itself tells us little. It may give us an overarching logical structure within which to work, but it gives us nothing else. History is a human product, and one must descend at least to the level of trans-social objectivity for the study of history to have any significance.

The problem lies mainly in the demarcation between the categorial, the trans-social, the social and the personal levels of objectivity. To the extent that historians are the product of their time and place – and the 'Whig' historians Macaulay and Trevelyan spring to mind – they are working at the level of social objectivity, and are the less reliable for it. To the extent that historians are aware of their social and personal objectivist limitations, so they strive to reach the trans-social level. To the extent that historians are aware of the prisms which distort their vision, so their subjectivity is the less, and their vision is therefore the more valuable and reliable. So the crucial question to ask is not why historians normally choose the Battle of Hastings rather than Wat Tyler's seventh birthday as an 'historical fact'. They do so because the Battle of Hastings is important within a particular conception of history – because of prior values about what is important. 'Facts' are plucked from obscurity to fame because of their contribution to an overall scheme. But the crucial question to be asked is at what level of objectivity is this overall scheme functioning.

Thus the prior scheme of values determines what facts count as being of significance. As Carr (1982: 23) put it:

> They are like fish swimming about in a vast and sometimes inaccessible ocean; and what the historian catches will depend, partly on chance, but mainly on what part of the ocean he chooses to fish in and what tackle he chooses to use – these two factors being, of course, determined by the kind of fish he wants to catch.

But he might also have added that what the historian catches will depend upon the depth of the ocean in which he chooses to fish – will he choose the more superficial levels of personal and social objectivity, or try for the much trickier depths of trans-social objectivity? He will almost certainly never completely reach them, but he needs to be aware of their existence to even aim for them in the first place.

The question to ask, then, is at what level historians have selected these values. Are they the values of a personalist, prejudiced nature, are they those of a particular culture or time, or have they attempted to transcend this time and place and select at the trans-social level? It is only by reflecting upon the place of values within the interpretative framework which each historian uses that one fully appreciates the value of his or her work.

SCIENCE

And what, then, of those supposed paragons of reason and detachment, the physical sciences? Do not these draw their facts exclusively from the levels of categorial objectivity, and moreover use these levels to falsify and validate them as well? The historian has the problem of always being intimately involved in the selection of data, of never being completely free from the trans-social, the social and the personal levels of objectivity. Cannot the scientist leave these levels completely?

The position at first glance would not seem hopeful. One line of attack on the objectivity of science would be that of Kuhn (1970), which locates its perspective at the level of social objectivity. Kuhn argues that all scientific theories are little more than the consensus of the group of scientists whose perspective holds sway at that time. In support of such a thesis might be quoted the rejection by the scientific community of anything to do with parapsychology. Look, for example, at the attempts described by Collins and Pinch (1979) of parapsychologists to legitimate their experiments in the eyes of the scientific community by adopting methodological procedures sufficiently stringent for them to become 'respectable'. Indeed:

> It seems likely that the best of modern parapsychology comprises some of the most rigorously controlled and methodologically sophisticated work in the sciences.
> (pp. 243–4)

And yet despite these attempts, many orthodox scientists deny their claims, citing grounds for dismissal never adopted by them with 'normal' scientific enquiries. Rejection is based upon prior social values, not facts.

This last example, it might be argued, is a little off the beaten scientific track. Scientists are human, and are naturally suspicious of claims to science from areas which seem to have little in common with 'normal' explanations. This, of course, is precisely how Kuhn (1970, Chapter 3) described the 'normal' scientist and his blinkered attitudes to anything outside his scientific paradigm.

But granting for the moment this objection, the same can hardly be said for the following example, which is to be found at the very heart of the scientific citadel. Miller's findings (see Polanyi, 1958: 9–14) cast grave doubt on the validity of the Michelson-Morley experiments, the supposed stimulus for Einstein's conception of relativity. However, the reaction to Miller's presidential address to the American Physical Society in 1925 has been described thus:

> by that time they had so well closed their minds to any suggestion which threatened the new rationality achieved by Einstein's world-picture, that it was almost impossible for them to think again in different terms. Little attention was paid to the experiments, the evidence being set aside in the hope that it would one day turn out to be wrong.
> (Polanyi, 1958: 13)

So much for the scientist taking note of all the evidence. Miller's material was so uncomfortable that despite the fact that it had all the experience of the Michelson-Morley work, and also the tremendous technical development in the intervening period, it was ignored simply because it did not fit in with the prevailing orthodoxy of the time.

It may, however, be possible to counter the Kuhnian thesis, at least in part, by advancing the following kind of argument used by Popper (1970: 56):

> it simply exaggerates a difficulty into an impossibility. The difficulty of discussion between

people brought up in different frameworks is to be admitted. But nothing is more fruitful than such a discussion . . . a critical comparison of the competing theories of the competing frameworks is always possible.

Popper is pointing to the fact that whilst people may well work, falsify and validate their concepts at the level of social objectivity, they do not need to. It is a moot point, however, whether Popper's argument takes one higher than the trans-social level, for a 'critical comparison of competing theories' could be validated at this level or at higher levels. His basic point, though, is that people may well be restricted for one reason or another to the level of social objectivity, but there is no logical reason, derived from the nature of scientific enquiry, why they should.

Far more corrosive to the notion of scientific objectivity is an approach which concentrates upon asking what would count as a valid method for achieving scientific knowledge. If science is a pursuit which rises above personal and social objectivity, by what standards at the categorial level of objectivity is it validated? Two main methods claiming this will be examined.

The first, induction, argues that the method of science is the accumulation of positive instances and the inferring of theories from such instances. But this will not do as a method of achieving scientific certainty at the level of categorial objectivity, for no number of positive instances can definitely confirm a theory: induction cannot claim the same kind of necessity which the other logical categories such as identity, non-contradiction and deduction claim. It only needs one instance to bring the pack of cards tumbling down. The sun has risen every day since the beginning of recorded time – but it need not tomorrow. Metal bars have always expanded when heated – but there is no logical reason why the next one should. Induction may make good solid practical sense in the everyday world, and be the foundation for the common sense belief in the solidity of scientific 'facts'; but it is no guarantor of certainty. Accepting induction is accepting that science is the province of social and personal objectivity by default.

The second method, the falsificationist approach (see Popper, 1982), at first sight looks a better bet: instead of concentrating upon certain knowledge, it suggests that one concentrates on dispensing with that which is no good. Science, then, is not about positive accumulation and inference, but about falsifiability. False things can be dispensed with. Of them we can be certain.

But then, anomalies do not always falsify theories – there might be something wrong with the initial conditions, there may be factors unknown which, once disco-vered, protect the theory. And if one cannot be sure of positive instances, why be so confident of the negative? They are, after all, different sides of the same coin. The history of science simply does not support the notion that one instance of falsification is enough to throw out a theory – and nor should it. Theories can and do protect themselves – they have protective belts which defend them against awkward instances. (See Lakatos, 1970: 134–8 and the example of continued protection, *ibid.*: 100–101.) The crucial comparison, Lakatos argues, is not between theory and instance, but between theory and theory, the extent to which they are 'progressive' (spur on further research, make predictions which are confirmed, have implications which link in with other theories) or 'degenerative' (result in little research, have few predictions confirmed, fail to link in with other currently successful theories) (*ibid.*: 116–22). To take a current example, is Kohlberg's cognitive-developmental theory a better one than Skinner's behaviourist theory? Here is a comparison between theory and theory, in which judgement will turn on the extent to which they spur on further research. Is a theory of progressive stages of justice reasoning more fertile ground for research than a theory of operant conditioning?

The ugly question which raises its head now, however, is 'when can a theory be discarded?' The answer must be 'almost never'. No matter how ridiculous, seemingly outdated or degenerative a theory may appear, there is always the possibility that some new finding will come along which winds it up and sets it going again. But if this is the case, how much further on are we from individual judgement and personal choice? On this account, the scientific enterprise is not a gradual approach to the truth, but rather as Feyerabend argues (1979: 30):

> an increasing ocean of mutually incompatible (and incommensurable) alternatives . . .
> nothing is ever settled, no view can ever be omitted from a comprehensive account.

On the levels of objectivity described in Chapter 4, this hovers somewhere between the personal and the social, never any higher. If this is the pinnacle of human objectivity, then what hope is there for humanity?

However, before accepting this description of science, it can be argued that there is more to falsification than this. There seem to be two parts to the theory. The first part, that falsifiability is the opposite side of the coin of induction, has already been dealt with. The second part, however, has much more mileage in it. It is of the essence of science that it encourages the public examination of an individual or social proclamation, and does so by inviting the use of the standards of the logical and categorial levels of objectivity.

Lakatos, however, is very aware of the lower levels of objectivity. Theories cannot be discarded, once appeal is made to the categorial levels, not because the pursuit of science does not reside at this level but because so seldom do people work completely at it. There must always be the lurking suspicion that a scientific statement (supposedly at the level of categorial objectivity) is in fact so infected by trans-social, social and personal objectivity that it never completely reaches this higher level. Because this happens so often – think of the rejection of the findings by Miller or the parapsychologists' attempts to be published in respectable journals – never completely discarding a theory remains eminently good practical sense. Scientists, aware of their own and their colleagues' fallibilities and failings, keep their options open.

CONCLUSIONS AND IMPLICATIONS

History, then, aims for a level of objectivity which transcends the merely socially acceptable. Science, on the other hand, aims for the highest level of objectivity possible to humanity. Both, however, must always be aware that their practitioners have feet of clay, simply because that is the nature of the human condition. There can therefore be *no* area of human knowledge which can claim total categorial objectivity. The lower levels of objectivity are necessarily involved in all human knowledge. All aspects need an element of tolerance and humility in their undertaking. If this is accepted, then the implications for the whole of the school curriculum are important and extensive.

Firstly, this suggests that all taught curricula should have an additional content inclusion, if it does not already exist, which concentrates on the degrees of subjectivity, the tentativeness and the temporality of human knowledge.

Secondly, it suggests that this content inclusion will, if pursued, have important ramifications for the hidden curriculum, for teachers' and children's attitudes to knowledge in general. It will prevent the attitude that there are simple facts to be learnt, that simple ingestion is acceptable. It will be a further step away from the 'banking' concept of education described by Freire (1972: 46–7) in which education is seen as the transmission of simple objective facts by an all-knowing teacher to passive, ignorant pupils, facts to be deposited and 'banked' in their heads. It will be a move towards an appreciation of human knowledge as a progressive, expanding but always limited endeavour. It will suggest even the expert's fallibility and make less likely the possibility of Milgram's (1974) experiments being repeated.

Thirdly, it provides a philosophical underpinning for all areas of the curriculum, and provides a defence against those who would limit a definition of education to the behaviourally observable and publicly testable. In so doing, it provides the teacher with a coherent philosophy which emphasizes the complexity of teaching and the professionalism and expertise needed. It also prevents the use and misuse of evaluation techniques which fail to come to grips with the depths and beauties of the learning process.

Fourthly, it suggests the destruction of the hard fact/value distinction so often assumed, the acknowledgement of the interdependency of fact and value and a correspondingly increased importance in the status of value considerations.

Fifthly, it suggests that the term 'contentious' issues might well need expanding from its present pigeon-hole of reasonably well-defined 'sensitive' issues.

Sixthly, it suggests that, in certain respects, it is the teacher's duty to educate the child away from his or her authority, and to help the child to develop his or her own style and understanding. The overarching authority of categorial objectivity remains the same for both teacher and pupil. The status of trans-social objectivity allows for principles at this level to be used as a base by which the practices at lower levels may be evaluated. However, an appreciation of each individual's limited attainment of these levels becomes a vital lesson to be taught and learnt. Each person will ultimately have his or her own picture of what categorial and trans-social objectivity are like. It is because of this, then, that:

> teaching is seen as a mode of being with, a positive mode of solicitude in which one leaps ahead of the other so as to open his possibilities for him, but never leaps in for the other, for this would be really to deprive him of his possibilities.
> (Macquarrie, 1972: 205)

Teachers must be aware of the limits of their authority, and of the place for neutrality.

Finally, it suggests that there is a need for a curriculum area which highlights the true complexity of other areas of the curriculum. One explicitly concerned with values can make this contribution. Far from being the Cinderella of the timetable, it can help other areas to a clearer appreciation of themselves. Instead of being perceived by many teachers as part of the school's soft underbelly, lacking clear definition and purpose, it can be seen as the one which enriches and redirects the perspectives of others. For it is through the appreciation of the levels of the subjectivity of knowledge, and the interdependency of fact and value, that comprehension of the depths and difficulties in the search for understanding can be gained. And it is *this* understanding which issues in clearer ideas about the demarcation between authority and autonomy and a tolerance of others and their opinions.

Chapter 6

Value Assumptions in Psychological Theories

So far, it has been suggested that the application of moral principles is complicated by the involvement of lower levels of objectivity. For as individual preferences, desires, experiences and perceptions and the accumulated customs of society interact with these principles, so they will become altered and, in some cases, perverted. It can then be predicted that their application in practice will always be problematical. Morality will always be an ongoing process of perception, reflection and action, in which the individual encounters new situations which demand the application of the same principles, but in different combinations and sometimes where they are opposed to each other, always with different veiling and obscuring factors.

This relationship between moral principles and practice is mediated at the personal level by psychological factors. However, these psychological factors are not isolated 'facts', but parts of complex psychological theories. So just as with other areas of human knowledge and understanding, it should not be assumed that psychological theories and practices are value free. They assume very different things about what a human being *is*, and consequently suggest very different factors and very different techniques for schools and teachers to use. An understanding of their different orientations, then, is crucial if a comparison is to be made between one's own picture of a moral being and that of a particular psychological theory. The use of an inappropriate theory and hence the use of inappropriate techniques could therefore be seen as not only counterproductive, but possibly immoral!

This chapter, then, will argue that psychological theories are not value free, but are in part a product of the value assumptions that psychologists and teachers bring to bear. This being the case, it will be suggested that whilst teachers must be aware of the variety of psychological strategies available to them in the practice of moral education, these value considerations must condition the degree to which they accept and implement the findings of the various theories. The teacher needs to be suitably cautious in the acceptance and implementation of psychological material.

By way of an introduction, please read the following eight statements about possible desirable classroom practices, and ask which of these approaches is nearest your own educational beliefs.

1. Rewarding children for good behaviour is the best means of ensuring correct moral behaviour.

2. Classrooms should be structured in order to show children the correct behaviour to adopt.
3. Moral development is basically the result of an interplay between the experiences children meet and their thought processes.
4. Classrooms should be structured in order to shape a child's behaviour in the desired direction.
5. One of the teacher's most basic tasks is to let the child know that he or she is liked, respected and secure.
6. Experiences must be provided for children which stimulate them to try to make greater sense of themselves and their relationships with others.
7. 'Do as I do' is more important than 'do as I say' in the teacher's moral education of the child.
8. A child's basic needs must be attended to before higher personal and moral development is possible.

The first group (numbers 1 and 4) are the kind of statements one might well expect a behavioural psychologist such as Burrhus Skinner to make in advocating desirable teacher behaviours in the classroom. The second group (2 and 7) are the kind of statements which a social learning theorist like Albert Bandura might be expected to espouse. The third (3 and 6) are the kind of statements a cognitive developmentalist such as Jean Piaget might make. And the last (5 and 8) are the kind a humanistic psychologist like Abraham Maslow might utter.

Two things should emerge from the emphases given. Firstly, any fairly large difference between the emphases indicates that more value is being placed on the statements of one group of psychologists than another. In other words, regardless of the fact that psychology is normally taken to be a science, and therefore impartial in its findings, some findings are seen as more important than others, and some findings would rather be applied in the classroom than others. Secondly, whilst one group of findings may be favoured more than another, all theories will probably still be seen as having *something* to contribute. It seems important, then, that one is aware of the variety of theories available, what they stress about human beings and what they tend to leave out.

Now look at the groups of statements again. These questions about their basic assumptions may now be asked:

(a) How free or how determined is the individual believed to be in his or her responses in each of the theories? Compare statements 1 and 3.
(b) How logical and rational are people believed to be in their behaviour in the different theories? Compare statements 4 and 6.
(c) To what extent is the person seen as a single unified trait, or as little more than bits and pieces joined together by genetic and environmental chance? Compare statements 1 and 8.
(d) To what extent are people seen as changing because of how they see the world, or because there are measurable factors outside themselves which change them? Compare statements 4 and 6 again.
(e) Are people seen as capable of being explained in objective scientific terms, or are they seen as deep creatures whose personalities will never be totally understood? Compare statements 2 and 5.

It will readily been seen that whilst some of the theories may share some assumptions they will differ on others. (For a more detailed treatment, see Hjelle and Ziegler, 1981.) Each theory starts with a particular selection of assumptions about human nature. It will probably be the case that some of the assumptions listed above are the root cause for an individual's liking or disliking of a particular theory. Being aware of these (generally unspoken) value assumptions is therefore immensely important. (Another very readable introduction is Stevenson, 1984.)

It is important to notice that value assumptions enter into psychological findings in at least two different ways. Both psychologist and teacher come to the findings with certain prior value assumptions. Both necessarily start off with a particular notion of what a human being is, of what particular aspects are seen, believed or valued as being those things which make a person distinctively 'human'.

Thus psychologists tend to devote their research to those aspects which they find most congenial to their intuitive notions of what constitutes the human being, and this tends to validate the approach they take. For example, the behaviourist will judge outcomes in terms of rewards and punishments, positive and negative reinforcement contingencies. If a particular psychological approach is used in teaching a particular topic, and the results are disappointing, it is unlikely that the behaviourist will recant and throw out his or her theoretical approach. Much more likely will be a reply that there is nothing wrong with the theory *in principle*: it is only that this particular experimental situation did not apply it well enough. In other words, behaviourist principles will work really well next time.

A good illustration of this can be seen when the views of the behaviourist and the cognitive-developmentalist come into conflict. Engelman (1971), for example, attempted to teach preschool children the concept of specific gravity using floating and sinking objects with behaviourist techniques. However, he achieved only equivocal results at best. His conclusion, though, was not that behaviourist techniques did not work, but rather that with more time the job could be better done: the rules could be better designed to cover a wider variety of situations and the subject taught to elicit a higher criterion of performance. Kamii and Derman (1971), developmental psychologists, argued however that the children had learned nothing more than a superficial verbal overlay and that deep-seated notions had not evolved. They supported this view with observations that seemed to show that when children were confronted with a result they did not expect, many of them hesitated briefly, searched their memory for a learned rule that might apply and vocalized it, whether it really made sense to them or not.

Now, as has been suggested, the problem seems to lie as much in the approaches as in the results obtained. Kamii and Derman use concepts like 'hesitate', 'search memory', and 'making sense' – inferential notions used in conversation all the time, but ones not admitted or attended to by Engelman, who instead concentrates on behavioural factors which can be isolated and then reinforced. Different paradigms are in use.

Even the results of another developmental psychologist, Greco (quoted in Duckworth, 1979), would not, one assumes, be sufficient to convince the behaviourist. Greco studied the effects of helping children work out which of three glass beads in a revolving tube would be at a particular end of the tube after a specified number of revolutions. He came to the conclusion that in no case did outside help characteristic of behaviourist approaches speed up the learning process. Greco says (*ibid.*: 302):

> the failure of these methods . . . shows that the discovery of the rule could not be the product of perceptual learning . . . it is the discovery of the law which makes possible the correct use of visual tracking.

The problem is, of course, that the behaviourist can always turn round and suggest that modifications to Greco's approach *could* produce the required improvements, or that more time spent on helping children would have done the same. And if next time doesn't work out too well either, there can always be found *some* aspect of the procedure which protects the central core of the theory. The theory tends to be self-perpetuating. This is not a criticism of behaviourist psychology as such, but of psychological theories in general. They all tend towards self-validation and protection of their central assumptions.

Indeed, this phenomenon is not restricted to psychological science. As was seen in Chapter 5, Lakatos (1970) has argued convincingly that this is the same for all scientific endeavours. Rather than rejecting the theory being worked with, the scientist will concentrate on those kinds of factors which surround the theory itself, but which can be modified or changed without affecting the more central assumptions. It does not take much to arrive at the position of a scientist like Feyerabend (1979), and find oneself believing that not only are different paradigms in use, but that these are esentially 'incommensurable' – that there is no criterion by which one may be evaluated against the other. The purpose here is not to enter too deeply into this debate, but to point out that the problem of objectivity and values exists even within the heart of the physical sciences. If teachers are aware of these arguments, then they can become that much more cautious in accepting the findings of a particular psychological school.

In many ways, the practising teacher comes to a much more complex situation than the experimenter. All practitioners worth their salt have to be aware of the findings in the area in question, of the transitoriness of these findings, and then use their value assumptions to decide whether or not to put them into practice before attempting the task of translating them into practical techniques. It may be that human beings are seen as very similar to other creatures, and that they should therefore be treated, in psychological terms, in much the same way. If they are seen as essentially passive creatures moulded by their environment in terms of positively or negatively reinforcing experiences, then the teacher can structure the classroom accordingly. If, on the other hand, human beings are seen as essentially active, always trying to interpret, structure and make better sense of their surroundings, then the teacher will probably take account of this and *not* over-determine the nature of learning experiences, for each child will be viewed as making a different sense of each situation. On this account, then, the teacher can provide the conditions, but cannot and should not attempt to predict the eventual outcome.

Non-specialist teachers who know little of the niceties in this area may tend to adopt the findings and applications of the theory most congenial to their own point of view, and reject or at least simply not take up those recommendations made by theoreticians with whose perspective no great affinity is felt. This explains why some teachers, given recommendations by an educational psychologist, or upon reading a psychological textbook on moral development, may feel uneasy with that which is prescribed. They may not be able to vocalize what is wrong, but may feel that the psychologist's underlying assumptions about the nature of a human being are not in harmony with their own.

However, and probably just as bad as adopting a theory simply because of its congeniality, some practitioners may accept a psychologist's educational prescriptions having never been given alternative prescriptions to try out or compare, simply because such alternatives stem from other theoretical viewpoints. It is therefore crucial that practitioners be aware of what is available, and then choose for themselves what is required in a particular situation with a particular child. The psychologist, generally speaking, is *not* an educationalist.

This is a point made at length by Egan (1983), who argues that many educationalists make the mistake of thinking that a psychologist like Piaget tells them what to do. But the point, Egan argues, is rather that Piaget describes a state of affairs which the educator can take up or not. Piaget describes a factual state of affairs; it is for the teacher to decide if such affairs are valuable and worth translating into practice.

This is one of the crucial difficulties and fascinations of the position taken up by the developmental psychologist Lawrence Kohlberg (1981a). Unlike Piaget, who was not particularly interested in the teacher or the application of his theories to education, Kohlberg is concerned with just this. On the basis of extensive cross-cultural research, Kohlberg suggests that people from all cultures may move through five or six stages of moral reasoning, each 'higher' stage involving a level of reasoning which makes more sense of moral problems than 'lower' levels. Such movement he believes to be universal in the form of reasoning, even though different cultures may give this form different content, and he also believes the movement through these stages to be invariant – once you move to stage 3, because it is more intellectually satisfying than stage 2, you will not return.

His theory of stages of moral development is not only a psychological theory in its own right, but also the basis for an explicit teaching programme in moral education. Even if one grants that Kohlberg's scientific findings are watertight – and there is sufficient controversy over this (see for instance, Bergling, 1981) – the problem still remains of on what basis his findings are to be used as the foundations for an educational programme. Fundamentally this must come down to a prior conception of what a human being is, and whether such a prior conception deserves to be implemented educationally. These are considerations which cannot be resolved by Kohlberg's findings alone. They are philosophical and ethical questions of a quite different order. And if this is the case, then Kohlberg has to stand as a philosopher as well as a psychologist. To his credit, he recognizes this and attempts to do so in numerous articles (1981a, 1981b, Kohlberg with Power, 1981), but the fact still remains that the case for the implementation of his findings cannot, on psychological grounds alone, be proven.

So whilst Egan's position cannot be completely supported – this chapter has so far been devoted to showing that even psychologists come to their work with prior values – yet an important point is being made. To put it bluntly, the psychologist is a purveyor of wares which the educator may buy or not, depending upon the educator's value theory of education. It is imperative, therefore, that teachers be aware of both their own standpoints and that of the psychologist. The teacher's job, dare it be said, if properly done, is much the more complex of the two.

Let us put this into practice. All teachers, whether they like it or not, are confronted almost from the first minute they step into a classroom with the ethical question of whether to punish or not to punish. 'Punishment' here means the use of any aversive stimuli. It does not mean only, or even mostly, the use of corporal punishment. Even where corporal punishment is prohibited by law, punishment – in the forms of detentions, lines, harsh words, frowns, etc. – goes on all the time. Let us therefore assume that before stepping into this classroom, they realize that they will be asking this question, and decide to do something about it. They decide to confront the question head on: do I use punishment as a disciplinary technique or don't I?

Their next question must surely be: what sort of things do I read, what sorts of issues do I consider, in order to decide? There is certainly no lack of psychological evidence on the subject (see Wise, 1979, Wright, 1972, Docking, 1987). There is a mountain of it in animal research, though less when it comes to human beings. (This is interesting in itself, because the reason seems to be essentially an *ethical* one: we regard it as fine to shock baby puppies, to make rats vomit and to submit white mice to intense and terrifying noise, but we do not think that we should do that sort of thing to human beings. In other words, values enter into our psychological facts even before we research them.) The evidence is not totally conclusive, but seems to suggest that while punishment undoubtedly works, there are so many side-effects that one can never be entirely sure that one can control the punishment and produce more good than harm. The psychological evidence tends to suggest: do not use it.

What, however, if an article were published in a journal next week which produced results to show that when using a particular technique, punishment could totally deter a person and none of the side-effects noted in the literature would appear? The question would still remain: should the technique be used? It is very plain what is happening. The facts cannot decide this issue on their own. There must be recourse to value questions in order to know whether those facts are required in the first place.

Put the matter another way. Imagine there is a person who abhors the notion of manipulating other human beings and of causing them actual physical or psychological pain, who espouses the notion of providing the child with a warm, secure and loving environment, in the belief that through this procedure the child will grow up to be healthy and well adjusted. This person is browsing in a bookshop one day and sees an interesting-looking book. It is entitled 'How To Control Your Child By Electric Shock, With No Side-effects – Guaranteed'. What is this person likely to do? The book may be flipped through out of curiosity (it is, after all, an incredible claim), but it is unlikely to be considered seriously. The facts may be available, but they will probably not be taken up and utilized. This individual's prior value scheme may well prohibit their application.

Now this is *not* to say that no facts affect or have affected this person in the past. Any value scheme is partly the product of personal experience, reading material and reflection. Factual evidence will go quite a long way in determining a value scheme, which then in turn will go a long way in determining the selection of facts, which then affect the value scheme, and so on.

This effect of values upon facts and behaviour can again be seen in an examination of different arguments for the use of punishment in schools. It seems simply not true that punishment is only used or has only been used by incompetent teachers. Such a statement suggests that only the inept, the inadequate and the thoughtless would use such a technique. This seems to be clearly contradicted by the possibility of the following ethical or philosophical viewpoints.

Firstly, there are utilitarians in the teaching profession who can see the value of punishment as one of deterring others from similar actions. There is a distinguished philosophical pedigree for such a belief. In the *Protagoras* Plato adopted a utilitarian/-deterrence posture when he stated that:

> he who decides to inflict rational punishment does not retaliate for a past wrong, which cannot be undone; he has regard to the future and is desirous that the man who is punished, and he who sees him punished, may be deterred from wrong doing again.
> (Quoted in Docking, 1980: 203)

The good achieved through preventing further bad behaviour, utilitarians would argue, outweighs the evil of the punishment itself. It could well be that this is not so much a moral argument as an empirical one, for if it did not deter, there seems little point in its continuation. Indeed some might argue that this point of view is downright immoral in that it admits that punishment is an evil, but is still prepared to countenance it. Whatever the value of such arguments, the fact remains that this belief in the validity of balancing present evil against future good can be a reason for the institutionalization of punishment.

Secondly, there may well be retributivists in the teaching profession who truly believe that at a certain age children can be deemed responsible for their actions, and therefore not only deserve punishment but also should be granted the privilege of it. This phrase 'granted the privilege of it' may seem a curious one to use, for it is hard to imagine anyone apart from the masochist who would enjoy such an honour, but retributivists believe they are making a very deep moral point. If one wants to accord responsibility to human beings, then with this attribution come certain assumptions, and the most central one is that a person can be praised and blamed. This belief in the possibility of responsibility leads the retributivist to the belief that punishment should be institutionalized.

Lastly, consider this remark by John Calvin, whose theology formed the basis of Puritan beliefs:

> Education is to be a complete regimentation of the child to suppress his evil nature and build good living and thinking.
> (Quoted in Piele, 1979: 95)

Calvin believed that his educational goals would and should be achieved by the 'rod of correction'.

Here, then, are three very different ethical viewpoints which would affect the perception of 'relevant' facts surrounding this issue, and from which could stem the institutionalization of punishment. In such a way is the circle of values affecting facts and facts affecting values created.

The point is not that people cannot change, but rather that to break the circle of self-confirmation, they must be aware that there is a circle in the first place. This circle can be a self-chosen one, as has been suggested above, or it can be one instituted and perpetuated by an inadequate grasp of the area. This, again, is why it is vital to be aware of the different standpoints within psychological theory and to treat them cautiously.

The teacher, then, has an immense task. Adequate practice demands a variety of things, among which is an understanding of the academic research relevant to education. Among *this* is a working knowledge of the psychological research. And adequacy of grasp demands an appreciation of each approach's relevance to the teacher's own practice, and the active selection and application of such findings. The teacher, to be truly professional, has to be immensely competent. The reward is in the excitement of the job. Where outside pressures reduce the status and professionalism of the teacher, they reduce the level of competence required. The results for education will be apparent.

One half of the thesis on psychological theories has thus been dealt with. Psychological theories are not value free, but are in part a product of the value assumptions that the teacher and psychologist bring to bear upon the area. The other half of the thesis – that the teacher must be aware of the tentativeness of psychological fact and theory – will be dealt with in the next chapter.

Chapter 7

Psychological Theories – Liberators or Jailers?

The previous chapter looked at the beginnings of psychological theories – their value assumptions. This chapter will look at their endings – the findings they produce and the effect of these findings on teaching theory and practice. It will attempt to do two things. Firstly, it will survey the cognitive-developmental literature and suggest that many 'moral' processes occur at an earlier age than is normally presumed. The work of Piaget is particularly highlighted because his thought has been so influential. Secondly, it will be suggested that the cognitive-developmental view is an incomplete model of the child's moral psychological functioning, and other aspects will be suggested for the attention of the educator. Thus, a major conclusion of the chapter will be that the manner in which such findings are viewed by the teacher will have important repercussions upon classroom practice.

By way of an introduction, look at a simple experiment which can be performed in any classroom. It takes the form:

> Edith is fairer than Susan.
> Edith is darker than Lily.
> Who is darkest?

It may well be that readers have some initial difficulty with the question. Certainly, Piaget is of the opinion that this sort of puzzle is strictly for teenagers and adults – it involves a stage of thinking (Piaget's stage of 'formal operations', Table 7.1) of which young children are simply not supposed to be capable. If the puzzle was put in the form of looking at and handling three dolls with varying shades of hair colour, the problem would not pose any difficulty: they would be dealing with concrete objects, and therefore be at Piaget's stage of 'concrete operations'. However, in the Edith–Susan–Lily question, they are handling little more than abstract ideas.

So the Piagetian explanation is one in terms of stages, and of children who cannot answer the question as having not gone through these stages yet. However, there are other explanations available. It may be the case that it is not the puzzle *per se* which is the difficulty, but its presentation. For instance, what if the children do not often come across other children called Edith and Lily, and do not often deal with words like fairer? Giving the children this puzzle as it stands might then cause this kind of (silent) reaction:

> 'Edith and Lily, they're funny names' and
> 'What does "fairer" mean? Oh yes, it's the opposite of darker.'

Table 7.1 *Piaget's Stages*

1.	*SENSORIMOTOR*	*0 to 2 yrs*	(Tied to immediate sensation, experience)
	Can	Act reflexively	Suck a breast if presented Cry if startled
		Act purposively	Cry to attract attention Attempt to grab objects
	Cannot	Think about actions, just does them Understand object permanence	Decide between action A or action B Will not follow you if you disappear one side of a screen, appear the other side
2.	*PREOPERATIONAL*	*2 to 7 yrs*	(Can't operate fully logical thought)
	Can	Think about actions Understand object permanence Attach symbols to objects, actions	Dolls stand for babies Can play at being mummy/daddy
	Cannot	Form genetic concepts Make transitive inferences See a situation from another's position (egocentrism) Focus on all aspects of problem (centration) Reverse	All men are 'daddy' A>B, B>C, ∴ A>C ? How does the mountain look from where you are? 2 equal plasticine balls, one rolled in sausage – sausage seen as bigger Liquid poured from flat glass into tall thin glass: same result $2 + 3 = 5$ but $5 - 2 = 3$?
3.	*CONCRETE OPERATIONS*	*7 to 11 yrs*	(Can reason logically, but tied to the concrete, previously experienced)
	Can	De-centre Reverse Infer transitively Form genetic concepts See situations from other positions better	Plasticine balls, water transfer – both OK A>B, B>C, ∴ A>C 'Daddy' is particular, 'men' is general term 'The mountain will look different from where you are'
	Cannot	Deal with hypotheses (needs to see them, deal with them concretely)	Edith is fairer than Susan Edith is darker than Lily Who is darkest?
4.	*FORMAL OPERATIONS*	*12 yrs onwards*	(Full adult reasoning)
	Can	Deal with hypotheses Evaluate as well as describe Deal with abstract questions/symbolic thought	Is your football team the best in the league? What do we mean by fairness?

In other words, the children's minds would be preoccupied with irrelevancies before they even begin.

The puzzle can be changed, whilst still retaining the same logical form. It could become:

John is smaller than Sam
John is taller than Fred
Who is tallest?

Of course, any combination of names can be chosen, depending upon which group of children are being dealt with. In informal little tests, I have found the results to be quite dramatic. When the Susan–Edith–Lily problem was given, only about one-third of the classes of nine-year-olds arrived at the correct answer. When the John–Sam–Fred question was given, three-quarters of the children replied correctly.

What this suggests is that problems with children's reasoning may lie as much with the experimenter as with the child. If the wrong questions are asked, or if they are phrased in such a way as to be incomprehensible to the child, then perhaps it should not be the child's ability which is questioned, but the experimenter's. It may be that the child *is* capable of quite sophisticated processes, but they can only be performed within a limited range of experiences. This would throw an entirely new light on teaching. For instead of the teacher feeling that there is little point in trying something out with children because 'they are not ready for it yet', it may be the case that the children *are* ready for it, as long as the teacher has the wit to put it in a form which they can understand. If this were the case, then the teacher's job would be infinitely more exciting because it would tear itself away from the mechanical stage-theory belief which many teachers bring to the teaching situation almost as an absolute.

These, however, are little more than suggestions and 'what ifs'. Where is the evidence, apart from one small puzzle? It is found if the literature is examined.

Piaget's ideas on children's moral development centred around a number of core ideas (well reviewed by Lickona, 1976), but the two listed below will serve the present purpose of assessing the adequacy of the standard cognitive-developmental model.

(a) Children are, for a considerable part of their early life, 'egocentric', not only in perceptual outlook, but in moral outlook as well. They are simply incapable of taking another person's point of view.

(b) Moral development is predicated upon cognitive development; the child cannot be expected to develop morally until he or she has undergone a related stage of the cognitive process.

In the purely cognitive domain, Piaget came to his conclusions about egocentrism after experiments like the 'three mountains experiment' (Piaget and Inhelder, 1956: 210–13). In this, a model of three mountains was utilized (Figure 7.1), each mountain being distinguished by such things as snow on the top of one, a house on another and a flag on the top of the third. The child was then seated in some position next to the mountains, and a doll at some other, and the child asked: what does the doll see? Rather than verbally describing what the doll sees, the child was asked to choose from one of ten pictures which the doll sees, or was given three smaller mountains and asked to arrange them as the doll would see them. Piaget found that children as old as eight or nine could not do this, and that they tended to pick out or build the view that they themselves saw. Piaget took this as evidence for egocentricity – that children are unable to place themselves in another's position because they think that everyone has their view of things.

However, there are now a number of studies which seriously call these conclusions into question. For example, Hughes (1975) set up a similar experiment but with some crucial differences. Hughes used two walls intersecting to form a cross, and two small dolls, a police doll and a boy doll (Figure 7.2). Hughes started his experiment by introducing the child to the dolls, placing the boy doll in different areas between the intersecting walls and asking if the police doll could see the boy doll in each of these

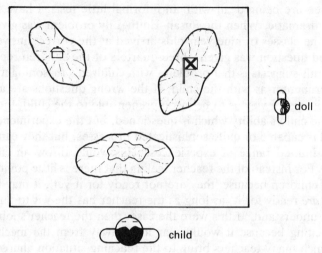

Figure 7.1   Piaget's 'mountain' experiment (from Piaget and Inhelder, 1956)

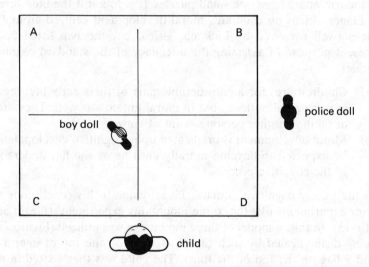

Figure 7.2   Hughes' 'hiding' experiment (a) (from Hughes, 1975)

areas, so as to familiarize the child with the set-up. After this, the experiment began, and the task was made more complicated by introducing another police doll (Figure 7.3). The child was asked to hide the boy doll from both police dolls, which in effect meant taking into account two different points of view. The task was repeated three times, and the results were quite dramatic: when 30 children of between 3½ and 5 years were given the task, 90 per cent of their responses were correct, a result totally at variance with Piaget's findings and predictions.

Donaldson (1978) came to the conclusion that the crucial difference between Piaget's and Hughes' experiments lay in the fact that the children could make sense of what they were asked to do in the 'hiding from the policeman' task, whilst they could not do this with the 'three mountains' task. This, she argues, is because children know what it is to hide from somebody – it is part of their experience, and they can

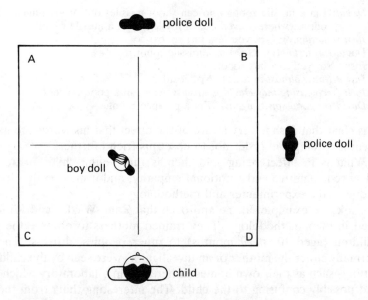

Figure 7.3 Hughes' 'hiding' experiment (b)

become involved in it. The mountain problem, on the other hand, is artificial, abstract and totally outside the children's experience. It provokes little enthusiasm, and cannot be understood.

This goes some way, then, to showing that children can understand some of the more complex mental processes if they are couched in language and situations within their experience. The emphasis is not so much on whether the child has the ability or not, but whether the experimenter or teacher has the ability to make the situation relevant. Indeed, it is possible to go further than this and suggest that one of the crucial roles of the adult is to provide guidance for the child in the structuring and facilitating of communication situations. Wood (1988), in an extensive review of Piagetian theory, suggests that there is considerably more room for the development of children's understanding of complex situations through adult help than Piaget allows. Development, both cognitive and moral, may well be more a product of social communication than of structural development *per se*.

Something further than this should be noted, however, and this is that the 'policeman' task is naturally interactive like a game, in a way in which the 'three mountain' task is not. In other words, the 'policeman' task asks the child to take another person's perspective, to empathize in a very natural way, much more so than the more austere 'put yourself in the place of someone looking at these mountains from another position'.

The type of empathy so far described could be called 'cognitive' empathy, in the sense that it involves comprehending another's perspective, without there necessarily being an emotional component to the subsequent action. But there is also a type of empathy which might be called 'emotional' empathy, in the sense that there appears to be a genuine feeling of concern for the other. This also can happen with the very young. For a humorous and warming example of an emotional empathy in four-year-old children look at this conversation recorded by Rubin (1980: 57–8):

> *David*: I'm a missile robot who can shoot missiles out of my fingers. I can shoot them
> out anywhere – even out of my legs. I'm a missile robot.
> *Josh (tauntingly)*: No, you're a fart robot.
> *David (protestingly)*: No, I'm a missile robot.
> *Josh*: No, you're a fart robot.
> *David (hurt, almost in tears)*: No, Josh!
> *Josh (recognising that David is upset)*: And I'm a poo-poo robot.
> *David (in good spirits again)*: I'm a pee-pee robot.

It is clear that Josh is very aware of the effect that his words are having, and adjusts them accordingly in order not to upset his friend further.

What is in effect being said then is that young children are capable of quite advanced cognitive and emotional empathy, and it may be that its lack of detection is due to the experimenter and methodology.

Look, for example, at the approach that Zahn-Waxler and Radke-Yarrow (1982) used in their methodology. They trained mothers to observe the reactions of their children (aged 10 to 29 months) to other peoples' distress. These other people, normally either the mother or an investigator, were seen by the children in naturalistic settings such as their own homes rather than in a laboratory which would be strange and possibly confusing to the child. The interesting thing from the present point of view is that the relationship between mother and child *did* make a difference to the child's behaviour. As they said (p. 130):

> prosocial interventions toward mother were significantly more frequent than those directed towards the investigator.

And they continue:

> If the study had used a relative stranger as the victim, the conclusion would have been that children between the ages of 1 and 2 are not capable of prosocial behaviour.

In other words, the methodology used significantly affected the results obtained. Foorman *et al.* (1984: 265) hit the nail on the head when they said:

> if researchers lighten task demands, children appear less egocentric.

This is precisely what Borke (1971) did when she suggested that one of the main problems for children of 3 to 3½ years was that of giving *verbal* replies to the experimenter. She reasoned that children would do much better in an experimental situation where they were asked to do no more than make a behavioural response. So Borke read stories to children from 3 to 8 years in which the characters had happy, sad, afraid or angry feelings, and then asked the children to match pictures of faces which also had happy, sad, afraid or angry expressions. This, then, required an empathic move on the child's part (what would a person who feels angry look like?), but asks for only a behavioural response. The results of the experiment showed that children of 3 to 3½ years easily identified the 'happy' faces correctly, but needed to be slightly older to correctly identify 'sad' and 'angry', and a little bit older still for the 'afraid' faces. Despite these slight variations, the main result – that very young children can empathize with others if the demands made upon them are simplified – stands, and Borke's comment (p. 268) is most appropriate:

> the task used to measure interpersonal perception, especially with very young children, significantly influences the child's ability to communicate this awareness of other people's feelings.

What Borke's experiment shows, crucially, is that the young child can recognize other people's emotional states – that is, he or she can empathize with them, and therefore the child should not be viewed as being totally egocentric. This is shown by the fact that the child has to listen to and understand what the main character is going through, and then correctly identify this feeling with a behavioural response (pointing to the happy or sad face).

Thus we have a situation where a simple cognitive-developmental model will not capture the full richness of the child's moral functioning. Whilst techniques stimulating the cognitive side (dilemmas for instance) would be of undoubted benefit, they are not half the story. Techniques must also be developed stimulating the empathic abilities, and especially the emotional type. Then not only will children understand a situation as another views it, but will also see how that person feels it as well, and so be motivated to do something about it.

Of course, it is one thing to empathize with another's situation: it is another to do something about it. Johnson (1982) has taken the empathic process even further back in the child's life, to 18 to 24 months, and has shown that as children develop their concept of themselves as distinct from others, so they will not only react to but also do something about other people's distress. In his experiment, Johnson took away a doll from either the mother or a stranger, in the laboratory or in the child's home, and had the mother or stranger act as if distressed. His results showed that children of this age respond to others in a positive manner, either by helping directly (giving them their doll), or by getting someone else to help (pulling someone's clothes and indicating).

It is worthy of note that whilst the small child's action may be inappropriate – not many adults would get comfort by being given a doll – the child is aware of another's need, and is doing its best to supply a remedy. The fact that the remedy is inappropriate is something which can be altered – one can begin the process of showing the child that some things work better than others, that some things are more appropriate for some individuals than others. There is undoubtedly a developmental sequence here, but not as normally conceived on the cognitive-developmental model. The foremost proponent of such a model of developing empathy with cognition is Martin Hoffman.

Hoffman (1982) argues that the development of such prosocial and altruistic motives is not a rather dry process, but rather a synthesis of empathic distress evoked in six different and non-sequential modes and the child's increasingly sophisticated sense of the other. The development of empathy is then seen as progressing through these six modes in five distinct phases (Figure 7.4).

1. *Global empathy* is the most basic empathic level. It is observed in the newborn child, where no distinction can be made between the self and another, and where there is little or no awareness by the newborn of what is happening. To this extent, any development in empathic abilities would appear to be dependent on cognitive growth.
2. *Egocentric empathy.* When the child develops sufficiently to realize that there are others in the world with feelings, then the level of egocentric empathy has been reached. Having said that, the child still has no awareness of the cause of others' distress, nor of the fact that different people may have feelings different from him or herself, nor that different people require different kinds of help –

	Level	Limits	Help possible
1	GLOBAL EMPATHY	No self—other differentiation No awareness of what is happening	Change largely dependent on cognitive growth
2	EGOCENTRIC EMPATHY	No awareness of cause of others' distress No awareness that different people need different help No awareness of different internal states	Adult direction to cause of distress Adult direction to use of different help Adult direction to internal states Feedback on effectiveness of help Use of models acting, verbalizing feelings
3	EMPATHY FOR ANOTHER'S FEELINGS	No awareness of long-term distress	Use of drama, literature, film, acts of role-play (plus all of 2)
4	EMPATHY FOR ANOTHER'S GENERAL PLIGHT	No awareness of distress of nations, racial groups, etc.	Use of drama, literature, film, role-play (plus all of 2)
5	EMPATHY FOR OTHER GROUPS, CLASSES OR NATIONS	? No empathy for other distant life-forms (trees, etc.)? for animal life-forms in ecological sense?	

General facilitating conditions

1. Experiencing many emotions at optimum level of arousal
2 Providing safe, secure, caring environments for such encounters

Non-sequential empathic modes

Reactive newborn cry	*Classical conditioning*	*Direct association*	*Mimic cry*	*Symbolic association*	*Role taking*
Another baby crying makes a newborn baby cry	Observing distress while feeling distress oneself allows others' visual distress cues to be conditioned to distress feelings	Observing others' distress reminds us of our previous distress feelings	Automatically imitating others' distress actions evokes distress in oneself	Symbolic cues (a letter, a description) evoke empathic distress	Deliberate acts of imagining oneself in another's place evoke empathic distress

Figure 7.4 A theory of empathy development (based on Hoffman, 1976, 1982)

hence the oft-repeated example of children at this stage either putting their thumbs in their mouths and sucking them, as this has comforted them in the past, or of them offering their teddy bears to others because this too has made them feel better in the past. As can be seen from Figure 7.4, there is a variety of means by which the adult may facilitate this process.

3. *Empathy for another's feelings* is a significant empathic development in that children now realize the existence of different internal states in others. They may, however, be aware only of short-term distress or passing moods or events, and not of long-term distress caused by living conditions, personality problems, etc.
4. *Empathy for another's general plight*, then, comes when the child is able to recognize the possibility of others' distress in the long term. There is at least one more step, then, in recognizing the existence and viability of group distress.
5. *Empathy for other groups, classes or nations* is seen by Hoffman as the final step in this development. This fifth step involves a well-developed grasp of long-term events, the co-ordination of information relevant to understanding particular groups', races' or nations' situations, and sensitive role-taking, and this demands a high degree of cognitive functioning.

Hoffman would be the first to accept that his theory is by no means complete, and it is possible to speculate that it may not be the final stage at all. Rather, there may be involved an empathy for distant life forms which do not present clear distress to the observer (such as plants), or an empathy for species of animals rather than for individuals on their own. This is necessarily extremely tentative, but does suggest a movement, almost a return to a 'global' empathy again, except this time it is not a case of thinking 'If I hurt, everything hurts', but rather 'If anything hurts, I hurt'. It appears to suggest a motivational link into the religious/mystical mode of thinking, a link made much more explicit in the next chapter.

Given these five levels of empathic development, what are the modes through which empathy is evoked? Hoffman suggests six, and describes them as non-sequential, suggesting that none of these six ways encompasses and replaces the preceding mode. Instead, he argues that different stimuli will produce different kinds of arousal. The mode of arousal is therefore dependent on the situation.

The earliest – developmentally – of the means by which a baby can be aroused, the *reactive newborn cry*, was found by Simner (1971) in 2 to 3-day-olds, and has been replicated by Sagi and Hoffman (1976) who reported that infants responded to a distress cry in others by experiencing distress themselves. This is obviously not a full empathic response as it lacks any awareness of what is happening and further, the concept of person permanence does not occur until 1 to 1½ years (Johnson, 1982). However, this lack of differentiation between self and other may actually facilitate the empathic process, because the child will be unclear as to just who is experiencing the emotional disturbance. Thus, via the second mode of arousal, *classical conditioning*, the child will connect his or her experience of distress with another child's experiences, and the gradual nature of the differentiation will allow the vital link to be forged.

The third mode of arousal, *direct association*, involves the observing of others' distress, which then reminds one of previous personal distress, and thus evokes distress feelings within oneself. The fourth mode, *mimicry*, is the automatic imitation of others' distressful actions, an act which it is claimed evokes distress in oneself. The fifth mode, *symbolic association*, is the action of symbolic cues such as a letter or verbal description evoking empathic distress. The final module, *role taking*, involves the deliberate act of imagining oneself in another's place, the act of which evokes empathic distress. These six modes of arousal suggest a number of different techniques which teachers can use to help the development towards empathic maturity.

Before describing some of them, however, it is important to point out that such techniques can be used in two very different ways. They can be read, digested and used when the situation arises in the classroom. In some cases this makes eminent sense. But on other occasions, they can be read, digested and then prepared for in the classroom – situations can be planned so that the techniques form the focus of the learning. In this way, the teacher is anticipating and utilizing them in a conscious proactive manner, rather than in a purely reactive way. The difference is crucial. The teacher would never consider providing the majority of language or mathematical concepts and skills on a reactive basis – these are carefully planned in advance. For the moral education of the child to achieve the same degree of proficiency (and status) its practice must have the same degree of proactivity. Teachers must come to the area with the same preparedness as they do for other areas of the curriculum. This being the case, it may be instructive to use as many methods as possible from the list following. The first three techniques can all be constructed through the use of story, drama, music and film.

(a)   The teacher can construct situations which permit the child to experience many emotions. It is worth, noting, however, that there may be an 'optimal' level of experience, and above this emotions may be so upsetting as to be avoided or repressed.

(b)   Attention can be directed to another's internal states. Calling attention to the pain or injury caused by a child's action and encouraging the child to imagine how it would feel to be in the victim's place are both examples of a reasoned rather than a punitive approach to discipline.

(c)   The teacher can devise situations for role-taking in order to sharpen the child's understanding of others' internal states.

The next two are essentially ongoing processes, though consideration of them in terms of the hidden curriculum of the school can sharpen awareness and suggest ways of countering inhibiting practices.

(d)   A warm and secure environment can be created, heightening children's self-confidence and self-esteem, thus helping to ensure that they are less preoccupied with their own needs and more open to those of others.

(e)   Teachers can and should act as models of prosocial behaviour, and also verbalize their empathic feelings in order to show children what to do and to establish that this behaviour is desirable.

The next three techniques involving helping have a natural unity. Helping can mean washing the paint brushes at the end of a lesson. It can also mean helping younger children in the school with their reading, providing assistance at the local old people's home or clearing up and beautifying neighbouring wasteland and gardens. A little time preplanning how instructions to children will be phrased can save a lot of misunderstanding later on. The personal appearance of those helped, or letters from them, or verbal reports by the teacher, or photos of and visits to the place where the help has been given in order to see results will all have a prolonged effect.

(f)   The child should be given the opportunity to help when he or she asks to. Whilst the empathic response is already there, Grusec's research (1982) shows that children given the opportunity to help continue to do so, whilst those not given the opportunity reduce the number of their offers.

(g)   The teacher can provide the child with clear directions as to what they can do in a situation. This will help to negate the possibility that the child will refrain from helping through feeling embarrassed or confused.

(h)   The child can be provided with feedback on the correctness or incorrectness of his or her attempts to solve a problem situation. This will not only provide extra cognitive input, but will also boost feelings of success, and hence confidence to help again.

The last is, of course, a hugely important ongoing process.

(i)   The teacher can facilitate as early as possible the acquisition of language by talking to, extending, rephrasing and helping children to rehearse their own thoughts. Such communication helps to prevent the disruption of children's thought processes through easing task loads and preventing misunderstanding, and so helps to further and structure complex thought.

Indeed, through this last factor, by late childhood or early adolescence children become more aware of others as having personal identities and life experiences beyond immediate situations. This leads them into the complex areas of judgement about helping people in a specific situation versus long-term effects and imaginative understanding of the distress of not only individuals but groups and races as well. It is at this level that empathy's limitations are most apparent, and when developed cognitive capacities come most into play. After all, whilst empathy may sensitize one to another's plight, it cannot on its own decide between competing moral claims; and even the most mature empathizers will be biased in favour of those people with whom they share interests and experiences. This, it seems, is a strength rather than a weakness of empathy theory, because it recognizes its limitations and draws on other areas in order to complement and strengthen its contribution.

This chapter, then, has argued for six things in particular. Firstly, it has argued for teachers to have a rather guarded approach to the theories of major psychological writers, and the validity of psychological findings, on the basis that even the most prestigious research can be flawed. Secondly, there is a continued need for psychologists to examine their methodologies, for it may be inadequacies of these which prevent our understanding of children's thought processes. Thirdly, the teacher's approach to the moral education of the child needs to become more anticipatory and less reactive. Only in this way can it be performed as professionally as other areas of the curriculum. Fourthly, a more optimistic view of young children's capabilities in this area is needed. Assuming that children cannot, at certain ages, think and act in certain ways ensures that they will not be given the opportunity to do so, and therefore will not. The teacher must be aware of this self-fulfilling prophecy. Older evidence is sufficiently discredited and newer evidence sufficiently suggestive for the teacher to give the child the benefit of the doubt, to dispense with 'they can't at this age', and instead assume that 'they can'.

Lastly, teachers need to take on board the findings for all theories of moral functioning and blend them into an approach which does justice to the fact that the human being, child and adult, functions at a number of different levels and in a number of different modes. By so doing, a model can be arrived at which provides an overall framework for the implementation of curriculum policy.

Chapter 8

Handling Content

It has already been suggested that the choice of content in this area has been an extremely thorny subject in recent years. Where absolutes can be accepted, as they generally were under the 'ruler and ruled' code, then content can be fairly simply described. One had unarguable principles, so one simply chose the content to attain understanding and obedience of these principles. This generally consisted of readings and exhortations of appropriate sections of the Bible, the teaching of one's place in society and the inculcation of the appropriate social manners. Where an 'objectivist' code is accepted, then, content is reasonably easily prescribed: one has a goal and content is part of the means to that goal.

When, however, such objectivist codes come into question, as they did with the rise of the 'self-chosen' code, then content becomes much more problematical. Teaching *what* is seen essentially as prescription, which runs counter to the notion of self-chosen principles. Some of the approaches taken to avoid this position have already been examined. McPhail *et al.* (1972) allowed their 'moral consumers' – the pupils – to choose the content. Wilson (in Wilson *et al.*, 1967) attempted to show *how* to tackle the moral area rather than *what* to tackle in it. Raths *et al.* (1966), with the values clarification approach, placed emphasis upon the virtues of individual choosing and cherishing, whatever the outcome one came to; Kohlberg (1981a) concentrated on the form of moral judgements rather than the content, and tried to draw applications from psychological research to the practice of moral education.

It was suggested that for a number of reasons these approaches, whilst valuable in many respects, failed to answer certain crucial questions, notably failing to justify the choice of the principles acted upon, and further failing to specify the kinds of content which a moral education curriculum must deal with.

The second of these shortcomings, failing to specify content, may be seen as one of the major reasons why implementation has tended to lack coherence both within and between schools. The practising teacher, naturally enough, wants something with which to get to grips, something rather more substantial than talk of form, of reasoning procedures, of how to approach the subject. These, the teacher will readily agree, are crucial, but there has to be meat in the sandwich as well – what is the teacher to teach *about*?

For the reasons given above, the answers have been few in number, and extremely tentative in their answers. Prescribed content is associated with objectivism, and most educational thinkers have wanted to avoid such content because of its associations with problems like indoctrination. Practising teachers, faced by so many demands, may be left with the uncomfortable feeling that they will be told how to 'do it', but the *it* is not defined. They are left to choose the content. But if educationalists will not prescribe content, what right have teachers to prescribe content for their pupils? In what are they supposed to bed reasoning procedures or forms of moral education? Without content, procedures and forms are dry, lifeless, uninteresting and just about unteachable. As soon as such procedures are bedded in content, are they not prescribing, in the sense that they are implicitly telling their pupils that this area is important and must be considered? Many teachers may well be left with the feeling that the buck has been passed to them. There has been much debate about how contentious issues should be dealt with (for two recent discussions see Stradling *et al.*, 1984 and Wellington, 1986), and this has been off-putting to teachers. How much more so when content is not suggested except in the most general sense of either 'these issues are of interest to present-day society' or 'what are the issues that concern you?'. Little wonder that the raising of values issues has not done too well with the uncommitted teacher. What is needed is an overarching scheme in which to bed such issues.

Is there a way of doing this? I believe there is. In just the same way as it is possible to suggest principles at a trans-social level, so it is possible to consider human experience at a trans-social level, based upon the origins of the experience, and divide it into five separate though interconnected areas of morality. These areas will be briefly described.

THE PERSONAL AREA

This first area could be described as moral claims from the point of view of individual human existence. This is the classic existentialist position of writers such as Kierkegaard, Sartre and Camus (for an introduction see Scott, 1978), which sees humans as potentially free but enormously responsible. It asks fundamental questions such as are there ultimate objective values? If there are not, what are we to make of this existence on earth? What foundation can one provide for a morality which may be purely a matter of personal choice? Themes of freedom, responsibility and meaning crop up constantly. The personal area, then, includes issues such as:

(a)   making sense of a limited life span
(b)   respect for one's body and mental health
(c)   problems of personal development
(d)   moods, emotions and self-control
(e)   facing problems and dealing with them
(f)   loneliness and shyness
(g)   problems of work and leisure
(h)   weighting values and value conflict
(i)   reasons for being moral.

This area clearly does not come within the working definition of morality given in the introduction to this book – that morality is *that area concerned with the ways in which people treat and affect other people*. Yet these issues are clearly ones of value and choice. This being the case, the original definition will now be expanded to be *that area concerned with the ways in which people treat themselves and other people.*

THE INTERPERSONAL AREA

The personal area can therefore be seen as separate from a second area, the moral claims of an interpersonal perspective. Such morality is naturally closely tied to the individual area, and can be produced from it – as with the thought of Heidegger and Buber (again, see Scott, 1978), who see meaning and morality stemming from the exchanges between people. It is the essence of Kant's moral position (for an introduction see Paton, 1978), postulating the existence of rational, autonomous beings who interact with other such beings. It is the classic position of the main stream of western thought on moral matters. The interpersonal area includes issues such as:

(a)   the nature of friendship
(b)   the need for affection and security
(c)   fairness and trust
(d)   getting on with others and personality conflicts
(e)   jealousy, bullying, hatred, conceit, prejudice
(f)   faults in oneself and others
(g)   sexual relationships and marriage
(h)   dependence, interdependence and independence
(i)   the rights and needs of the very young and very old
(j)   the rights of the unborn
(k)   roles and attitudes.

This interpersonal aspect of morality is already embedded in the definition of morality given in that it is about how 'people treat other people' so there is no need for alteration at this stage.

THE SOCIAL AREA

The interpersonal area is, however, at odds with a third area of morality which stipulates that social groups create moralities, and that it is only by understanding the power and influence of the group that one understands the forces upon the individual. Certainly, it is impossible to understand how individuals can be engaged in a war, play football with each other on Christmas Day and return to their trenches at night only to kill each other the following day. The obscenity of that – which occured in 1914 during the First World War – can only be understood and thereby to some extent countered by becoming aware of this social element. It is the essence of Durkheim's (1961) conception of human beings, and of the Marxist (for an introduction see Kamenka, 1969) position as well. The social area, then, includes such issues as:

(a)   roles and attitudes
(b)   conflicts between personal and social wants
(c)   loyalty

(d)   problems of authority and freedom
(e)   the need for rules
(f)   the individual's responsibility to society
(g)   society's responsibility to the individual
(h)   the effects of social institutions upon the individual
(i)   the 'hidden curriculum' of school and society
(j)   types of groups and their demands upon the individual – family, school, work-place, unions, nation
(k)   the problems of minority groups – the handicapped, ethnic groups, homosexuals, gypsies
(l)   problems of society – urban/rural, poverty/affluence
(m)   our society and its relation with other societies
(n)   society and its relation with the natural world.

The inclusion of the social area means that an alteration must be made to the definition of morality given above. It will now be *that area concerned with the ways in which people, individually or in groups, treat and affect themselves and other people.*

THE NATURAL AREA

Fourthly, there are the moral claims of the natural world, the belief that the natural order of the world, its ecology and its inhabitants, have a right to exist, without any reference to the interests of humans. The inclusion of this area is much more contentious than the last three, and it has had a poor time of it in the western philosophical tradition. It is however increasingly being recognized that not only is it important for human beings to be aware of and to have regard for their environment, but also that other living things have certain claims of their own (see, for example, Singer, 1981). Thus pollution, overpopulation and usage by humans in the forms of hunting and factory farming have all to be balanced, it is argued, by the moral rights of the world's other inhabitants. The natural area includes such issues as:

(a)   the natural world and its relations with human society
(b)   pollution
(c)   world resources
(d)   overpopulation
(e)   ecological and ethological insights
(f)   the rights of other creatures on this planet
(g)   hunting
(h)   factory farming.

The acceptance of this as an area of moral concern will mean that a final revision can be made to the definition of morality. It becomes *that area concerned with the ways in which people, individually or in groups, treat and affect themselves and other living beings.*

THE MYSTICAL/RELIGIOUS AREA

There is a fifth area, sometimes in accord with the fourth, more often not, which argues that all life is precious. As Schweitzer puts it:

> in world- and life-affirmation, and in ethics I carry out the will of the universal will-to-live
> (1949: 245)

Yet this area of morality argues that we have become conscious of this precious life ethic in a way which other animals and plants of the natural world have not:

> The world is a ghastly drama of will-to-live divided against itself. One existence makes its way at the cost of another: one destroys the other.
> (1949: 245)

It is then the combination of the understanding of the unity of all life with the realization of the tragic situation of the world which exists which impels us to unite all life, and it is this ethic which should guide human conduct.

This fifth area, however, can also be generated from within the other areas as well. It has been seen by some as being generated through the personal area by reflections of our finiteness (see Heidegger, 1962), through the interpersonal area by seeing the eternal 'Thou' in friendship with another (see Buber, 1958) and through the social area by the sublimation of oneself in the group identity (see Durkheim, 1961). The mystical/religious area includes issues such as:

(a)   reasons for being moral
(b)   the limits of our understanding
(c)   the many meanings of love
(d)   the problem of evil
(e)   the significance of death
(f)   coping with personal tragedy
(g)   people's quests for transcendent meaning
(h)   the nature of friendship.

This generation from within other areas suggests that a crucial element of the religious/mystical approach is the way in which people come to re-view themselves, other people and life as a whole upon taking on this perspective. Their commitment to these other areas is reinformed. A concluding definition of morality can now be: *that area concerned with the ways in which people, individually or in groups, conceptualize, treat and affect themselves and other living beings.*

This, then, can be the final definition, because it takes on board the insights of all these different areas.

It is precisely because there are these autonomous areas that principles generated by them are contradictory at times, and lead to problems in ethics in everyday life which seem quite unresolvable. Table 8.1 gives examples of how the conflict between these five moral areas can generate moral dilemmas. Each area, having a different genesis, emphasizes a right, a duty or a need which may at one time or another come into conflict with the rights, duties or needs of other areas. This conflict suggests a number of insights which are of value to the educator.

Table 8.1   *Dilemmas generated by the conflict between moral areas*

	Personal	Interpersonal	Social	Natural
Interpersonal	The right not to wear a seat belt versus the duty to dependants to take all precautions to stay alive to support them			
Social	The right to life versus the duty to maintain laws punishing theft (Heinz dilemma, see Chapter 2)	The duty to help one's friends versus the duty to tell on those who steal		
Natural	The right to profit from one's labours (e.g. start a gold mine) versus the duty to maintain an ecological balance	The duty to maintain a family by exploiting the land (e.g. by farming) versus animals' rights to live and the duty to maintain an ecological balance	Society's need for new land for an expanding population versus the rights of other creatures	
Religious/mystical	The right to take one's own life versus the duty to maintain *all* life	The duty to maintain a family by killing for food versus the right of other living things to stay alive	Societies' exploitation of the biosphere versus the duty to maintain all life	The need to maintain one's own life by taking other life versus the duty to maintain all life

Firstly, it suggests a coherent overarching policy for content planning. Five areas are identified to which teachers may refer either for help in planning a comprehensive approach, or for checking to what extent materials already in operation present a fair balance.

Secondly, the conflict between these areas presents a means of entry for the teacher into this area. Whilst focus upon such conflict between areas cannot be a comprehensive policy for dealing with aspects of value, as much material is non-conflictual in nature, nevertheless it can generate moral dilemma situations which provide intriguing and exciting teaching materials in all curricular areas. Appendix 1 describes one possible use of such dilemmas – their translation on to computer, providing structure and background strength to the lesson.

Indeed, dilemmas may be generated from *within* separate areas. Table 8.2 gives examples of such generation which the teacher may utilize as a stepping-stone to the question of the scope of morality within one area alone.

Table 8.2   *Dilemmas generated from within one area*

A.   PERSONAL
Individuals have the right to make what they will of their lives. If they wish to become a drug addict, or an alcoholic, they have that right. But what of their duty to maintain their self-respect?

B. INTERPERSONAL
Your friend is desperately keen to remain young looking, and has begun to look like mutton dressed up as lamb. You don't want to hurt him or her by telling the truth, but you feel you ought to, even if he or she is very upset. What do you do?

C. SOCIAL
You feel duty bound to obey the rules of the society you live in. But it is in the grip of a dictator, who is committing all kinds of abuses. Rational argument and peaceful protest will only result in your imprisonment, or worse. You feel it is your duty to help to produce a better society. What do you do?

D. NATURAL
You feel a duty to help to maintain the ecological balance of nature, especially when a particularly virulent form of pest is destroying the local vegetation, and therefore much of the wildlife. On the other hand, you feel it is a duty to let nature take its course and not interfere in these natural processes. What do you do?

E. RELIGIOUS/MYSTICAL
You feel a duty to maintain all life, and yet your mother is suffering terribly from an incurable disease and asks you to put her out of her misery. What do you do?

Thirdly, it places Kohlbergian dilemmas in an entirely new perspective. Rather than being the vehicles for a controversial theory of propelling individuals through stages of moral justice reasoning, they instead become the instruments for focusing upon a conflict between moral areas which because of its very nature is never entirely resolvable in an objective sense.

Fourthly, it points one back to and supports the argument of previous chapters which stated that the nature of morality need not be seen as a battle between absolute objectivism and absolute relativism, but rather might be viewed as the acceptance of the possibility of different levels of objectivity.

Finally, the subjectivity of the individual will affect not only the judgement of such moral dilemmas but also the very value placed upon the respective moral areas. Thus, to the extent that there is a concentration on individual human beings and living within societies, the personal, interpersonal and social areas will tend to occupy moral awareness. However, as awareness and knowledge of the world in which we live increases, as our interdependency and our species' frailty is realized, as these move into our 'subsidiary awareness', so the last two areas force their way into consciousness. Solving moral problems therefore is much about the business of the relative weighting of the importance of the claims of the different areas involved.

This helps us to understand the fact that the topics on which morality dwells shift their ground through the centuries, and so what are seen as moral concerns in one era are not in another. Take, for instance, the fact that people can be aware that animals feel pain to the same degree that they do, and yet it simply does not gain entry into their sphere of moral action. Midgley (1983: 14–16) gives a striking example of this phenomenon when she quotes from a book written in the last century by R. Gordon Cummings, a traveller and hunter in Africa in 1850. He encountered a magnificent specimen of an elephant, shattered its shoulder bone with a bullet, thus rendering it lame and unable to escape, and then proceeded to make camp, have a drink and reflect for a time on what a fortunate man he was, before performing the interesting experiment of seeing in how many places he could shoot the elephant before killing it. Now this was no prototype SS guard: this was (to his own eyes, and, one presumes, the reading public of the time) a jolly decent fellow. He really saw nothing wrong. There was just no link up in his mind between animals feeling and it mattering that they do.

Why, then, is there this moral blindness at times? It can, it seems, suggest two very different things. Either it could mean that moral relativism is true, that morals vary from society to society and are no more fundamental than the culture's rules; or it could mean that there *are* levels of objectivity, but that the line between the social and the trans-social is extremely blurred and, at times, is difficult to perceive. The line becomes clearer with respect to cruelty to animals when such factors as an increased understanding of animals' lives, the studies of ecology and human genetics and the threats from pollution and population growth all make us stand back from our position and empathize with other beings beyond our normal perspective. But, to repeat, because the level of trans-social objectivity is perpetually influenced by levels of social and personal objectivity, one can never be totally certain of the level one has attained. Teachers, then, must help their pupils to make the difficult balancing act of assuming that all values are not relative, that there is a way of deciding between them, whilst at the same time not assuming that the moral truths they arrive at are timeless certainties. Only by a clear appreciation of the value – and difficulties – of trans-social values can stability and tolerance both be provided.

One has, then, an understanding of how areas and levels of morality can interact. The significance and importance of areas can be distorted by the influence of lower levels of objectivity by particular cultural beliefs and personal experiences. This is an important point for teachers to remember in their construction of a curriculum, not only in terms of how 'objective' are the pronouncements being made, but also in terms of the emphasis being given to each area within the moral curriculum as a whole.

What kinds of justification can be given for dividing content in the manner described above? I would suggest that there are at least six.

The first justification is that such a division corresponds well with the concept of trans-social objectivity already discussed. The five areas, in other words, all seem to derive their existence at a level beyond the social or personal. It would be hard to imagine a society which found that experiences from these areas did not impinge on its consciousness. This is no conclusive proof on its own, of course, for there may well be other ways of dividing up such trans-social experience, but it is at least highly suggestive.

The second justification may be purely intuitive – to the reader they may simply look and feel right. This hardly makes the grade as a justification, but whilst it is not sufficient as a reason, it may well be necessary – if something is not intuitively satisfying it is hardly likely to be taken up.

The third justification is essentially pragmatic in nature. It stems from noticing that morality asks all kinds of different questions which do not fit happily together until some division of them into separate groups has taken place. What, for example, has the problem of loyalty to do with that of pollution, or the 'hidden curriculum' of the school and society to do with the nature of friendship, except in the most general terms? What reason could we have for placing the problems of minorities next to that of respect for one's body and mental health? The point being made is that whilst there *is* a sense in which all share some common feature which is usually called 'moral', the commonality is so distant and weak that the making of these common links would generally fail in the school and society unless some more detailed division were carried out. The five areas provide this detailed division which can give coherence and structure to a child's (and a teacher's) understanding. At its bluntest, this pragmatic argument simply states that if divisions are not made in the area as a whole, then it will be seen as too large and confusing; teachers will not teach about the area, and so children will not get taught.

Table 8.3 gives an example of how a spiral curriculum derived from these five areas might look in practice. It is suggested in this table that such topics are applicable at both primary and secondary levels, their level of conceptual difficulty being adjusted to the capabilities of the pupils involved. Needless to say, each school and its teachers will have additions and different emphases to such a scheme, but the presentation of such a curriculum provides a valuable device for conceptualizing the handling of value and ethical issues in school. More detail about its possible implementation will be discussed in Chapter 10.

The fourth justification stems from the fact that an acknowledgement of the existence of these five groups goes some considerable way to explaining the difficulties which some theories have of incorporating uncomfortable facts or moral areas into their arguments. Having already examined some of the kinds of questions which do not sit comfortably together, indeed which on occasion directly clash, it may now be worth looking in a little detail at a complete theory.

Take, for example, the philosopher John Rawls' monumental work in political theory, *A Theory of Justice* (1971). A criticism of some force of his work is that there is no place in it for the rights of animals or non-rational creatures. This is because the work is premised upon the notion of an 'original position', in which human beings, in possession of rational faculties but with no knowledge of their personal circumstances in the world, attempt to design a system of government most favourable to themselves.

It would be most unfair to say that Rawls is unaware of the difficulty. He explicitly states (p. 512) that consideration of the rights of animals or non-rational creatures is:

> . . . outside the scope of a theory of justice, and it does not seem possible to extend the contract doctrine so as to include them in a natural way

So the problem is recognized, even if it is not resolved. A theory of justice, as he describes it, cannot accommodate the rights of animals, babies or mental defectives. As they cannot fight their corner, they have no voice. This at face value seems a terrible indictment of Rawls' theory, and yet, looked at from another angle, shows both the strengths and weaknesses of his position, and throws an interesting light on the structure of moral thought as a whole.

This criticism, that Rawls' theory only takes account of the rights of articulate, linguistically rational creatures, only has force if it is seen as the total extent of morality. And yet Rawls' account, and contract theory in general, being concerned as they are with what constitutes a fair and just society, are interested in only one area of morality. This being so, they cannot account for the rights of other kinds of creatures, or of the nature of some interpersonal exchanges (like friendship), or of the feeling of reverence of the sanctity of life, or of other transcendent urges. It cannot incorporate the other areas of morality. It is clearly not meant to do so, and this points, not to Rawls' theory being wrong, but to it only being applicable to and possibly correct for that part of morality dealing with social justice between human beings. It points to the conclusion that if a conception of morality starts off with an

Table **8.3** *A spiral curriculum in values education*

	Personal	Interpersonal	Social	Natural	Religious/mystical
LOWER	1. Hygiene 2. Dealing with change 3. Dress 4. Self-reliance 5. Safety	1. Fairness 2. Games and taking turns 3. Co-operation 4. Sharing 5. Identifying others' needs 6. The need for politeness and manners	1. Roles of members of the school and family 2. People in society who help us 3. Different groups in society and how they live 4. The need for rules in school 5. The functions of people in school	1. Respect for the environment 2. Care for pets and animals 3. Life, growth and nurturance	1. Religious practices in the local community 2. Stories from the holy books 3. The wonder and mystery of life 4. Problems of religious language
MIDDLE	1. The uniqueness of each individual 2. Dealing with moods 3. Possible abuses of the body 4. Diet 5. Dealing with change 6. Decision making	1. Other people different from ourselves 2. Friendship 3. Sharing 4. Fairness 5. Helping others	1. The roles of members of the family 2. The functions of people in society 3. Different groups within this society 4. Different societies	1. Preservation and conservation of nature 2. Things which spoil or pollute the world 3. People and their environment	1. Comparative religious practices 2. Examples set by famous people 3. Stories from the holy books 4. The many meanings of love 5. Problems of religious intolerance
HIGHER	1. Being truthful to oneself 2. Bodily abuses 3. Physical and emotional development 4. Dealing with change 5. Self-reliance 6. Personal hygiene	1. Different people, different needs 2. Sympathy and empathy 3. Care 4. Fairness and justice 5. Arguments and how they are caused	1. The rights and duties of individual and family 2. The rights and duties of individual and school 3. Societies with other social arrangements and rules 4. How people in society help each other	1. The dangers of pollution 2. Respect for one's environment 3. Preservation and conservation of life	1. Religion, indoctrination and fanaticism 2. The limits of understanding 3. The lives and teachings of central religious/moral figures 4. The significance of birth and death; the rites of passage 5. Why be moral?

inadequate base, then it will have difficulty accounting for people, beings or things to whom or to which moral status would normally be ascribed.

Such an account naturally spells out the limitations of a theory of moral development such as that of Kohlberg (1981a). This is for two main reasons. For a start, any theory which uses Rawls' conception as part of its philosophic base must, on the preceding analysis, be too limited. Any theory which does not acknowledge the existence of five different areas is bound to find itself in difficulties. It is little wonder, then, that there have been so many other theories of morality over the centuries. So often, the whole of moral experience is squeezed, like an occupant of Procrustes' bed, into one perspective, one area of production, with the result that it looks and feels wrong and fails to satisfy as a complete explanation. Morality, it is being suggested here, was never meant to be so squeezed. The limits of each area have to be recognized, and it be accepted that morality is not all of a piece.

The other reason for the limitations of an inadequately conceived theory of moral development is the scope of its questions. What it is looking for, what it will ask, will be grossly limited by its initial assumptions of what it takes morality to be. If morality is generated by five separable areas of experience, it would be expected that children's thoughts and judgements would be considerably more diversified early in life than has generally been thought to be the case. Instead of a rather simplistic view of children's thought processes, capabilities and interests, one would expect to see a much richer picture. This accords much more with findings produced by, for example, Williams and Williams (1969), Steward (1979) and Huntsman (1984), who have found that children's moral attitudes and thought processes show a considerable complexity from very early ages, and further suggest that developmental sequences found by other researchers may be as much a function of adult socialization processes as any physiological maturation. Research at the young child's level has just the same dangers as those at the level of moral theory: if one starts off with an inadequate conception, one ends up with an inadequate theory.

The fifth justification derives from the fact that the division of morality into five areas would go some way to explaining one of the thornier problems in moral philosophy – that of the naturalistic fallacy. As mentioned in Chapter 3, the naturalistic fallacy is that principle which states that one cannot derive ethical conclusions from factual premises, that one cannot derive an 'ought' from an 'is', that descriptive and evaluative languages inhabit different linguistic universes. To give an example: one cannot say that garrotting cats is wrong because nobody does it. Estimating and reporting how many people garrotte cats produces a factual statement: deciding that such actions are wrong is an evaluative one. In order to make a correct transition to the statement that garrotting cats is wrong, one would have to have an initial evaluative premise to the effect that causing pain to cats is wrong, or that garrotting is not a pleasant occupation, or some such thing.

In this sense, adherence to the naturalistic fallacy is, it seems, correct. But it would be absurd to assert that *no* factual statements are taken into account when making evaluative judgements. For instance, one must know both what 'garrotte' means and also various facts about cats before being able to make any evaluative pronouncements upon an act of this nature. If future scientific research were, incredibly, to prove that partial garrotting was actually beneficial to cats, in that it increased their life expectancy by causing the flow of some age-retarding hormone, or some such thing, then evaluative attitudes to such acts would no doubt change substantially. What would we think of dentists if their occupation had no beneficial effect?

The problem is essentially one of deciding when facts have a place and when they do not. If it were possible to decide upon their relevance, then the job would be enormously simplified. This is where the place of a division of morality into five areas may make much sense. If morality is not seen as some monolithic entity, but deriving from five distinct areas of experience described above, then such an approach could locate moral attitudes of the natural, the personal, the interpersonal and the social in the 'facts' of existence on this planet, as naturalistic philosophers have done, whilst still acknowledging that there is another area of morality – the religious/ mystical – which explicitly states its distancing from any naturalistic grounding, and yet which undoubtedly is a very potent force in many people's moral attitudes. To exclude this last area from a consideration of the functioning of morality as a whole is simply to fly in the face of experience. Thus a foot is being placed in both camps, simply because there is truth in both camps. The naturalistic/non-naturalistic argument (i.e. whether morality is a product of natural events or is in some sense transcendent) and at least part of the is/ought debate, then, are examples of the difficulties which are encountered when people fail to recognize that morality has its genesis in five different areas. A belief that is located in only one or two of these areas – perhaps the personal and the social – may lead to a naturalistic attitude which cannot do justice to the mystical; whilst a non-naturalistic attitude which locates morality solely in the mystical/religious has great problems accounting for the fact that many people do not have mystical experiences, and claim not to have a religious orientation, and instead assess morality in the light of the perceived facts of this world. If five areas are crammed into one or two, and their different geneses are not taken into account, then is/ought problems are created which need not occur.

The final justification lies in that this division into five areas has implications which agree with previous chapters in this book. Thus, having argued that morality is not all of a piece, but comes from five separate areas, it follows that each individual, throughout his or her life, is faced with a complex of moral decisions and different demands. These are generated firstly by the five different moral areas previously described and secondly by the levels of objectivity attained by each person. So to the extent that individuals believe in the importance of principles generated from one or more of these areas, so they will give emphasis and take action in ways which make their judgements unique.

Such an approach then takes, as a basis for moral reflection, humanity's predicament in this world – our personal relationships, our roles as actors in society, our views of the claims of other living things on this planet, our perennial desire to make sense of the reason for our existence and of the meaning of life and death – all of this wrapped up in a biological and physical framework of constraining and determining ideas which impede the development of our understanding of the different levels of objectivity. It is to such an understanding that much of a moral education should be devoted.

Yet this cannot be enough. The practising teacher needs more. How is he or she to approach this area and implement it? Some beginnings have been suggested, in terms of such things as focuses of attention, moral areas, and dilemma situations. This process will be continued in the next chapter when one major area of concern, that of co-operation, will be addressed.

Chapter 9

Furthering Co-operation

Three of the four focuses of attention highlighted in Chapter 3 as needing urgent consideration by the school are in fact the major psychological factors so far dealt with in this book. The three dealt with are:

(a) the fostering of the child's self-esteem
(b) the promotion of rationality
(c) the heightening of the child's empathy.

The final focus, then, is the promotion of co-operation. All four of these focuses were seen as being important for the remediation of pathological tendencies arising in society at the present time. Thus, it was argued in Chapters 1 and 2 that it was possible that a too-vigorous pursuit of the GNP code might produce certain deleterious effects in society and in the climate of the school in particular which schools would do well to recognize and combat. One reason, then, for the fostering of the child's self-esteem was seen as the necessity to counteract the effect on pupils of an increased emphasis on overt assessment (which is fine for winners, but most people will of necessity be losers). Similarly, one reason for the promotion of rationality was seen as the necessity to counteract the tendency for simple answers to be demanded for complex issues; whilst one reason for the heightening of empathy was seen as the necessity to counteract the effect of the simplistic belief 'if I can do it, so can they'.

In like manner, one reason for the promotion of co-operation is seen as its necessity in an era which is tending to see education as a competitive activity. Where education is seen in the GNP manner – as having explicit aims and objectives, identifiable ends and quantifiable assessment, as being concerned predominantly with a training for introduction into the job market – then it will be viewed as essentially a question of providing children with the skills to fill particular vacancies when they leave school. When this is the view, then the most efficient (and indeed the fairest) way of filling such vacancies is via competition between the potential employees. Some form of assessment – probably examination success – will be seen as the means of facilitating such job placement, and so inevitably this must mean competition between pupils within a school. Pupils are then seen as pursuing independent, individualistic routes through their educational careers, ones in which other pupils are seen as at best irrelevant, at worst in competition.

Indeed, one does not have to dwell on present tendencies to argue for the existence of these effects. Piaget (1932: 286) came to much the same conclusions as to the reasons for cheating in class. As his analysis takes one a little further, it is worth quoting at some length:

> Cheating is a defensive reaction which our educational systems seem to have wantonly called forth in the pupil. Instead of taking into account the child's deeper psychological tendencies which urge them to work with others . . . our schools condemn the pupil to work in isolation and only make use of emulation to set one individual against another. This purely individualistic system of work, excellent no doubt if the aim of education be to give good marks and prepare the young for examinations, is nothing but a handicap to the formation of reasonable beings and good citizens. Taking the moral point of view only, one of two things is bound to happen. Either competition proves strongest, and each boy will try to curry favour with the master, regardless of his toiling neighbour who then, if he is defeated, resorts to cheating. Or else comradeship will win the day and pupils will combine in organised cheating so as to offer a common resistance to scholastic restraint.

The saddest part of this, to the present writer, is that the source of the child's 'immoral' practices, or its antagonism to the school's authority, is located precisely within the school's own procedures. Rather than aiding the child in its moral and ethical development, schools are at best hindering the process, at worst reversing it.

However, in addition to the effects of such social and political pressure on the school, there are other important reasons for establishing a more co-operative situation in the learning environment. Where there is still a generally didactic approach to teaching, competition will probably be the norm as well. Where this didactic approach is standard, a number of hidden – and probably unwanted – lessons may be learnt by the pupils.

Firstly, the student may learn that there is one and only one expert in the classroom – the teacher. Secondly, the student may also learn that there is one and only one correct answer to any question the teacher may ask: the answer that the teacher has in his or her head. The task is to figure out what the teacher expects. Thirdly, and most importantly from the present chapter's point of view, the students may also learn that they succeed by others' failing. Where competition is the form of interaction between two people, one must lose if the other is to win. Those who succeed may well look down on those who fail, while those who fail may be envious of those who succeed, and may be alienated from the school.

It must not be assumed, however, that co-operation is being recommended in a purely medicinal manner. Society may have its ailments, and it may need medication for them, but it would be wrong to see self-esteem, rationality, empathy and co-operation purely as counteractive strategies. They have undoubted positive benefits as well. Thus co-operation can promote friendliness and understanding between children in a unique manner. It would therefore be valuable to improve basic teaching processes so that children learn to like and trust each other not as an extracurricular activity, but as part of the actual activity of learning.

Further, co-operation must not be seen only as an asset for promoting sociability and learning in the classroom. It can also be claimed to be fundamental to future adult associations, particularly in business. This statement may come as something of a surprise when directed to such a competitive ethos, and yet *within* the business team, co-operation is vital if the team is to succeed. Belbin (1981) has found that a balanced team works better than any other form of team, and this is because co-operation is made that much easier. A team of all the talents fails because of clashes within the group. As Belbin says (p. 13):

> Overconcentration on becoming top boy in the class provides an unconscious training in anti-teamwork.

This, he suggests, may be due to the present nature of the education system, which not only stresses competition between pupils but also places a high premium on analytical criticism as the distinguishing mark of intelligence, and places much less premium on creative, synthesizing abilities, the kinds which propose solutions rather than merely analyse problems. Analysts may be needed, says Belbin, but other talents are needed as well (p. 77):

> The useful people to have in teams are those who possess strengths or characteristics which serve a need without duplicating those already there. Teams are a question of balance. What is needed is not well-balanced individuals, but individuals who balance well with one another. In that way, human frailties can be underpinned and strengths used to full advantage.

Belbin does well to point back from the adult in management to the child in education, for the school is undoubtedly a heavy influence in the kinds of behaviour which children will adopt as desirable, behaviours they will carry into adult life.

Table 9.1 *Eleven arguments for and against competition in education*

FOR	AGAINST
1. It encourages an appreciation of others' perspectives (if only to beat them).	1. It encourages it for the wrong reasons – to put other people down.
2. It provides motivation for learning – and so encourages better performances.	2. Motivation should ideally be intrinsic to the subject; if it is not, can it be achieved by other means (co-operation)?
3. It is a natural desire.	3. Anthropological evidence suggests it is not.
4. It is character forming. The child must come to understand it is not the winning and losing that matter, but the taking part.	4. If we have a competitive society, then this is a valid aim. But should education be working towards a co-operative society?
5. It helps understand the need for rules in a society, and the need to play by those rules.	5. This does not mean that education should further that need.
6. It is cathartic – a channel for aggression.	6. It is not – evidence suggests it provides modelling and reward for competition, but punishment for co-operation.
7. It boosts self-confidence and self-esteem in winners.	7. It reduces self-confidence and self-esteem in losers – and there are more losers.
8. It is a fair way of deciding between people in competition for jobs.	8. It is not – genetic and environmental differences prevent such fairness.
9. It helps children to think for themselves and be independent. It furthers autonomy.	9. It reduces their ability to see others as friends and learning resources. It reduces interdependence.
10. It is essential training for living in our society.	10. Perhaps society should change. Perhaps it is not essential.
11. It is the only way of ensuring high academic standards.	11. Co-operation can produce the same standards.

Co-operation is therefore propounded as not only a necessary antidote to present problems within schools, but also as a positive good in both schools and society. However, it has to be acknowledged that it does not have the stage to itself. There are certainly enough advocates of competition in education. Table 9.1 provides a summary of what the author believes to be the major arguments for and against competition in education. Some are undoubtedly more powerful than others. Thus, some may be dismissed pretty summarily. For example, competition is *not* a natural desire (argument 3), as there is enough anthropological evidence (see, for instance, Graves and Graves, 1982 and Turnbull, 1976) to show that many societies get on very well without it. It is rather that western society has become so used to its practice that practical alternatives to it cannot be imagined.

Similarly, it is simply wrong to say that it acts as a cathartic release for aggressive tendencies (argument 6). Rather, it provides modelling which suggests that those who win are best and most popular, and those who lose are not worth bothering with, and it similarly rewards those who compete whilst punishing those who lose or co-operate (see Orlick, 1978). Finally, it may well boost the self-confidence and esteem of winners (argument 7), but its general effect upon losers (of whom there are incomparably more) is precisely the opposite.

On the other hand, some arguments are not dismissed so easily. Thus, it may well encourage an appreciation of others' perspectives (argument 1), which we have already said is a 'good thing'. If this can be done in a friendly, fun-like way, then competition may well be of benefit to the individual. However, as we shall see, this appreciation of others' perspectives can be equally well accomplished by co-operation.

Similarly, it is undoubtedly the case that it provides motivation for learning (argument 2), and with some children it may be seen as a necessary preliminary step to a motivation derived from intrinsic interest in the subject. What will be argued shortly is that such motivation can be accomplished just as effectively by co-operation, without the harmful side-effects competition can have.

For those who believe it helps children to be more independent (argument 9), problems of competition reducing *inter*dependence may not seem as important in the short term. However, any proper consideration of such an effect may well come to the conclusion that being able to get on with others and work with them, pooling ideas and effort, is at least as important as pure undiluted independence, which could very easily become an unwillingness or inability to work or socialize with others or appreciate their points of view.

Finally, there is a last group of arguments which are very difficult to completely dismiss. The argument that the existence of competition helps children understand the need for rules and the need to play by those rules (argument 5) is one which presumes the continued existence of a competitive society (for who needs rules where all co-operate?). However, it is unlikely that utopia is around the corner, and this argument must in some measure be conceded.

Again, it is generally seen as a fair way of deciding between people when they are applying for the same vacancy, etc. (argument 8), and though a sound argument can be made for saying that *no* competition is ever totally fair because of different genetic and environmental inheritances, yet it would be difficult to suggest fairer methods which were also time saving and efficient.

The argument that competition can be character forming if used correctly (argument 4) – the child must learn to lose as well as win – is undoubtedly a worthy aim within a competitive society. And, whilst such competition exists, it may be seen as a very strong argument.

The final two arguments, I would suggest, are probably at the bottom of many arguments for the inclusion of competition within the school. Because they appear to be so important, complete sections will be devoted to them.

ARGUMENT 10

The first argument that competition is essential training for living in our society (argument 10) is usually grudgingly acknowledged by co-operative educators, who do not like the fact that they seem to be faced by a dilemma. Either they pursue co-operative aims in the school and thereby disadvantage the co-operatively taught child, or they acknowledge the need to ground the child in the ways of the world and thus unhappily use competitive processes. What will probably happen is a reluctant compromise, a bit of competition, a bit of co-operation.

The individual who helps others is faced, in evolutionary terms, by the simple question – what is the selective advantage in helping others? How, in other words, does the act of a man jumping into a river to save a drowning child square with the principle of 'the survival of the fittest'? How does this benefit himself? Robert Trivers (1971) first put forward an argument to explain this when he suggested that it would be of benefit to the man *in the long term*. Even if he was putting himself in some danger by his altruistic act, he was not actually sacrificing his life, and the result would probably be that the boy would grow up to help him in the future. A question of balance of costs, when viewed in the long term, results in a view that there is less cost in helping the boy now and insuring help later on than there is in leaving the boy to drown and having no-one to help you in future times.

What, however, of the 'cheat' – the individual who accepts help but then refuses to repay? This surely benefits the cheaters, and will eliminate the helpers. Or does it? Richard Dawkins (1976) suggests that a 'grudger' – one who gives help, but doesn't have it reciprocated – will remember the cheat and never give the cheat help again. So the cheat may benefit in the short term, but will quickly lose out. Grudgers, on the other hand, will help each other and so gradually eliminate the cheaters. In essence, then, one has the basis of social co-operation – which is why the anthropologist can argue that competition is no more natural than co-operation. They can both be behaviours of choice.

It may well be, then, that the co-operative educator does not have to feel so despondent about the chances of the co-operatively educated child in a competitive world. Further, the insights of Trivers and Dawkins have recently been taken up in an extremely elegant and fascinating piece of research by Robert Axelrod (1984) which demonstrates that even within an egoistic, competitive society, co-operation is the best strategy for securing the best results. Axelrod comes at the problem from a slightly different angle from Trivers and Dawkins, his research being based upon the classic problem of the soldier's dilemma. The dilemma is very simple. In it, two soldiers have to defend a wall guarding a narrow pass against an oncoming army. It will be very dangerous. They both know that:

(a) if they stay together on the wall they both have a pretty good chance of surviving;

(b)   if one stays and the other runs away, the one's chances of survival are fairly minimal;

(c)   if one runs away and the other stays, the other may delay the oncoming army for a sufficient length of time for the one fleeing to escape completely.

What should they do? The soldier's dilemma is easily turned into a game by having two players with counters, C (co-operate) on one side, D (defect) on the other. The rules are:

(a)   try to get the highest score you can
(b)   don't reveal your intentions until your counter is displayed
(c)   score as follows:

> both co-operate   = 3 points each
> both defect   = 1 point each
> one defect, one co-operate   = defect=5, co-operate=0

Axelrod asked computer experts to design a strategy which would gain the maximum number of points for the player. The unexpected result, after the first round of pairing strategies off against one another, was that a simple co-operative 'tit-for-tat' strategy beat all comers, even the aggressively selfish competitive ones. The same occurred when, on the second round, Axelrod asked all comers to design a strategy which could beat 'tit-for-tat'. Not one succeeded. Being co-operative in the 'tit-for-tat' manner as a long-term strategy for doing well worked better than any competitive strategy which could be devised. When examined closely, 'tit-for-tat' revealed four winning principles:

(a)   be nice – never be the first to be nasty: be optimistic about human nature
(b)   be provocable – always respond to nastiness with nastiness
(c)   be forgiving – always accept peace offerings from the nasty with forgiveness
(d)   be clear – always allow the other side to know exactly what you will do.

In addition to these four principles, Axelrod also teased out of the situation these further four factors which affected the behaviour of interactors:

(a)   There must be predictability in the situation – knowing what the other will do greatly increases co-operativeness. The simplicity of the 'tit-for-tat' strategy allowed precisely this.

(b)   There must be certainty of future interaction – for where this is not present, the future holds no threat to defection.

(c)   There must be frequency of interaction – the more frequent the interaction, the more predictability of strategy is assured, and the more the certainty of future interaction.

(d)   There must be an identifiability of the partners with whom interaction is taking place, and the more identifiable, the more co-operative behaviour will be encouraged.

How, then, can one improve co-operativeness? Specific strategies will be suggested in the appendices to this book, but for the moment some more general strategies will be offered. Firstly, one can, as Axelrod describes it, 'enlarge the shadow of the future' – make what happens after one acts at least as important as the immediate pay-off for defection. Secondly, one can change the pay-offs – make it more profitable to co-operate, less profitable to defect. Thirdly, one can teach people to care about each other – through such things as socialization, empathic activities and social ethos. Fourthly, one can teach reciprocity – actually show people how 'nice' strategies benefit everyone all round. Fifthly, one can improve recognition abilities – not only of what the person is actually doing, but also of who is doing it.

It must be remembered that Axelrod placed the whole of the exercise within a basically egoistic, competitive environment. One would naturally expect co-operative behaviour to be successful within an already existing co-operative environment – those who tried to make personal capital at the expense of the co-operating group could expect to make a short-term gain, but would then be ostracized by the group. But for co-operative behaviour to be the most successful strategy within a *competitive* environment is, I would suggest, nothing short of astounding. It may then be the kind of argument one needs in order to persuade others that one does not need to start with large-scale co-operative behaviour for it to gain a toehold. Rather it can have very humble beginnings and still prosper.

ARGUMENT 11

This argument states that competition is needed in education because without it there would be a decline in academic standards. On this argument, it may be acknowledged that co-operation has certain beneficial social effects, but these are gained at the expense of academic rigour, and in an age such as ours, the maintenance of such academic standards is crucial to the country's future economic prosperity.

One could of course immediately argue that such beneficial social effects should not be given second place to anything, including academic standards. The prioritization of academic standards is another assumption of the GNP code, and one which need not be accepted. It could be argued very strongly that having an economically prosperous nation counts for nothing if its inhabitants have no ability to get on with each other, and see each other as rivals or threats to their well-being. It might well be that a certain amount of economic prosperity should be sacrificed in the pursuit of the goals of understanding, friendliness and co-operation. At the very least, this kind of argument should be given thoughtful examination. At the moment, the 'economic' argument appears to be an accepted assumption by parties of all persuasions.

However, it may not even be necessary to argue this. One can take the argument on its own terms and show that similar or better academic results can be achieved by co-operative techniques. The most impressive findings in this area come from the work of Aronson *et al.* (1978) in their research on the 'jigsaw technique' in classrooms.

The 'jigsaw' classroom works by the teacher taking a topic and writing that lesson for the day in such a way that it now consists of four, five or six passages. These passages are then given out to each child in the learning group, one passage per child. Each child in the group has the job of mastering his or her passage, and then teaching it to the others in the group.

The children then go back into their groups, where they have a certain amount of time to teach the material in their passage to each other. They are also told that at the end of that time each person will be tested on his or her understanding of all the passages. Clearly the students have to depend upon one another to learn all of the material. The process is highly reminiscent of a jigsaw puzzle, with each student possessing a single vital piece of the big picture, which is why the system is referred to as 'jigsaw' teaching. The children then begin to learn two important lessons: firstly, that none of them can do well without the aid of every other person in that group, and secondly, that each member has a unique and essential contribution to make.

The findings by Aronson *et al.* were quite consistent, and consisted of five major benefits. Firstly, students in jigsaw classrooms increased their liking for their group-mates without decreasing their liking for other people in their classroom. Secondly, both white and black children in the jigsaw classrooms started to like school better (or hate school less) than white and black children in competitive classrooms. Thirdly, the self-esteem of the children in jigsaw classrooms increased to a greater extent than that of children in competitive classrooms. Fourthly, children in the jigsaw classrooms co-operated more and saw their classmates as learning resources more often than children in competitive classrooms did. Lastly, and most importantly for the present point of view, in terms of mastery of classroom material, children in the jigsaw classrooms performed as well as or better than children in competitive classrooms. Specifically, Aronson and his colleagues found that white children maintained the same standard of academic achievement, whilst black and Chicano children achieved a higher standard.

The initial technique was designed with secondary students in mind. As it stands, it is not appropriate for the primary classroom. Adjustments are needed if the strategy is to be used with younger pupils. This work was undertaken by the present writer (1987) in an inner-city primary school in the north of England to classes of 6- to 8-year olds. (A full description is given in Appendix 2.) Briefly, however, the results gained here replicated those of Aronson in the United States. The academic results from the tests given after the jigsaw lessons were consistently high, showing an average score of 75 to 80 per cent, with very few scores dropping below 50 per cent. There was then an undoubtedly – and in some cases unexpectedly – high retention rate of materials used. The enjoyment of the children in this experience transferred to the learning of the topics and stories chosen. However, the benefits could be seen in three other ways as well.

Firstly, the increased focus on co-operative behaviour between children in the classroom allowed for the practice of such behaviour, and because of the positive feedback from such co-operative behaviour improved the chances of its repetition. Secondly, the almost total absence of 'chalk and talk' by the teacher allowed the children to feel much more active and important in the learning process, and gave the teacher a chance to take a more guiding and advisory role. Finally, all readers, both good and poor, were given real reason and motivation for attempting to compre-hend materials. The feedback – by way of results of tests afterwards, and verbal responses (see Appendix 2) – strongly suggests that all readers felt this greater relevance.

Argument 11, then, that competition is needed in education because without it there would be a decline in academic standards, does not appear to be proven. There are other, co-operative, techniques which appear to do the job as well.

However, we need not leave the matter there. There are also areas which co-operative techniques may explore and exploit which would be of considerable benefit to the moral development of the child.

One such technique is a vehicle not only for co-operation but also for the explo-ration of the subjectivity of judgement and tolerance and the construction of rules.

The 'subjigtive' technique is described in greater detail in Appendix 3, but may briefly be described here. Like the jigsaw technique, it consists of a total problem situation, only one part of which is known to each group member. Their task is to co-operate in order to construct a total picture of the problem, and then move on to attempt to devise rules which would solve the dilemma posed. By so doing, pupils come to appreciate that they need all points of view in order to gain a less subjective perception of the situation. They also begin to realize that tolerance of others' opinions is no bad thing, for many situations in real life have precisely this subjective element to them. And lastly, they begin to realize that rules are created because of and in order to legislate between the competing claims within such dilemmas.

Another co-operative technique, the 'pooling' technique, described in Appendix 4, demonstrates that not only do co-operative efforts produce better results than individual ones, but also the judgement of 'better' can be very much of the subjective nature described in earlier chapters. Judgement in many situations may not be ultimately proved by any 'objective' criteria, but it is still undoubtedly better than other judgements. It was originally taken from a NASA exercise on deciding what is most valuable to have with you when stranded on the moon's surface (see Appendices in Aronson *et al.*, 1978). However, the NASA exercise, having provided a list of possible objects, then contrasts individual choice with group choice by means of an 'objectively' correct order. The 'pooling' technique, on the other hand, deliberately provides no objective criteria for contrast. It allows individual and group to compare opinions, and attempt to validate priorities in the same way as people do most of the time in ordinary life – by a combination of scientific knowledge, common sense, intuition, logic and values. It offers no final solution, but demonstrates that even without this, making a choice still makes sense.

A further variation, 'creative pooling', takes this process one stage further by posing a problem but providing no items at all for prioritization, thus leaving not only the assessment of the value of items to the individual and the group, but even their selection. Such a variation leads naturally to the fostering of creative and divergent thinking, and the use of 'brainstorming' techniques.

A fourth technique, 'co-operative squares', has wide popularity, and justifiably so for it is an excellent stimulus to children to actively perceive others' needs, rather than waiting to be asked. Briefly, it involves the cutting up of squares into various shapes which are then distributed between members of the group. They all have different parts of different squares, but are informed that they may not ask for parts to complete their square, but must wait until another perceives their need and gives them a piece. All parties thus experience both need and help. The game is completed when all members have a square each. Appendix 5 describes this game in greater detail, and also suggests ways in which the game may be modified so that even the youngest members of the school may play it.

Finally, Appendix 6 is a list of games and activities which can be performed during PE lessons, or purely for the fun of it. They emphasize that co-operative techniques are as simple to implement as competitive ones, are as much fun, and have markedly beneficial effects on children's self-esteem.

It therefore seems fair to say that co-operation between pupils can lead not only to generally better than average academic performance, but it can have significant beneficial effects upon the ways in which pupils see each other, how they get on in class and how they perceive themselves, as well as being capable of linking in with concepts like divergent thinking and creativity, tolerance, subjectivity and the mutual creation of rules. Competition, on the other hand, has a rather different effect. Through the necessity of seeing others as fellow competitors, pupils may channel feelings towards others into antagonistic and aggressive channels. And further, competition, by its focus upon there being clear winners and losers, may boost the winner's self-concept but may lessen that of those who do not win.

The conclusion must be that such a competitive environment is not inevitable in school. Where an environment can be created which not only boosts each individual's self-esteem by demonstrating that there is something to be valued in each person's performance, but also creates an ethos in which each person sees each other person as friend and ally, then surely this latter environment is more to be favoured. What is the point of a competitive environment where the same academic results can be gained by other means, and better social results can always be produced?

Chapter 10

Implementation Throughout the Curriculum

The complexity of the school's involvement in moral education can be immensely off-putting for the non-specialist teacher. The task of the educator may seem a daunting one indeed. Yet this should not be seen as prohibitive. It is doubtful whether the ultimate aims of any area of the curriculum are ever achieved, and yet this should not prevent the attempt. What is needed, once an idea of the aims and complexity of the area is understood, is some relatively simple procedure which gets things going. This is the aim of this chapter.

It is important at this stage to recapitulate on the perspectives already suggested in previous chapters. There have been two main ones so far. First, there has been the suggestion that there are four focuses of attention which need to be addressed in schools at the present time, in part at least because of the prevailing social and political ethos. These are:

(a) the fostering of self-esteem
(b) the heightening of empathy
(c) the furthering of co-operation
(d) the promotion of rationality.

The second perspective has been that morality is generated from five separate but interpenetrating areas, which were described as:

(a) the personal
(b) the interpersonal
(c) the social
(d) the natural
(e) the religious/mystical.

The first perspective suggests to the teacher the kinds of processes which should be concentrated upon and developed. The second perspective suggests to the teacher the kinds of areas within which these processes might be bedded. This immediately gives the teacher 4×5 areas in which to develop teaching materials. This may be represented in a grid such as that in Table 10.1.

However, there is one more perspective to be added which can greatly facilitate the development of an overall conception of this area for the school. If it is accepted that the linkage between morality and the school is to be a proactive one – one where the school actively works towards a desired conception of the moral society –

Table 10.1 *A grid for co-ordinating two perspectives*

PROCESS AREA	Self-esteem	Empathy	Co-operation	Rationality
Personal				
Interpersonal				
Social				
Natural				
Religious/mystical				

then this relationship between morality and the school should be translated into curricular terms. This has been begun by means of the grid in Table 10.1 between the focuses of attention and areas of morality. It can be substantially completed by the addition of one more perspective – a curricular perspective which describes the various 'layers' of school practice which can influence the relationship between morality and the school. This can be thought of in terms of the 'curriculum onion' of Figure 10.1.

Each area of the 'curriculum onion' raises different questions and different strategies. Each will be examined in turn.

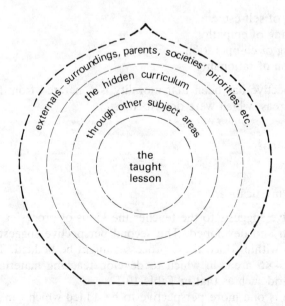

Figure 10.1 The curriculum onion

EXTERNAL FACTORS

(a) Questions on the school's surroundings might be:
   – are they affluent/depressed? urban/rural?
   – is there unemployment? racism? a high crime rate? drug-taking?
(b) Questions on the parents of the school's pupils might be:
   – are they a multi-ethnic group?
   – what are their views on value issues?
   – what attitudes do they transmit?
(c) Questions on society's priorities might be:
   – what is transmitted to the young as being of major concern? Is it justice? care? equality? freedom? wealth?
   – are its educational aims closely tied to economic priorities?
   – what is its hidden curriculum?

HIDDEN CURRICULUM

Roland Meighan (1981: 52) suggested that a working definition of the hidden curriculum might be:

  all the other things that are learnt during schooling in addition to the official curriculum.

However, he goes on to point out that the term is highly ambiguous, a 'porridge' word, which lacks precision but stimulates further thought. It can be used in a variety of ways.

The hidden curriculum as the manipulative curriculum

It can be used to suggest that much of what goes on in schools is hidden in order to manipulate the unwary. Thus, seating in classes might be deliberately arranged in rows and children trained to sit quietly in these rows until asked a question. If this was done precisely to socialize children in class into a particular way of behaving which they could be expected to replicate on the factory floor, then this might be a case of the hidden curriculum as manipulation.

The hidden curriculum as the informal curriculum

It can be used to suggest that part of what goes on in schools which is not part of any formal timetabling, but is seen as the manner in which the formal timetable is conducted. It is not regarded as manipulative in that practitioners are aware of its existence and are prepared to defend its use. Examples might be the use of co-operative strategies as a means of encouraging greater understanding and self-esteem in pupils. It will be readily recognized that one person's 'manipulative' hidden curriculum could well be another person's 'informal' curriculum.

The hidden curriculum as the forgotten curriculum

It can be used to suggest that much of what goes on in school is now practised in an unthinking way, and so has an effect which is simply not noticed or recognized. Thus, to take the example given above, if the original reason for sitting children in rows, training them to sit quietly and only speak when spoken to, is forgotten, but the practice continued, the effect will remain, even if the resulting pattern of socialization is not intended.

The hidden curriculum as the unrecognized curriculum

It can be used to suggest those activities in school whose effect, far from originally being designed for a particular purpose and that purpose having been forgotten, was never recognized in the first place. Thus, to take a simple example, it might be pure administrative efficiency which induces a primary school to have different children collecting registers and dinner books. It might however do wonders for children's self-esteem in that they are given what they perceive to be a responsible job.

Two things become clear from this brief discussion. One is that the hidden curriculum is not necessarily something that has 'bad' effects. The second is that the hidden curriculum can be either covert (manipulative or informal) or unintended (forgotten or unrecognized). However, to the extent that it is covert, it bypasses the critical faculties of pupils (and sometimes teachers) and may come close to indoctrination. To the extent that it is unintended, it can have effects which both pupils and teachers may find disagreeable. Crucially, then, whatever one may wish to say about its definitions, it is the effects of the hidden curriculum which must in the end be the major concern. Table 10.2 suggests the ways in which the hidden curriculum may influence the moral activity of the school, ranging from the effects of society in general through to the teaching style used in a particular lesson.

Table 10.2 *The hidden curriculum of the school – some questions*

Goals
1. Who has most influence in defining the goals of the school?
2. Are the goals well defined or fluctuating?
3. Are there regular meetings for such goals to be discussed?

The head
4. Does the head present a model to the staff?
5. Does the head appreciate the work of the staff?

The staff
6. What is the morale of the staff like?
7. What is the proportion of staff regularly attending courses?
8. What is the average reading matter of the staff room?
9. What is co-operation between staff like?
10. How do staff regard their pupils?
11. How do the pupils regard the staff?
12. Where do the staff, in general, locate the major cause of pupils' behaviour problems?
13. How are non-teaching members of the school treated?
14. Is the staff room for all members of the school, or just the teaching members?

The children
15. Is a child missed when absent?

16. If he or she is missed, why?
17. What is the school policy on children without PE kit?

Racism
18. What proportion of senior management posts are held by teachers of minority ethnic origins?
19. What image of the Third World is presented in the school?   •
20. Is there a presentation of other cultures' customs, views and beliefs?
21. If there is, are these integrated across the curriculum or performed as a separate lesson?
22. Is the presence of ethnic minorities in the school seen as a problem or as a possibility?
23. Are children from ethnic minorities treated differently in disciplinary matters?
24. To what extent do the staff see the problem lying with the minority or majority culture?

Sexism
25. What proportion of senior management posts are held by men/by women?
26. *Which* senior management posts are held by men/by women?
27. What are the relative proportions of boys/girls taking optional subjects?
28. What proportion of time in a lesson do teachers spend answering and dealing with boys/with girls?
29. Are boys and girls treated differently in disciplinary matters?
30. Do the girls do the tidying up after a lesson?
31. Are the boys' names always called first on the register?
32. Does grouping within class enhance sex mixing?
33. Are games lessons organized on the basis of sex differences?

The parents
34. What part do parents play in the running of the school?
35. What part would the staff like to see the parents play in the running of the school?
36. How are letters home to parents addressed?
37. What account is taken of parental expectations?

Visitors
38. How are visitors to the school treated?
39. What are visitors' first impressions of the school?
40. Are visitors' views noted and taken account of?

Community, society and environment
41. What account is taken of society's expectations?
42. Do the school facilities and the surrounding environment make any difference to the implementation of the goals of the school?
43. Are school facilities viewed as shareable by other members of the community?

Teaching styles, topics and activities
44. What teaching styles are regularly used?
45. How are project topics selected?
46. Is there co-ordination between staff on teaching styles and topics?
47. What are the number and type of outside activities?

Competition and co-operation
48. What proportion of time is spent on co-operative as opposed to competitive activities?
49. Does the school have school teams, and if so why?
50. Are trophies valued highly, and if so why?

Achievement and assessment
51. What stress does the staff place on academic achievement?
52. Is there selection and streaming in the school?
53. If so, how many pupils transfer classes each year?
54. What subjects are regarded as important, and why?
55. What form does marking take?
56. What function does marking perform?
57. What other forms of assessment are there, and what functions do they perform?

Democracy
58. What is the head's view on the involvement of staff in decision making?
59. What is the staff's view on the involvement of staff in decision making?
60. In what areas are the staff most involved in decision making?
61. In what areas are the staff least involved in decision making?
62. Does the school involve pupils in the decision-making process?
63. If so, in what activities is this participation seen?

Rewards and punishments
64.   When are rewards and punishments used?
65.   What rewards and punishments are used?
66.   Is withdrawal from certain lessons used as a punishment?
67.   Is compulsion to do certain lessons used as a punishment?
68.   What is the relative proportion of rewards and punishments in the school?

The beginning and end of the day
69.   What time do head and staff arrive at school?
70.   What time do they leave?

A profitable way of approaching this list would be for a staff to deal with the questions one at a time, using the following procedure:

(a)   Ask the hidden curriculum question.
(b)   Provide an answer.
(c)   Ask whether the staff are happy with this answer.
(d)   If they are not, why not?
(e)   How could the situation in the school be changed?

Each question could be the topic of an entire staff meeting (or several!), and its repercussions could go on indefinitely in terms of action taken and the evaluation of such action. There is probably enough material here to occupy a school from its inception to its closure.

MAKING THE LINKAGE BETWEEN MORALITY AND SCHOOLING THROUGH SUBJECT AREAS

It will have been noted that the lines dividing the different layers of the curriculum onion in Figure 10.1 are broken rather than solid. This is to indicate that the layers are not to be seen as separate and discrete but continuously interactive. Thus, whilst one may talk of making a linkage between morality and the school through curricular areas, this should be expanded by taking on board the perception that the other layers will provide stimulus and enrichment for this layer, and may indicate that final implementation could be through a taught lesson. However, within this layer, it appears possible to distinguish two complementary approaches.

(a)   Using subject area content. Examples might be:
   – story and drama – developing an understanding of others' thoughts and feelings
   – science – value issues behind scientific research, e.g. nuclear energy, foetal experimentation
   – history – consideration of value issues facing historical figures and their reaction to them
   – religion – examination of religious value systems, examples of great model behaviours
   – social studies, geography – how different living conditions affect cultures, value systems and behaviours
   – physical education – competition versus co-operation in sport, commercial pressures in professional sport.

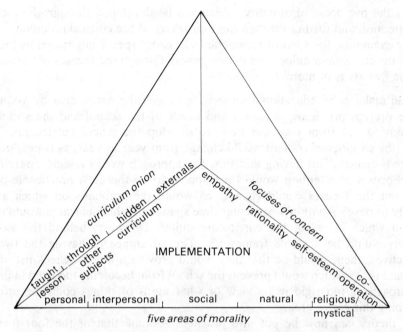

Figure 10.2 The implementation pyramid

(b) Using subject area process. One particularly good idea, as mentioned in Chapter 9, is that of the jigsaw technique in which selected material is divided into four, five or six parts. Each part is learnt by one member of a group of pupils, who then teaches his or her part to the others. In this way, each member of the group has an important part to play in the overall understanding of the material. A simple test for comprehension at the end of the lesson may aid as both a stimulus to learning and an assessment technique for the teacher.

THE TAUGHT LESSON

One might use the kind of moral dilemma devised by the American psychologist Lawrence Kohlberg. As described on pp. 23–4, he believed that human beings think about moral issues in six qualitatively different stages. It is then possible, by confronting the individual with such dilemmas and by suggesting arguments at a higher stage of development than their own stage, to move them on to more advanced moral reasoning. Now whilst there has been considerable criticism of the existence of such stages, the construction of such dilemmas does undoubtedly stimulate more sophisticated moral reasoning. With a little ingenuity, such dilemmas could be given an empathic component by means of drama and role play (and see Appendix 1).

If the layers of the curriculum onion are then added to the focuses of attention and the five areas of morality, there is produced a three-dimensional implementation pyramid (Figure 10.2) by which to approach this area in the school. This pyramid can be entered either:

(a) by the four focuses of attention, which can then be developed within each of the five areas of morality and through the four layers of the curriculum onion

(b)   by the five areas of morality, which can be developed through the focuses of attention and further through the four layers of the curriculum onion
(c)   by examining the sorts of techniques and issues specifically raised by the layers of the curriculum onion, and develop these through the focuses of attention and the five areas of morality.

It would make good educational sense to approach the entire area by asking what are the present problems, demands and needs of the school and the society, and then moving out from such questions to develop the school curriculum. To this extent, the specifics of content would change from year to year, as issues, problems and needs change. But having said this, the approach would remain essentially the same. Focuses of attention would then appear to be the most practicable point of entry, but the focuses would change, as would the emphasis on which areas of morality to develop within a particular time span, and which teachers would concentrate on which layers of the curriculum onion. However, behind this necessary flexibility would lie a stable framework. The advantage of having the two other perspectives, then, would be that they would provide a kind of check-list of areas, topics and issues which would prevent the school from becoming too fixed in direction of approach or too rigid in its view of what kinds of things could be utilized in developing this entire area.

This theory can now be put into practice. Assume that of the four focuses of attention just described, the two on which it is decided to concentrate are rationality and empathy. The next question is: through which areas of morality? Perhaps through the interpersonal and the natural. The question after this is: and what layer of the curriculum onion shall be utilized? Perhaps one has a social studies teacher at the secondary level who would be more comfortable tackling these through his or her curriculum area. In such a situation, a dilemma of the following sort might well be part of the answer.

NEGRITA'S DILEMMA

'Negrita's dilemma' is read to the class as a whole. It goes like this:

> Negrita is a country which is very poor. Its people can't grow enough food to live. The government wants the people to grow coffee on the land so that they can sell it abroad and pay back money that the government has borrowed.
>
> There is spare land in Negrita. It is jungle. Many wild animals live in the jungle. If the trees are cut down, to grow food or coffee, the animals will die because they will have nowhere to live and nothing to eat.
>
> Just at this moment, an oil company has found oil in the jungle. They want to chop the jungle down and make themselves and the country rich.

Once the situation is read out, the class are assigned to four different groups. Each group is given one of four characters with an initial 'set' behaviour.

Farmer: I want to grow food where the jungle is.

Game warden: I want to keep the jungle and the animals safe.

Oilworker: I want to drill for oil where the jungle is.

Government minister: I want the farmer to grow coffee where the jungle is.

The dilemma provides for rational discussion and empathic commitment. It provides for the examination of competing personal, interpersonal, social and natural claims. It allows for the investigation of an area of social studies which would prove stimulating and enriching for the pupils. (It needs little pointing out that such a dilemma will only have full impact where it is used as part of an overall conception of both the social studies *and* moral areas of the curriculum. There needs to be considerable background work in social studies for the children to be able to deal competently with the complex issues involved in this dilemma; at the same time, one dilemma on its own will do little to increase rational or empathic capacities. Would one expect children to develop mathematical capabilities on the basis of a one-off lesson?)

In the curriculum onion, no one layer is seen as being more important than any other; the relevance of each will be a function of the subject matter, the situation encountered and the post of the teacher. For a primary teacher or a secondary teacher with a post in pastoral care the taught lesson may be a central concern. For a secondary teacher in history, biology or economics, for instance, an approach through his or her subject area will almost certainly be seen as more possible. All teachers, I would suggest, should be aware and take account of the layers of the hidden curriculum and the external factors affecting the school. Consideration and use of such a model, then, should not only help teachers to consider the focuses of attention and all the possible content areas which schools should deal with when considering the moral education of the child; it should also focus attention on the various ways in which these may and do manifest themselves.

The initial groundwork, then, is done. Here is a framework which a school may adapt to its present purposes and needs, from which a school may borrow to highlight particular perspectives and issues. It provides the kind of overall strategy, the safety net, to which a school may refer when embarking on a schoolwide and years-long curriculum policy. What now of the stages of implementation?

FIVE STAGES OF IMPLEMENTATION

The first things needed are co-ordinators within schools, people with expertise and interest in the area. Their task will be different for the different type of school in which they find themselves. The primary school co-ordinator will be largely concerned with facilitating a developmental flow between different ages and abilities. The secondary school co-ordinator, on the other hand, will be largely concerned with developing a co-ordination between different subject specialisms and attempting to provide for the pupil a continuity of experience in terms of topics offered.

There is a rising tide of opinion that primary schools should move away from a child-centred, class-teacher, developmental orientation towards a more subject specialist one, what Campbell (1985) calls the 'collegial school'. At the other end of the age range, secondary schools, through GCSE, may be taking on board rather more of the primary schools' insights through an emphasis on relevance and interest to the pupil. To the extent that primary and secondary schools swap their identities, so the subject co-ordinator's task will become both more similar and more complex.

However, there can be little doubt that the co-ordinator's role is crucial if implementation is to be effective and not merely a matter of practice within the isolation of individual classrooms. Leadership and guidance must be provided by at least one member of staff. This consists of five separate stages.

1. Fostering discussion

It is perhaps worth stating the obvious: nothing of any use will be accomplished without the genuine support of the staff. This would seem to involve the co-ordinator in carrying out much of the initial hard work. The first part of this must be to create and provide information/materials/discussion papers on this aspect of the curriculum and, by personal visits, see that these are read, thought about and discussed. It may well not be advisable to have these discussed initially in staff meetings. Staff meetings can be good as final get-togethers. However, as a discussion forum they can be less than ideal for a variety of reasons. Some people, for example, become wallflowers in large meetings, and fail to make contributions which might prove extremely valuable, whilst others enjoy nothing so much as an audience for their (possibly poorly thought out) opinions. Staff meetings may also have the unfortunate effect of preventing flexibility of attitudes; some people may find themselves unable, due to personal pride, to admit in a public meeting that they might be wrong. This can lead to the strengthening of initial opinions, intransigence, bad temper and a subsequent lack of progress in implementing ideas. For these reasons, it is suggested that staff meetings are *not* the place for most of the discussion. This should be done in ones and twos or in small groups. Only when something approaching a general staff consensus is perceived should staff meetings be used to solidify implementational arrangements.

2. Deciding upon ideal content

The discussion papers and discussion by the staff should ultimately be aimed at the production of an ideal description of where they as a staff would like to go in this area; what they see as being the essential ground to cover. In its simplest form, this amounts to a description of the focuses of attention for the school, a developmental description of the five areas of morality for the primary school or a subject-connected description for the secondary school. Undoubtedly the best practice is for the final description to be a staff-produced document; but with demands upon time as they are, it is much more likely to be a document which is in fact produced by the co-ordinator, upon the advice and opinions of the staff, which is then discussed, criticized, revised and finally accepted by the staff. The preferred description can then be used as a contrast with the present state of play and for help with proposed additions.

3. Deciding on present content

A further statement of the obvious is that it is almost never a good idea to start with completely new subject matter or materials. Not only would this mean that new techniques would have to be learnt in total isolation from previous experience, it would also implicitly say that what teachers had been doing before is not worth keeping. What was done in the past might well have been of good quality, but produced in an unsystematic and unco-ordinated manner. The role of the co-ordinator then is to provide this system and co-ordination, not to try to sell brand-new ideas on their own. Any new ideas can be fitted into a system which recognizes the good work that has already been going on.

This being the case, the third step is to find out what kinds of content the staff are covering at the present time. This probably means that after the initial discussion and explanation of the focuses of attention, the five areas of morality and the use of the 'curricular onion' to help this description, each teacher can be invited to fill in what they are actually teaching in terms of these areas in each layer of the curricular onion.

It has already been noted that this usually means slightly different things for primary and secondary teachers. For the primary teacher it would mean selecting from all their available practices, both formally taught and as part of the 'hidden curriculum', what they teach at the present time. For the secondary teacher, it would mean more a setting out of the ways in which the focuses and five areas touch their specialisms, and how and whether any of these connections are being covered at the present time.

4. Bridging the gap between present and ideal content

Having assessed what is being done, it is then time to assess what can be done further. As the teachers involved now have the benefit of step 2, a 'master plan' of where they want to go, this step involves a subtraction sum – taking away what they are presently covering from what it was agreed they should be covering. This will leave what else needs to be covered. Reflection upon this will probably prompt four questions:

(a) Am I interested?
(b) Have I the time?
(c) Am I qualified?
(d) Am I professionally obliged?

All four of these questions are interconnected.

'*Am I interested?*' In an era of decreasing teacher autonomy, interest is a vitally important issue, both because there is still leeway for implementation of curricular materials and because without interest there is no motivation. Without motivation, the exercise will be sterile and unappetizing and will fail to capture the students' imagination. The co-ordinator can engender interest by doing the spadework, as already suggested, and by being an available source of enthusiasm and information. The commitment of the headteacher to the project and the professionalism of the teaching staff being dealt with also help. These are variables for which there are no ready-made answers.

'*Have I the time?*' This, again, is a function of co-ordinator, head and teacher. The co-ordinator can cut down on the time teachers need by being prepared to do the hard slog of producing discussion and summary materials; the headteacher can help in this by taking classes and so easing the burden of this work; and both of these can help to enliven teachers' enthusiasm and encourage them to give up some of their time to produce a better education for their students. Again, though, this is not a situation for simple answers. Much depends on the individual touch that is given to the project. It is part of the art of organization, not something which can be prescribed in detail.

'*Am I qualified?*' There is no short answer to this question either. Ability to do the job is only determined in part by paper qualifications. It also comes from reflection, preparation, commitment to in-service training and help from more experienced colleagues. There is no magic point when a teacher is qualified in this area. Commitment to its implementation, hard work to back this commitment and an aptitude for diplomacy are as sure qualifications as pure academic ability.

'*Am I professionally obliged?*' This can only be answered in terms of what one considers 'professional' to mean. If it means, as present trends already discussed in previous chapters suggest, an attitude of working to a contract, where rules, regulations and conditions are laid down, which a centralized curriculum and benchmark assessment procedures could well induce, then the answer might well be 'no'. If, however, teaching is seen in its more traditional sense as the education of the whole child, a process which seeks to make the child responsible, critical, autonomous and productive, and in which the teacher is seen and sees him- or herself as creative, responsible and interdependent-minded, then the answer must be 'yes'. The manner in which teachers see themselves critically determines how this question will be answered, and this is fundamentally a function of government and local education policies, implemented by the headteacher.

Not all or even most of the bridging between present and desired curricula can be done immediately. The pace of improvement will be determined by a host of conditions which vary from school to school. Setting limited realistic objectives, teacher by teacher, is far more sensible than a blanket agreement that everything will change, but with no agreed plan of action.

5. Assessing and evaluating change

This will be examined in much greater detail in Chapter 12, but a few words need to be said here.

Firstly, there needs to be both formative evaluation (the kind that is undertaken as the implementation takes place) and summative evaluation (the kind that is undertaken at the end of the implementation). It will almost certainly be the case that the formative evaluation will drastically affect the conception of the summative, simply because ongoing evaluation has the opportunity of diverting and changing the course of implementation, so that the summative evaluations of projects run with formative evaluations will be much different from those of projects run without.

Secondly, certain aspects of the evaluation process need to be made very clear. In particular, teachers should be extremely careful in deciding what aspects of the process they are evaluating – gross behavioural or more delicate attitudinal changes by the students. They require very different assessment procedures. Moreover, it should be clearly stated at the beginning at what specified times evaluation is to happen. Whilst the unpredictable must be catered for, there must be a timetable of procedures clearly posted so that all know when and what is happening. This can only benefit communication and co-ordination between staff.

Thirdly, and following from this, the co-ordinator again has a crucial role to play in co-ordinating and systematizing insights from teachers on present stages of implementation. It is all too easy for the end part of an implementation project to be neglected, even when the earlier parts have been performed very professionally. It is the co-ordinator's job to ensure that these later stages are performed to the same standard.

Fourthly, evaluation is not a once-and-for-all procedure. Even the summative evaluation is evaluation for the end of one cycle of implementation only. Perhaps this cycle consists of the first year's running of the course. It will have to be run in the second and third years as well, and each year will require refinements as new insights and new demands are made. This is then part of an ongoing process which does not end.

Lastly, the production, implementation, assessment and evaluation of a moral curriculum content by a school staff, if properly performed, is the finest answer to those who would deny schools the opportunity to do precisely this. By showing that external imposition is unnecessary, and indeed produces poorer quality ideas, materials and products than those produced within the school, school staff display a professionalism which not only rewards themselves and the pupils, but in the long term must be in the best interests of education as a whole.

Chapter 11

What Stance Shall I Take?

This book has tended to argue for an approach to value issues which facilitates reasoned, balanced and tolerant discussion. This supports the idea that there must be room for variation in opinion, not only of teachers but of students as well. Part of the notion of a just and moral school lies precisely in the acceptance and tolerance of differences of viewpoint.

There are, however, those who would argue that there are situations where society meets problems which are so dangerous that they threaten its very existence. If this is the case, it is argued, individual variations in response are worse than a luxury, they are a positive menace. Where the evidence for a particular attitude or viewpoint appears to be completely one sided, and the demand for uniformity in response derives from the sheer urgency of the situation, then it is the lesser of two evils to present only one point of view. The greater evil would be to present pupils with alternatives and allow them room to choose a viewpoint which might endanger themselves and others. Is there any doubt, it might be argued, that individuals must exercise some kind of change in their behaviour to deal with the threat of AIDS? Should an acceptance of sexual licence be permissible? Is there really any doubt about the unacceptablity of a racist stance? Should society allow the possibility of the development of bigotry and intolerance within its educational institutions? In both these cases, it might be said, the evidence is so overwhelmingly one-sided that there is little need to present another side to the argument.

Thus, it is argued, when problems are so urgent and there is extremely strong evidential support for one particular course of action, there can be little question as to what a teacher should do. To do less than indicate in the strongest possible terms what particular course of action should be taken by the students would be to abnegate one's responsibility. It is this kind of acute and very real question which brings one face to face with the question of teacher stances. As Stradling *et al.* (1984) have found, in real life the stance a teacher takes when dealing with an issue is not just a theoretical but a practical problem, and tends to vary depending upon a number of pragmatic factors. These certainly include:

(a) the urgency of the issue – to what extent is conformity to a particular position seen as essential to personal and social well-being?
(b) the 'objectivity' of the material involved – to what extent are the 'facts' of the matter seen as being clear cut?

But practical considerations will go on to include the following as well:

(c)   the knowledge, values, personality and experience of teachers – what do they know about the issue, what is their initial commitment, can they cope with an open-ended discussion, have they run such things before?

(d)   the organizational arrangements of the school – does the timetabling facilitate or hinder an open-ended discussion, does classroom and furniture design encourage or hinder the process, what is the status of the course and methods adopted?

(e)   the approval or disapproval of other colleagues and the head

(f)   the approval or disapproval of governors, LEA and DES

(g)   legal prescriptions on stances teachers may take – are there laws specifically against the adoption of a particular attitude by a teacher, even if only to be a 'devil's advocate'?

(h)   the knowledge, values, personalities and experience of the pupils – are you in a mixed-sex school when discussing sexism, are you in a racially mixed school when discussing racism, are issues close to the sensitivities of the pupils involved, do they know much about the issues to begin with?

(i)   the teaching methods normally used – are these normally teacher directed, question and answer and didactic, or group based, open ended and pupil directed?

(j)   the perception of the sensitivity of the material under consideration – is this sensitive because of sociopolitical controversy (nuclear disarmament, homosexuality) or because of the nature of the student group (sexism, racism) or because of the closeness of the issue to the teacher and institution (authority, punishment, the value of education)?

In real life, then, there will be constraints upon practice which need to be anticipated and allowed for when more theoretical perspectives are considered. With these caveats in mind, it seems possible to suggest at least six stances a teacher might adopt when involved in value issues. These would be:

(1)   The teacher attempts to be totally neutral in the presentation and discussion of material.

With this stance, the teacher facilitates the student debate as much as possible, but deliberately avoids any intervention in the discussion which might suggest his or her own stance on the issue.

A first problem with this stance might be to ask whether it is ever possible to be completely neutral. After all, the constraints of time within the school day mean that there must be some selection of the topics to be discussed, and which materials within this subject matter are to be used. Further, it has been argued in previous chapters that the very subjectivity of human beings must negate any attempt at complete neutrality. However, it does seem fair to say that there are degrees of neutrality; whilst one cannot get away from some selection, one can, to some extent, deliberately refrain from expressing commitment.

Accepting these initial conditions, this would then mean that the teacher could deliberately repress his or her own opinions. This was the approach used by Stenhouse (1978) with the 'neutral chairman' approach. The use of such methodology is quite clearly to prevent the inhibition of the expression of students' opinions, and the possible biasing of them by the teacher's own. There were occasions, however, when this procedure was used for discussions of racism which moved to ever more intolerant attitudes, and the teacher, because of his or her stance, being unable to intervene. It is doubtful whether any teacher would feel that an educational activity had been of benefit where racist attitudes had been allowed to harden.

It will be clear that such a statement suggests that there are certain overriding values which must be included within discussions, and that the teacher must intervene if they are not being adhered to. This will be developed later.

(2)   The teacher attempts to present every side of the argument with equal fairness.

Unlike the first stance, this approach does not require teachers to deliberately repress their own attitudes. All that it requires is an attempt at impartiality. Personal views may then be presented just so long as they are counterbalanced by an equally perceptive, lengthy and committed presentation for the other side(s). This of course is easier said than done. It may be the case that the teacher is simply unaware of all the sides in a disagreement. And even if this initial problem is overcome, it is unlikely that equal enthusiasm can be mounted for all sides, just as it is unlikely that students will not be moved by the fact that the teachers hold particular views. In some cases, the fact that the teacher does hold certain views may well predispose the children to adopt them simply because the teacher holds them. With others, of course, it may have exactly the opposite effect, and motivate the children to hold the contrary opinion!

A further problem for teachers comes in that they may feel that even though an impartial account might be possible, it still might not be desirable. For example, it may well be perfectly possible to invite two equally plausible opposing speakers into the school, but would one want to invite an articulate and attractive member of the Nazi party? Even if legal proscriptions against the incitement of racial hatred were not a major consideration for the teacher, would an educationalist feel happy about inviting a skilful weaver of unpleasant but clever arguments – particularly if certain sections of the class were likely to be influenced? Again, an implicit reference to certain overriding core values is being made which will be brought out as the discussion proceeds.

(3)   The teacher presents his or her own views, but qualifies them with the admission that he or she is no expert in the area.

In the course of a lesson, a value issue crops up – the use of nuclear power, for example. One member of the class asks the teacher's opinion. The teacher has little or no background in the subject, and her understanding is limited to what she has seen on the television or read in newspapers. She admits to this limitation, but then says 'for what it's worth, I think . . .'.

Certainly, the admission of ignorance is vital, and a crucial lesson for the students to learn: teachers aren't authorities all the time; the validity of their opinions varies with the topic at hand. Moreover, the students may well feel cheated if no personal opinion is forthcoming. Much of the magic of teaching comes in the development of personal relationships between teacher and student, and the withholding of opinions by the teacher hardly fosters this development. The problem still remains, of course, of whether the students will react simply because of the personal qualities of the teacher. Given a high positive or negative personal rating, the teacher's opinion could be immensely influential in the formation of a point of view.

A further question to ask is whether the teacher must always take such a stance. Are they always that limited in their authority? This then leads into the next possible stance.

(4) The teacher presents his or her own views, not as the final statement in this area, but as someone who is an expert in the field.

The question of nuclear power is raised with another teacher, who happens to be actively committed to the development of power generation in this country by other than nuclear means. What stance should he or she take? Certainly, there is more expert knowledge here than in the last case, and it could be argued that the commitment to a particular side is due precisely because of the greater degree of knowledge. Should not such teachers then express their own points of view?

One of the problems with this approach begins with the observation that facts and values are not distinct. It is unlikely that commitment is due entirely to a study of the facts, but to a prior value commitment in the first place, which led to the study of these particular facts and the possible appreciation of some and rejection of others on the basis of this prior value commitment. A simple 'I'm an expert in this field, and here are the facts that led me to my beliefs' is probably not an accurate description of the real situation. Any teacher professing to be an expert would have to acknowledge firstly their value orientation which led them to a consideration of these issues in the first place, but secondly the simple fact that experts disagree. There *are* levels of subjectivism, but these are still subjective levels. No expert opinion is necessarily the correct one. This must be clearly understood by the 'expert' and communicated to the children as part of his or her own particular stance.

(5) The teacher presents his or her own view as the truth.

It will be apparent by now that the present writer would generally consider such an attitude untenable and harmful. If the arguments of the earlier chapters are accepted, it can be argued that it is untenable because all human opinion is subjective in nature. Even were one to accept the claims of those who believe they have 'the truth' by way of revealed texts – religious or political – one would still be able to argue that the application of these 'truths' in the world is one which requires human perception and judgement, and thus entails an appreciation of the subjective nature of human action.

Furthermore, such a stance would be harmful for two reasons. Firstly, because it would prevent the use of rationality, the commitment to which is an essentially *moral* act, for such a commitment involves one in following the rules of the game – a game which has, as part of its structure, the notion of equal respect for people and impartiality. The decision to adopt either rationality or irrationality, as Popper (1945: 232) says:

> will deeply affect our whole attitude towards other men, and towards the problems of social life.

Faced with resolving any sort of problem, rationality is the safest and surest way, the way which guards against fanaticism, bigotry and totalitarianism. Its surrender invites them.

The second reason for believing this approach to be harmful is the related point that it prevents the growth of an understanding of the subjective nature of the human condition, and thereby inhibits the development of those qualities which are essential for a tolerance of others and their opinions. Only when one is convinced of the fact that *nobody* can be certain of objectivity in their actions can one really appreciate that others with differing opinions may well have some truth and justification for what they do.

If one accepts this, though, what is one to make of those situations – particularly to do with AIDS and racism – where it might be argued that the urgency and seriousness of the situation demanded a committed and one-sided approach from the teacher? Is this not a case for presenting particular views as 'the truth', and is the simple training and instruction of pupils not only sufficient but also the correct thing to do?

To answer this question one needs to reflect on the meaning of 'education', and the implication of the adoption and practice of those meanings. Stenhouse (1978) has argued that education comprises at least four different processes:

(a)   training – acquiring skills for performance
(b)   instruction – learning information for retention and reproduction
(c)   initiation – familiarization with social values and norms for interpretation and anticipation
(d)   induction – introduction into a thought system leading to autonomous judgements within and upon that system.

Many have seen the adoption of a particular level as at bottom an ethical one. Kliebard (1968: 246), for example, talking about training and instruction, argues that:

> from a moral point of view, the emphasis on behavioural goals, despite all the protestations to the contrary, still borders on brain-washing, or at least indoctrination rather than education. We begin with some notion of how we want a person to behave and then we try to manipulate him and his environment so as to get him to behave as we want him to.

He thus identifies the ethical issue as one of individual freedom. Training and instruction, it is therefore argued, cannot be the ultimate goals of education. Rather, it must be that of providing the individual with the intellectual equipment to think for him or herself. If this is the case,

> Education as induction into knowledge is successful to the extent that it makes the behavioural outcomes of the students unpredictable.
> (Stenhouse, 1978: 82)

This does not mean being totally unpredictable in the sense of random outcomes, but rather in the sense of using the modes of thought within that thought system to manipulate the material at hand in an individual manner to arrive at an original, interpretative judgement. Fundamentally, the argument goes, one must ask whether anyone has the right to deprive the individual of this freedom. Those who adopt the stance of 'this is the truth', and those seeking stability and clarity in aims, evaluation and accountability, are, whether they intend to or not, doing precisely this.

However, this book has been at pains to argue that morality is composed of at least five areas, each with their own rights and duties, which must inevitably conflict at some time or another with the rights and duties of another area (see Table 8.1, p. 78). It would seem that this is precisely what is happening at the present time.

Those arguing for individual freedom as an ultimate aim in education argue from the personal area of morality, but it must be questioned whether aims for education might not derive from other areas as well. For example, an ultimate aim for education from the interpersonal area might be that of furthering the well-being of others close to oneself, whilst an ultimate aim for education from the social area of morality might be the furtherance of social harmony. These may well coincide for most of the time with individual freedom, but they need not. Thus what if the individual was allowed to decide by the education system that sexual licence was a 'good thing'? Such an attitude might well have been viewed unfavourably in the past because of the psychological traumas such licence might have upon that person's sexual partners, or because of the likelihood of the spread of venereal disease. Today, the situation is even more urgent because of the potentially fatal consequences for those who contract the AIDS virus. Is not that person's freedom in conflict with demands from the interpersonal area of morality? And if that is the case, does not the school have the duty to take account of this interpersonal demand and limit personal freedom, which may mean not leaving the question of preferable sexual behaviour to the individual, but rather strongly recommending an approach which stresses the need for care and preparedness?

In similar vein, has the school not the duty and the right to promote an attitude towards racism which runs counter to the individual right to hold racist attitudes, not only because of the rights of other people but also because of the needs of society as a whole?

If this is the case, it might well be argued that there are occasions when Stenhouse's 'training' and 'instruction' stages can be viewed as more appropriate than his 'initiation' and 'induction' stages.

This is an interesting argument, but seems to be unnecessary. The choice does *not* need to be between:

- training and instruction in approved information and behaviours, and
- a free choice of whichever behaviour, attitude or selection of material the pupil wishes to adopt.

After all, as was argued at length in Chapter 4, there *are* levels of objectivity and subjectivity, and if this is the case it is surely part of the teacher's professional duty to guide pupils in the discussion of contentious material in order that they adopt the highest level of objectivity possible. This, then, becomes our final teacher stance:

(6)   The teacher presents his or her own views as an example of the process and product of a reasoned choice.

Thus it is perfectly right and proper for teachers to acknowledge and make the pupil aware of the subjectivity of knowledge, but equally right and proper for them to acknowledge and make the pupil aware of the fact that some materials and evidence are less subjective than others: the dangers of AIDS and the arguments against racism are cases in point.

Similarly, it is perfectly right and proper for the teacher to have as an educational aim the achievement by the pupil of individual interpretation and judgement, but it is equally right and proper for the teacher to ensure that such interpretation and judgement are performed at the highest level of objectivity possible, which means not only being aware of lower levels of subjectivity and pointing them out, but using the canons of reason and the use of valid evidence as the way of approaching and dealing with issues. Where pupils do not, where they decide upon an issue irrationally or take no account of their own or a particular group's bias, or attend only to one source of information, then it is the teacher's duty to ensure that the rectification of this takes priority over arriving at an individual opinion. So, for example, where the dangers of AIDS are discounted through ignorance, or where racist attitudes are taken on faulty evidence or through biased opinion, it is the teacher's duty to influence the pupil to take account of the process by which more objective opinions are arrived at.

Two things are thus being argued. Firstly, that some degree of subjectivity is inevitable in anyone's opinion, and this should be acknowledged by the teacher. But secondly, and notwithstanding this, the teacher has the duty to appear and behave as an educational model of reasoning, a model in dealing in an unbiased manner with the evidence, a model of how to arrive at an opinion. This is radically different from the view that it is the teacher's job to merely influence pupils with his or her opinion. It is the process which is as important as the product, though the fact remains that in many situations, by following the process, one can be fairly certain that the teacher will express the opinion that it is felt vital to express. In this situation, the voicing of opinions is an essential educational lesson.

If this is the case then the use of a simplistic teacher stance which suggests that an opinion is 'the truth' is unnecessary. Similarly, the suggestion that training and instruction are necessary aims for education in a time of urgency and crisis is also unnecessary. Only when training in rationality is an ultimate aim for education can training ever be considered an *educational* aim. Even in times of crisis, the higher aims of education may still be seen as worthy ultimate goals. What needs to be added, as has been suggested, is the crucial element that there is nothing wrong with the teacher acting as the model of a trained professional in rationally arriving at an opinion, and expressing that opinion, in order to shed light on the process of its construction.

What, then, are the insights to be gained from this discussion of teacher stances? There appear to be five.

Firstly, parents, politicians and teachers should remember that education is more about induction than instruction. It may start off as instruction, but to be worthy of the name, it must rapidly become more than that. It must enable individuals to think for themselves.

Secondly, it must be accepted that as one moves from the instructive to the inductive, one moves from the objective to the subjective. This takes courage, for it involves a gradual relinquishing of the reins of control. As Downey and Kelly (1986: 124) put it:

> The teacher's authority must contain within it the seeds of its own destruction.

Thirdly, it involves another kind of courage – not just the courage to let go, but also the courage to let education deal with the unpredictable. It involves moving beyond the stable and the secure and making of education the intellectual adventure it should be.

But fourthly, it involves the understanding that freedom in education involves responsibility by both teacher and pupil. It cannot mean licence. It involves the understanding that freedom is exercised the more one becomes more rational, less subjective. It is the teacher's duty to help in this by being a model of the process. Thus the teacher's utterance of opinions likely to influence pupils is desirable just so long as they are the end products of such a process. This is very different from opinions influencing at the end of training or instruction. The former allows for flexibility and interpretation of the final opinion using the process itself; the latter provides for nothing other than the parroting of the opinion.

But lastly, one must have not only courage and responsibility, but also belief in a new generation. This belief in part derives from optimism, but also derives from the education given, in that by acquainting pupils with the higher processes of education, by modelling the use of rationality and the attempt to deal with issues as objectively as possible, one can be confident that when one lets the reins go and gives pupils their heads, they will not abuse this responsibility and freedom but will grow into them. Parents, politicians and teachers must not allow a lower level of education to become the primary aim. If they do so, they deprive children of a fundamental right. A school system so depriving children cannot be educational and cannot be moral.

Chapter 12

Evaluation and Accountability – Problems and Prospects

Evaluation is related to the morality of the school in at least two different ways. The first relationship is at the curricular level, in the evaluation of any teaching materials or lessons which deal with values education. Questions like 'did the materials work?' 'did the children enjoy the lesson?' 'was there any change in their attitudes or behaviour after the lesson?' may all be posed in evaluative procedures. To this extent, evaluation of values education shares the same kinds of problems as the evaluation of an English or science lesson, or any other area of the curriculum.

However, evaluation is related to the morality of the school in a deeper and more subtle way. This is at the level of the hidden curriculum of the school, because values impinge upon the very topic of evaluation itself. After all, evaluation is the process of forming judgements stating value or worth. Thus how a school views evaluation, what it sees as appropriate evaluative techniques, says a considerable amount about the general value orientation of the school, about where it places its priorities. Take two very common views of evaluation. If a school sees evaluation as (a) the process of testing the outcomes of pre-specified objectives, in a tight quantitative manner, it will have a very different picture of what education is from the school which sees evaluation as (b) an ongoing multifaceted qualitative procedure which cannot pin down educational outcomes in quantitative terms, but should try to understand the process in order to better inform the practice. As Eisner (1985: 46) puts it:

under the rug of technique lies an image of man.

Accountability is also related to the morality of the school in two ways. First of all, there is the fact that just about all calls for accountability are at bottom moral in nature. If one uses Barton *et al.*'s (1986) analysis of accountability, one can see that there are at least three modes of accountability:

(a) moral accountability – to clients
(b) professional accountability – responsibility to oneself and colleagues
(c) contractual accountability – to employers and political masters.

On this account, *moral* accountability is a call to teachers to prove that they have honoured a contract – the contract being the agreement that they nurture the intellectual and emotional capacities of children whilst *in loco parentis*. *Contractual* accountability is similarly moral, though the emphasis this time is more upon making sure that teachers, having been paid to do a job, give value for money. These two forms of accountability are the two modes most often discussed at the present time, and yet there is much to be said for an increased emphasis on *professional* accountability, a responsibility to the teachers themselves and their colleagues. This demands self-respect for oneself as a teacher, and places an obligation upon the individual to support the other members of the team within the school.

Table 12.1 *Accountability and human nature*

Place an 'x' on the line at the point you feel most accurately reflects your own opinion.

Theory X		Theory Y
People generally dislike work	————————————	People generally like work
People must generally be directed	————————————	People are generally capable of self direction
People are best managed by threat and compulsion	————————————	People are best managed by the prospect of personal achievement
People generally lack imagination and creativity	————————————	People generally possess creativity and imagination
People tend to avoid responsibility	————————————	People can learn to actively seek responsibility
People are generally not to be trusted	————————————	People are generally to be trusted
Moral and contractual accountability produce the best results	————————————	Professional and intellectual accountability produce the best results

(Based on McGregor, 1960)

There would also appear to be a fourth kind of accountability not mentioned so far, which relates to one's responsibility to one's own teaching subject. This might be called:

(d)   intellectual accountability

– a perception by teachers that they are under a discipline imposed by the intellectual criteria and structure of the subject which they teach. (I am indebted to Dr D. H. Webster for this insight.) Misuse or abuse of such subject material reflects upon teachers as disciples of that subject. They are then accountable to their discipline, and to themselves.

It will readily be seen that both professional and intellectual accountability involve self-respect, individual integrity and self-motivation, and to the extent that people respond to calls to self-respect and integrity, and enjoy being self-motivated rather than being externally driven (see Table 12.1), professional and intellectual accountability may be the more effective means of producing a better teaching force – not to mention moral imperatives of treating teachers as people and not as factory units.

However, to the extent that moral and contractual accountability are to do with the assessment of contractual obligations, and to the extent that these contracts have been freely entered into by teachers, such contracts are morally binding. Accountability is something to which in principle they cannot object.

What they *may* object to, of course, is that they may appear to be the only ones

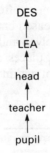

Figure 12.1   Bureaucratic accountability I

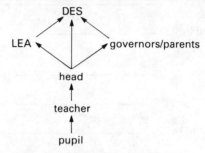

Figure 12.2   Bureaucratic accountability II

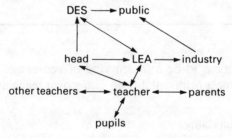

Figure 12.3   Democratic accountability

being held accountable, or at best, somewhere near the bottom of a hierarchy of accountability. Lawton (1983: 97) describes this as 'bureaucratic' accountability (Figure 12.1), a situation where only the pupils in the school are accountable to teachers.

It is interesting that this model, produced in 1983, can afford to make no reference to the accountability due to parents. The situation in Britain, after recent legislation, would be much more like Figure 12.2.

A less hierarchical relationship would be that described by Lawton (1983: 97) as 'democratic' accountability (Figure 12.3). In this model, most parties are seen as accountable to somebody else, as all are parties within the one enterprise of educating the young.

At the moment, the bureaucratic model is much the more accepted, and has consequent effects upon teacher morale. Why, after all, should teachers be viewed as bottom of the pile? Could it not be argued that they deserve much more respect, being the expert practitioners? As noted earlier, Lawton (1980: 12) suggests that the metaphor for the relationship between government and teachers has changed from 'partnership' to 'accountability'. The reasons for this will be investigated shortly.

The second way in which accountability is related to the morality of the school is to do with the way in which it interacts with evaluation. At the simplest level, all forms of accountability need some type of evaluation, for one assesses whether people are fulfilling their contracts by evaluating what they are doing. The relationship between them however is not a simple one, though there may well be demands for simplicity, not only in terms of accountability and evaluation but also about schooling in general. Why is such simplicity demanded? It is important to understand this because understanding the social and political climate in which this debate is taking place enables one to see the prisms through which people are looking, and further enables one to see what is being selected as important and unimportant, and why this selection is taking place.

The present educational debate is taking place within a social and political ethos of a need for security and certainty. This was not the case a few years ago. Being on the winning side in a world war, and then moving into the economic boom time of the 1960s, society could afford to see education in an expansive manner. Practitioners were allowed – encouraged even – to use much creativity, freedom and experimentation in their teaching methods. Ambiguous, qualitative techniques of measurement and evaluation were developed, and tolerated by those in power. Accountability could be and was left in the professional mode. All was well in society's garden, economically at least, and little need was felt to make schools externally accountable.

However, with the early 1970s came the oil crisis, followed by economic recession, unemployment, race riots, political extremism and social discord. Society's optimism began to evaporate. No longer did it see exploration, discovery, creativity and experimentation as 'good things'. What were needed instead were things such as certainty, security, stability and continuity. Where better to look than the past? As Eisner (1985: 218) put it:

> When conventional values are threatened . . . people seek a rock on which to stand, something to stabilise them in the flux and flow of social change; and they look to the schools as one such rock

Educationally, this comes out in a number of ways. Firstly, in curricular terms, there is an increase in the 'back to the basics' movement, notably in a stronger demand for concentration on the three Rs. Parents and politicians know what these are. They are tried and trusted, there is universal agreement as to their necessity and utility, they are something to which one can anchor schools. With them one is safe and secure.

Secondly, there is a corresponding return to tried and trusted values – those which can be instructed, such as good manners and obedience. The curricular projects of the McPhails, the values clarificationists and the Kohlbergs seem no longer quite so exciting and forward looking, but unclear in their aims and their results and so more threatening and destabilizing. There is a general feeling that there is enough social instability without encouraging it in schools by introducing schemes whose primary aim is to develop children's own ideas and viewpoints. This may have appeared tolerable, even laudable, in earlier more confident times, but is not so now. Personal, social and moral education is given a different path to follow. Instead of the self-chosen path, it is urged to follow much more a transmissive path which dovetails with society's economic needs.

Thirdly, when people find themselves in trouble, they usually need someone to blame. Education and its practitioners have been good scapegoats. If society is in economic and social trouble, then it is far simpler to blame an institution and change that than acknowledge that the ills of society are pervasive, historical and trans-national in nature. That would mean that the problems are not readily identifiable and quickly soluble. Instead it is far easier to blame education for not providing the correctly educated manpower, regardless of the true problem, or the fact that they have been trying to accommodate completely conflicting prescriptions from above.

Finally, security, confidence and stability are heightened when people 'know where they are'. Qualitative judgements are necessarily not of this kind. They are elusive, subjective and difficult to pin down. Quantitative judgements are then seen as much the more palatable. Similarly, pre-specified objectives are cleaner, more straight-forward, more controllable and safer and thus provide greater security than a process-oriented teaching approach. As Stenhouse (1978: 77) says of the demand for objectives:

> It is not about curriculum design, but rather an expression of irritation in the face of the problem of accountability in education.

The social and political ethos of a country, then, may determine the nature of educational evaluation and accountability, regardless of the long-term effects these might have.

Three things will be apparent. The first is that evaluation and accountability are not interchangeable terms. They do not mean the same thing, they do not refer to the same procedures. The second is that there are different forms of both terms of which one must be aware. The third, and following from this, is that the relationship between them is not a simple one.

Who, then, is to do the evaluating? Evaluation is not a neutral affair. MacDonald (1987) has argued that it is possible to classify evaluation into three main political types, these varying on who calls for the evaluation, and who performs it. He describes them as

(a) bureaucratic evaluation – the evaluation is produced to satisfy government bureaucrats, it is performed by an employee and essentially it is there to give them what they want.
(b) autocratic evaluation – the evaluation is produced as part of the activity of the academic establishment, it is performed by an expert and is validated in terms of academic standards.
(c) democratic evaluation – the evaluator is the impartial provider of information, the report is provided for the plural community and is non-recommendatory; it aims purely to inform for better debate.

We might also add a further category:

(d) professional evaluation – the evaluator is the person actively involved in the project, who performs it not principally for the benefit of government depart-ments, nor to advance academic understanding in the area, nor to provide information in an ongoing debate, but to help improve his or her teaching ability, and thereby provide a better education for the students.

It will be clear by now that each evaluator must be asking very different questions. Bureaucratic and democratic evaluation are essentially concerned with moral and contractual accountability, in that they seek to provide information on the effectiveness of schools, the bureaucrat to the government, the democrat to society at large. The autocrat, on the other hand, is in a curiously ambivalent position, for his or her research can be used in a variety of ways. It can be utilized by the bureaucrat or democrat for their own ends; it can be used by the professional as an aid to teaching; or it can be purely a form of academic exercise, adding to the body of conceptual understanding in this area. The professional is concerned with his or her practice and with his or her students. With such diverse interests, evaluation can and does ask very different questions, and will accordingly use different tools and come up with different results. Crucial, therefore, to the understanding of the results of any form of evaluation are the prior questions of who performed it, what they were looking for and what questions they asked.

The results of evaluation, then, very much depend upon who is asking the questions. Evaluation cannot escape from the social and political ethos of the society in which it is conducted. However, not only are the results of evaluation nor even just the type of evaluation subject to the social and political ethos. Even the *timing* of the evaluation may be forced.

Consider, for instance, a curriculum model which suggests that evaluation comes at the end of a sequence of activities, looking something like Figure 12.4.

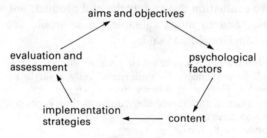

Figure 12.4

On this model one states what is aimed for, one takes into account the capabilities of the students involved, one selects the appropriate subject matter, designs suitable teaching strategies and then evaluates all of this to see how the materials, students or teachers have done. But should evaluation be left until the end of the cycle? Isn't much valuable insight to be gained during the lesson, or sometimes even before it? For example, what if one states one's aim, but then finds that the strategies cannot be matched to the capabilities of the students? Is the lesson still run in that form? Of course not. Aims, objectives and content are reworked to fit the students' capabilities, so that implementation strategies *will* work. In other words, *summative evaluation* – that gained at the end of the exercise – may not be the most appropriate form of evaluation; *formative evaluation* (see Scriven, 1967) – that gained during it – may be of much greater use to the student and teacher.

The opportunity to change course before the end of a lesson or sequence of lessons is obviously very useful if one wants to avoid wasted time and energy. Part of the art of teaching is precisely this: to be sufficiently alert and intelligent to know when to move from the prepared to the unprepared, to strike off at a tangent because it is proving more fruitful. This is not a weakness in teaching but a strength. Jackson (1968: 166–7) put it rather well when he said that:

> the path of educational progress more closely resembles the flight of a butterfly than the flight of a bullet.

If the science of teaching is the preplanning and structuring of lessons, the art of teaching is knowing how to adapt these whilst on the move. Formative evaluation, then, may well be a more intelligent, adaptable and accurate form of assessment than summative.

Teaching and education, then, do not exist in a vacuum. They exist in a social and political context. Teachers cannot be – should not be – totally independent bodies who go their own way just as they want (though this has certainly tended to be the case in this country in the past). Others want to know what they are doing. These others may be non-specialists in the field of education, but may still demand evidence of good practice, for whilst being non-specialists they still have concern for the good of the children, the future well-being of the country, or have a desire to know that the millions of pounds poured into education are being spent wisely. The kind of evidence at a premium will generally be evidence that is clear and explicit to these outside bodies, and evidence that does not take too long to assimilate. In this kind of situation, summative evaluation may be the most attractive. It shows the end result of a process, it is usually recorded in a clear quantitative form and is usually quickly digested. The dangers, though, are clear to see.

Firstly, summative evaluation shows only the end product, not what went on during the lesson or course, and so much valuable (some would say the most valuable) material is lost. As MacDonald has said:

> The impact of an innovation is not a set of discrete effects, but an organically related pattern of acts and consequences. To understand fully a single act one must locate it functionally within that pattern. It follows from this proposition that curriculum interventions have many more unanticipated consequences than is normally assumed in development and evaluation designs.
> (Quoted in Stenhouse, 1978: 110)

Crucially, then, the summative model may assess an effect without explaining it, thus preventing the teacher from replicating the result in the future.

Thus, secondly, if teachers have to concentrate on summative forms of evaluation, they may fail to spend as much time on the kind of evaluation of most benefit to the students. This is one danger with accountability that those demanding it must be aware of: they may distort the educative process in their demand for comprehensible products.

In terms of the education of pupils in ethical matters, this poses really serious difficulties. What would be clear evidence of good practice in this area? Such a rich, diverse and subtle field does not easily lend itself to evaluation. The pupils' self-esteem is not something which comes across on an examination sheet. The ability to empathize with others' predicaments takes time and patience to observe and record. The readiness to co-operate with others is something best assessed over days or weeks rather than hours. And the ability to deal rationally with a host of difficult and complex issues in one area of the moral domain is not, despite Kohlbergian attempts in this direction, something which can be readily recorded on a developmental six-point scale. Indeed, it might well be argued that the only meaningful way of recording development in this area is in an interactive context: rather than being the observer, the evaluator may well need to be involved with the students over a considerable time span to see how they feel, behave and consider. Much of the most valuable part of the educative process is simply not amenable to quantifiable testing.

Now, as we have seen, those who feel that they must be accounted to may not only have little time to assess this complexity, and so settle for something much cruder, much more behaviouristic in orientation, but they may also believe that the function of the school in the moral education of its pupils need not be anything as complex or rich as is suggested in this book. What is needed, it may be felt, is not a variety of different personal and social experiences which stretch the students' empathic and reasoning abilities, but rather a dose of old-fashioned values, such as obedience, politeness, good manners. The problem today, it may be argued, is not that children have too little experience of others' problems and dilemma situations, but that they have too much choice and freedom in making up their own minds. Rather than expanding the moral brief of the school, it should be retrenching its operation to a reduction of the area to a few, easily comprehensible virtues. Here we have a critical conflict about the aims of the school which has been discussed at considerable length in previous chapters. The point here is that arguments for simplistic accountability need not derive solely from a need for clarity or for simple convenience. Arguments for simplistic accountability may derive from the belief that nothing more complex is needed. It may be favoured on ideological grounds. If one believes that all children need is a course in obedience, politeness and good manners, then simple behaviouristic tests will do.

Such a viewpoint requires a reply on two quite different levels. Firstly, it needs a reply which questions whether *any* education should have as its ultimate aim a clearer series of behavioural objectives. And secondly, it needs a reply which suggests that children and society need an education in more than obedience, politeness and good manners.

To begin with, then, does the teacher always know exactly what is desired as the outcome of a lesson? Bruner (1977: 51) has argued that:

> While one benefits from clarity about the ends of education, it is often true that we may discover or rediscover new ultimate objectives in the process of trying to reach more modest goals.

Imagine, for example, that an instructor on a YTS course is explaining to the students the order in which a car engine must be stripped down. The outcome of the lesson will be fairly clear: the students must know clearly what is the sequence for the operation to be performed correctly. Here is a lesson with what Eisner (1985: chapter 2) calls clear 'instructional' objectives, a lesson where what is to be taught is clear from the very beginning, the products are pre-specified, the outcomes non-controversial. With such a lesson, clarity of goals, predictability of outcome and objectivity in assessment make excellent sense.

Rather more difficult, I would argue, would be the citation of unproblematical moral training and instruction. Perhaps the inculcation of good manners and politeness might be seen as relatively unproblematical if such training did not interfere with the development of critical faculties. Most moral instruction would probably be seen as a form of indoctrination, but certain fundamental moral ground rules, like co-operation, empathy and care, if encapsulated in moral homilies, might also be seen as relatively non-controversial. They too might provide predictable outcomes and clarity in assessment. And yet can they be the ultimate aim for the moral education of pupils?

What, however, if, in the non-moral curriculum, the lesson is one on *Macbeth*. What are the objectives for this lesson? Surely not merely that the story of the play be known by the pupils? This undoubtedly *is* a non-controversial instructional objective, but it is clear that the teacher will usually be aiming for much more than this. He or she will be aiming for an appreciation of the subtleties of the drama, the nuances of interpretation, and through the drama, the transforming insights into the human condition. It is not to be expected that all the students will take out of the play the same elements of appreciation, for each will come to the drama with their own thoughts, their own backgrounds, their own interests, their own interpretative schemas. Indeed, if all the pupils did vocalize the same insights in the same way the teacher might well feel that he or she had failed. This is not to suggest that all insights and interpretations are of the same validity, for they must all refer back to the play and be grounded on evidence which all can understand. But their weighting of what are to be regarded as significant features of the play will be different. The teacher, then, will be using 'expressive' objectives – objectives which are, of necessity, open ended, which allow for the participation and contribution of the learner in the process.

The same must be said for the moral dimension of schooling. If, as Stenhouse (1978: 82) says, education provides a 'structure to sustain creative thought and provide frameworks for judgement', then pupils must be given the opportunity to exercise this judgement. They must come to have opinions of their own. Just as some people would like to see curricula 'teacher-proof' – packages so well planned and constructed that the teacher cannot undermine them, so some would like to see education 'child-proof' – packages so transmissive and objective that children are not able to change their form by any kind of contribution. But just as the development of education is dependent upon the qualitative judgement of the practitioner, so it is dependent upon the interaction and negotiated agreement between teacher and pupil. Any other approach misunderstands or ignores the higher natures of education – the initiation and induction of the learner.

The type of evaluation used, then, is clearly determined in this context by the types of objectives adopted. Where education is seen as instructional in orientation, clearly defined behavioural objectives can be employed. If the youth manages to strip down the car engine in x number of minutes, using procedures a, b and c, then he or she has clearly understood the lesson on engine stripping. If the child behaves politely and shows appropriate manners, he or she has internalized his or her moral training. However, where education is seen as more expressive, more creative, more unpredictable in its outcomes, evaluation will be that much more subtle and difficult to apply. How does one measure the degree of appreciation of *Macbeth*? How does one measure the degree of empathy attained? the capacity for judgement on controversial issues? It is clear that expressive evaluation cannot be as unambiguous, 'objective', predictable and precise as instructional evaluation. It cannot be, simply by the nature of the educational enterprise.

However, this is where accountability may again play a dangerous and perverting role. Just as those demanding accountability may ask for summative as opposed to formative evaluation in order to facilitate their clearer understanding, so also may they demand instructive as opposed to expressive evaluation. For whilst expressive evaluation is almost invariably time consuming, difficult to interpret and demands a considerable depth of educational knowledge for the 'results' to be interpreted, instructive evaluation is much clearer, seemingly more factual and usually considerably more simple to test. Those who demand accountability may then settle for second best in terms of evaluation, which must inevitably mean second best in terms of educational quality. 'What is counted, counts' (Eisner, 1984: 138). What will teachers do who know that what is to be evaluated is the instructional side of education? If their jobs, the esteem of the public or government finance depend on their producing instructional objectives, then that is what their teaching will tend to concentrate upon. And by so doing the roles of aims and objectives, and evaluation and assessment, are reversed. Whereas previously it was the aims and objectives which determined the types of evaluative procedures to follow, now it is the types of evaluative procedure demanded by accountability which have determined the aims and objectives at the outset. The tail is now viciously wagging the dog.

By so doing, by constraining the types of possible educational outcomes, we constrain children's possibilities. As Eisner says (1985: 129):

> In education, we need to catch many fish, but we have used nets that let many of the most interesting ones slip through.

By letting many of the interesting ones slip through, we teach an impoverished curriculum and so produce impoverished minds.

Chapter 13

Education, Management and Morality

A crucial area of the moral influence of the school on both pupils and teachers is the way it is run, the management of the school. Indeed, this is perhaps the most pervasive aspect of the hidden curriculum; how a school is managed will have profound effects upon the institution.

This being the case, a first question must be: what kind of approach are headteachers and their deputies being asked to adopt in their management strategies? This chapter will argue that the GNP model of morality has had its effects here as well. It will maintain that there is a section of the management literature in education at present which is fundamentally flawed and ethically unpalatable. Its current stress upon effectiveness deflects attention from the more central question of what normative ends education should be engaged in pursuing. Its concentration upon treating teachers as resources in a national economic plan reduces the art of teaching to a functional and uncritical application of hierarchical directives. In so doing, it suggests that educational practitioners and recipients are to be viewed in an essentially manipulative manner – the manager/headteacher manipulating the staff, the teacher the pupils. It is argued that not only is such an approach ethically unacceptable, it also has grave practical consequences for education as a whole.

What, then, might make one uneasy with some of the notions used in school management? There are a number of themes which cause disquiet, and a central one is that some authors do not see morality and ethics as having a role of any central importance in the subject. Take, for example, a well-known book on the subject entitled *Effective School Management* (Everard and Morris, 1985). The first thing which may strike one is what it is *not* called: it is not called 'Acceptable and Effective School Management'. So two preliminary questions about the book might well be:

(a) Does the book devote any discussion to the ethics of such effectiveness? For does not the question of the morality of the methods decide whether such methods be included in the book?

(b) If education is an essentially *moral* exercise in that it is totally impregnated by judgements of what is or is not to count as valuable and worthwhile, can we even begin to talk of effectiveness if we have not determined what is to count as valuable in educational terms?

What do the authors reply to questions of ethicality? To be fair, they are aware of ethical criticisms, and on p. 11 of the introduction present a list of eleven possible criticisms to their approach. Their answer, however, is rather more abrupt:

> This is not a book about educational and managerial philosophy and ethics: it is about effective practice. Hence all we need do at this point is to outline how we perceive the school as an organisation, and what its mission is.

But is this all they need to do? Certainly, if their perceptions of the school as an organization and its mission encapsulate their aims and in so doing go some way to justifying their approach, then the inadequacy of this reply may be diminished somewhat. But the actual description is hardly satisfactory. They make a number of points to this end, but the points raised compound the problem rather than clarify it. Their central concerns are with the promotion of pupils' learning, the meeting of organizational ends efficiently and cost-effectively and a description of possible conflicts within the organization. These conflicts are to be resolved by referring 'to a set of values outside of and greater than those of the individuals in the organisation', whilst the recourse to such transcendent values is common to educational and commercial organizations, and acts 'as bridges between the two' (pp. 11–12).

This, however, is not an argument but a stipulative definition: individuals' values are less important than those of the organization, and this (acceptable) situation is a commonality between commerce and education. Behind even this definition one gets the feeling that there are other unstated assumptions, such as:

(a)   whoever is in charge of the organization has the right to dictate its aims
(b)   these aims can be relatively easily decided upon and implemented
(c)   as the organization's aims and values are more important than those of individuals within the organization, it is perfectly acceptable to treat people as means to the organization's ends.

Such unstated assumptions would appear to be present. Page 66 of the same book suggests:

> In many ways we should treat people as any other resource, selecting the best for the purpose we wish to accomplish, and maintaining, improving and adapting the resource as we would a building or piece of equipment to ensure that it meets our needs.

There is an anti-Kantian perspective here which being expressed in such bold and clear language many will find repulsive, and yet which is equally discernible though perhaps a little more guarded in other sources. Take Handy's best seller *Understanding Organisation* (1976), a compulsory book on many educational management courses. Talking of motivation, Handy says (p. 73):

> If we could understand, and could then predict, the ways in which individuals were motivated we could influence them by changing the components of that motivation process. Is that manipulation – or management?

Handy does not say, and we are left to form our own opinions.

Such clear terminology gives one a target at which to aim which does not move in one's sights. Rather more difficult to pin down and probably more dangerous because of this is the insidious and pervasive use of language which creates a prescriptive ethos of hierarchy and manipulation. It is precisely because the users of such terms slip comfortably from the original meaning of the terms to their manipulative/hierarchical connotations, and back again to the original meaning when challenged, that this dual use should be highlighted and disputed. Whilst not for a moment wishing to suggest that all or even most speakers and manuals on the subject do misuse words in this way, terminological perversion is not only possible but evident. For the cynical, a 'Devil's dictionary' of such terms (à la Ambrose Bierce) might include the following:

effective management: the head getting his or her own way in the quickest and most convenient manner.
employees: teachers.
good practice: what the head/DES/LEA wants.
inputs: pupils, children.
living resources: teachers.
managing conflict: making sure that disagreements within school end up with the head getting his or her own way.
management style: changing behaviour to get what you want.
managing the curriculum: making sure that the head gets his or her own way on curriculum aims, methods, implementation and evaluation.
motivation: manipulation.
negotiation: the head getting his or her own way without raising his or her voice.
outputs: pupils, children.
participation: getting members of staff to really want to do what the head/DES/LEA wants them to do by making them think that they are actually being consulted over the best course of action.
pedagogic material: pupils, children.
resourcefulness: the head using all the bribes at his or her disposal.
resource power: those bribes available to the head to get the staff to do what he or she wants them to do.
school management: the head getting his or her own way.
staff appraisal: determining if individual staff are working towards what the head/DES/-LEA wants.
staff development: getting members of staff to really want to do what the head wants them to do by making them think that the head is really interested in them and their personal interests and problems.
teaching units: teachers.
teamwork: getting together a staff who will work towards what the head/DES/LEA wants.

Besides this misuse of terminology, two other trends in the management literature should be noted.

Firstly, there is a restriction in what education means. Handy (1978: 300–301) defined the functions of education in these terms:

> The first function is to equip the young person with the essential knowledge and skills for survival in his society; the second is to nurture in him the values and behaviours desired by society . . . and a third is to provide the young adult with the special skills and knowledge which he will need to earn his living.

Very few would disagree with these functions, but it is not what is there which causes concern but the fact that so much is left out. What of the intrinsic worth of education, the pleasure of learning, the education of the autonomous, rational, critical and moral pupil? If one of the key writers in this field omits these objectives, how must this affect the types of management procedures advocated?

Such restriction is not just seen by the theoreticians. In 1983, David (now Lord) Young asserted that:

> Training should not be confused with education. Training is about work-related skills and is intimately connected with employment.
> (Quoted in Holt, 1987: 108)

However, in 1985 he was saying that there must be a 'determination to break down artificial barriers between academic and vocational learning' (*ibid.*).

In the same year the DES said in its White Paper 'Better Schools' that

> It is vital that schools should always remember that preparation for working life is one of their principal functions.

And in case one were to think that such prescriptions are confined to the secondary sector, it is worth noting that in the same year one of the HMIs said of primary schools:

> Consciousness of the work process cannot start too early, and it is enriching for young children to learn how the world earns its living.
> (Perry, quoted in *Times Educational Supplement*, 29 November 1986)

Now admittedly, preparation for working life and knowledge of how the world earns its living *are* two of schools' principal functions, so it is perfectly possible to conclude that belief in the prescription of limited and limiting education is somewhat paranoid. But if one takes into account the general sociopolitical ethos of the present time, it does not stretch belief too far to think that what is being written here is the suggestion that a focus on preparation for working life is *the* principal function of schools. Such a view would probably find many supporters so, one would have thought, it is not a belief to be ashamed of. But again, as with management terminology, a clear statement of its pre-eminence in the hierarchy of the functions of the school is hard to find, and so that much harder to tackle. As with so many other policies which are perceived by their creators as possibly contentious it is being introduced as death by a thousand cuts, the death that of a rich and developed education and quite a few of those cuts provided by present initiatives in educational management.

The second trend in management literature is a complementary restriction. If the concept of the curriculum is to be restricted, so is the concept of the teacher and the pupil. The teacher, no longer concerned with such concepts as autonomy, creativity and morality, is reduced in both status and perception. Teachers, Holt (1987: 7) says:

> must become passive agents by which change is to be brought about, and freed from moral involvement: they become not people, but functionaries – 'educational personnel'.

It is easy then for Everard and Morris to talk of treating teachers 'as any other resource' (1985: 66), for according to this view of management and education this is precisely what they are reduced to.

And as with teacher, so with pupil. On this restricted view of education they become inputs and outputs, assessed in crude 'objective' scientistic terms, evaluated by a criterion of whether they fit society's future requirements or not. As Jonathan says (1983: 6), the individual, whether pupil or teacher, becomes:

> primarily a cog in a given socioeconomic machine, and the education system as an arm of the Manpower Services Commission.

It must be stressed again that this is *not* the underlying principle of all management literature. More heartening is the approach taken by Day *et al.* (1985: 5) when they say:

> Adults, like children, cannot be developed; they can only be given opportunities to develop. This is a crucial principle, for it points the way to the consultant's role in the

process of curriculum and staff development. In essence, he or she cannot enforce change, only promote it.

This kind of approach stresses the professionalism of teachers as a community, recognizes the fact that a staff cannot be run like a line organization, for each teacher has his or her professional expertise to contribute, and points towards an essentially democratic form of school system. Les Bell (1988: 17) likewise suggests that:

> power and responsibilities within the school should not be centred on one person, but divided among as many of the staff as possible so that all feel involved in the decision making process and understand the rationale behind school policies.

This approach similarly suggests a collegial form of organization in the school. Within it, the head acts as raiser of issues, general school policy developer, consulter of experts, facilitator of implementation and co-ordinator of evaluation. The head's role is one among many, and all are vital. This at least is where such an approach is heading; but in theory and practice it tends to fall short. Why is this so? There are, I think, four reasons which converge to produce the same problem. The first reason is historical. The second is legal. The third is pragmatic. The fourth is theoretical. It is necessary to be aware of all four if comprehension of the bind which heads find themselves in is to be understood.

HISTORICAL

Bernbaum (1976) describes headship in the early nineteenth century as generally consisting of one teacher (the head) attempting to keep order and drum a few facts into 150 to 200 boys, all in the same room, assisted perhaps by one or two adults who would be given small groups of only 60 or 70 and who had had little more education than the boys they were instructing. Management consisted of being the jack of all trades who kept the ship afloat. The arrival of the great public school headmasters like Arnold saw little difference except in an added perspective – the head as the great moral leader, with the head as the academic or administrator lagging some considerable distance behind. The need for fee-paying students gave the head considerable licence in other areas, including 'selling' the school to parents, which might consist of working out the most acceptable curricula, which in turn meant hiring and firing the required staff, as well as being the 'front man' for the institution. The head came to be seen as the embodiment of the school, and he came to enjoy a status and prestige both within and without the school which made for a peculiarly British conception of headship and organization in the school. This was naturally transmitted to the state schools. In an era of moral, social and political consensus this presented few problems. In an era of cultural pluralism, of large schools where it is impossible for the head to know a majority of the pupils and of knowledge explosion which has been translated into profound curricular expertise, the historical conception becomes less and less tenable. Yet there is little doubt that the historical conception has considerable hold even now. Bernbaum (1976) has shown that even heads of comprehensive schools tend to think of themselves in an authoritarian, paternalistic manner, and the situation is even more pronounced in the primary school. If one thinks of three possible conceptions of headship as being on a continuum, ranging from (a) the historical paternalist to (b) the modern manager through to (c) the administrative democrat, then the inertia of tradition appears to have slowed movement down from the historical paternalist to a conception closer to the modern manager than the administrative democrat. It is hard to throw off the shackles of authoritarianism when they are so historically inbred, and when there are other factors for their retention.

Two relatively new and crucial factors have recently entered into the equation in Britain. The first is the advent of a national curriculum and testing. This considerably restricts the movement of both head and staff in what they may do in schools. It certainly reduces the power of the head, but it does not increase that of staff. Power has been moved out of the school to the DES. The second change is that of the increased powers of the governing body and the parents. This again is clearly a move away from the paternalistic conception of headship, but poses its own problems. In that the locus of authority is moved to a body outside the actual practice of teaching, it could be argued that it does even less to promote collegial organization. The head is at least in day-to-day contact with what goes on in school. Now, with much of the final say removed to an external body, prospects for greater staff involvement may well depend upon the interest and commitment of the governors. It will therefore be of interest to chart the course of relations between the different interests in British schools. Will the notion of collegial organization flower? Will the head be able to turn a governing body to his or her (or the staff's) own ends? Will a governing body adopt and use the powers given to them to their ends? Whatever is the outcome, the short-term view does not suggest that collegiality is any nearer.

LEGAL

The head's legal authority is mediated through the LEA and the boards of governors, but the head is *de facto* responsible for the internal activities of the school. This assumption of legal power works in three ways to restrain moves towards more participative involvement of staff in decision making. Firstly, where the head has a governing body looking over one shoulder and the staff over another, and the governing body has the ultimate power of veto, the head is more likely to take note of the governing body when pushed into a corner. Secondly, where the influence of the governing body is not apparent, the simple fact that heads have this *de facto* power makes it very tempting for them to use it. It is an unusual human being who, when presented with the authority and the coercive power to carry out procedures in his or her own way, does not feel a certain attraction in using it. But thirdly, it is a very brave, confident or foolish head who releases the reins of decision making to such an extent that major decisions are reached which run counter to his or her own judgement. When the responsibility for decisions ultimately lies with one person, then naturally that one person will normally make sure that he or she is sufficiently in control of the situation to prevent things going wrong for which he or she will take the blame. Thus by giving legal authority to heads, the ability to use it is presented but the desire to avoid any kind of mistake is magnified. These tendencies, then, militate against the genuine devolution of decision making to the staff.

PRAGMATIC

What prevents the existence of the democratic head? Legal factors have just been mentioned. But probably just as important is the inertia caused by historical precedent. Heads have to disengage their thinking from their own upbringing, their relationships with other heads and the ethos which surrounds their professional thinking. They must convince *themselves* that this is what they want. It presents no easy solution. The textbooks may tell them that this is the way to engineer real change. Heads may be convinced ethically that this is the only way an educational institution should be run. But experience as assistant teachers, as postholders and as deputies will tell them that it is much easier in a period of immense pressure on time and resources to at most consult the head of governors, but then to do the job themselves. Consultation with staff may be fine, but they may see it as having to be sacrificed. They must then convince themselves.

After that, they must deal with the expectations of teachers and parents. Nias (1986) has shown that teachers do not value their autonomy as highly as educational commentators do. As she says of primary school teachers:

> If these teachers are representative of the profession, it is clear that many would be willing to sacrifice a good deal of their autonomy in goal-setting in return for a greater sense of cohesion and teamwork . . . maximum job satisfaction went hand-in-hand with humane but positive leadership.

Hoyle (1975) described this as the difference between the 'restricted' and 'extended' professional: it is all very well to encourage participatory democracy in the staffroom, but what if the staff do not want it? What if they see an attempt by the head in this direction as an abrogation of his or her job? Let the head get on with managing the school whilst we manage our classrooms. White has argued (1984) that staff must be brought by selection and training to believe that not only do they have moral rights to participation, but also moral *duties*. This is inevitably a long-term project, and cannot be brought about in a negative or discouraging atmosphere.

Other factors, such as parental attitudes to school democracy and the attitudes of the LEA and the DES, must be positive as well. It is doubtful if this is so. As already noted, since the Taylor report (DES, 1977), and particularly with the 1986 and 1988 Education Acts, there has been a considerable increase in parental interest and involvement in education. It could still be argued, however, that this has been generally within an ethos which continues the notion of paternalism rather than extending real democracy. Bacon (1986), for example, found that the creation of boards of governors had actually increased the power of the head since an astute head could ally the governors against other potential trouble sources. Bacon found that the governors generally accepted the existing paternalist framework and worked within it. One must, however, wait for the full implementation of the 1988 reforms to see whether anything changes substantially in this area.

What of the LEA and the DES? It could be argued that management initiatives deriving from these sources are essentially democratic in nature, as they certainly call upon heads for greater staff involvement, and at the primary level the call for greater subject specialization seems to suggest that a model be adopted of professionals working together in a co-operative venture (see, for example, Campbell, 1985). However, there are good reasons to doubt that the call always goes this far.

As we have seen, greater staff involvement does not have to be an ethical call to heads but a pragmatic one – if you want to get something done in schools, the most efficient way of getting it done is to get a committed staff. The ethical notions that the staff have a right to involvement, and that it makes little *educational* sense to have a hierarchy (what does this say to children about the hidden curriculum of the school?) do not come across strongly. Indeed, hierarchy seems a central concept in DES thinking. As Lawton (1980: 12) has pointed out, in recent years the metaphor for the relationship between the DES and schools has moved from 'co-operation' to 'accountability'. This accountability is seen as only one-way, and thereby instantiates hierarchy. What appears to be emerging is an impossible position for the heads. On the one hand, a management course tells them that participation and consultation are to be their watchwords with staff. On the other hand, it is made abundantly clear that this is *not* to be the case in their relationships with their LEA and the DES. But then heads are caught in a vice. They follow the democratic decisions of their staff and put these to outside bodies, only to be told by outside bodies that heads will now implement and be accountable for what those bodies tell them. Management theory on the surface tells them one thing, but orders from elsewhere tell them another. Is it surprising if they interpret management theory in the manipulative manner described above? To avoid schizophrenia they must surely do so.

THEORETICAL

So from a pragmatic point of view heads will probably interpret management theory in a manipulative manner. But theoretically they must have their reservations too. Management theory in education is a derivative of management theory in commerce and industry. This must immediately cause problems. Jonathan (1983) has suggested that embedded in such a theoretical perspective lie three major social and moral assumptions about the nature of education which are easily identified with much of the above:

(a)   preparing pupils for life is identified with preparation for their economic role
(b)   educational benefit is to be assessed in social not individual terms
(c)   collective welfare implies the adaptation of the individual to social circumstance.

All three conspire to produce a hierarchical model of education and a management philosophy to go with it. However, the analogy with industry breaks down in a number of ways.

For a start, management theory in commerce and industry is based upon clear means and ends. The ends are the profitability of the product involved. Means are interesting, but not central to the activity. If one set of means does not work, another set can be instituted. Evaluation of the procedures is straightforward as well. How well is the product selling? Ethics and morality only enter into the subject peripherally, when some means outrage social decency. But many means are accepted because they achieve the goal of profitability. In the final analysis, in industry, the immorality of treating people as means to ends may be seen as offset by the profit to the company. If it is believed that the only way to achieve profitability is within such a hierarchical organization, then it may be the lesser of two evils – the greater being the bankruptcy of the company, and ultimately, for the society, starvation in a banana republic.

If an educational institution is viewed in this manner, as an input–output machine, where children are transformed into working units who can service the technology of society and help *it* to make a profit, then the commercial analogy holds water and business management techniques make sense. Children, then, on this model, are merely means to an end, just as teachers are. The children are the future parts for the industrial machine, the teachers are their shapers and oilers. And the head is the director of one factory which is ordered by central management (the DES) to produce units of so-and-so shape because this is how the industrial machine is going to look in *x* years' time. On this model, then, educational management *is* authoritarian, hierarchical and manipulative, and the headteacher has little more than a higher-grade part in this societal machine. This correspondence between the social relations of production and the social relations of the school has been extensively explored by writers such as Bowles and Gintis (1976), and one does not need to be a Marxist to see an unconscious espousement of such correspondence by the non-reflective headteacher, or the use of business analogies by politicians who have expertise in industry but little knowledge or regard for educational values. In the political climate of the present time, it is easy to see that current pre-eminent values of efficiency and cost-effectiveness could be dangerously over-used or misused.

The basic premise, then, of much of management theory is that schools are there to adopt policies formulated elsewhere. They are not in the business of being a creative part of the enterprise. The teacher is more and more defined in managerial terms as an effective agent rather than a responsible being.

However, it is highly debatable whether education should or need be viewed in this manner. It is a crucial moral question whether one should countenance *any* organization which treats people as means to ends. There may be some kind of economic justification for industry, but it is hard to see how an educational institution, viewed as one comprised of specialist professionals, either should or need be viewed in this light.

What if one views education as an essentially value-laden activity, in which each action must be questioned as to its ethicality? If one views the educational organization as not primarily a breeding ground for the future needs of society's technology but as a place where children are given the opportunity to question through examining existing practices, learn through rational constructive criticism and practise through genuine involvement then it is difficult if not impossible to view the school in the 'industrial' manner. Its being is antithetical to such a viewpoint.

However, and perhaps crucially for some people, the effect of the 'industrial' approach also must disqualify it even in the minds of those who favour the view that the prime function of the school is industrial provision. For one must ask what such an approach does to the school, its pupils and its teachers in the long run. The ultimate effect is surely the opposite of that planned, in that by de-professionalizing the schools, centralism ensures the production of poor quality time- and rule-servers. This is no mere educational insight. In a survey of the business methods of 75 highly successful American companies, Peters and Waterman (1982) come to just this conclusion. As one executive said to them:

Substituting rules for judgement starts a self-defeating cycle, since judgement can only
be developed by using it.

One would have thought that empirical insights from American business would have
been noticed in American education at least. The results have been disappointing.
Passow examined the perspectives of those advocating school reform in the 1980s,
and concluded that the emphasis, as in the UK, has been on achievement, raising
standards, concentrating on science, technology and mathematics at the expense of
arts subjects and generally adopting the hierarchical model described in this chapter.
What is missing, says Passow:

> is a meaningful discussion of the intrinsic worth of education, the pleasure of learning
> . . . the building of polity and community . . . the current stress is on producing persons
> who will enable America to compete industrially and commercially with other nations.
> (Quoted in Holt, 1987: 138–9)

So in the USA, so in the UK. What is perceived as the 'effective industrial' model
holds sway (even if now there is cause to doubt that it is the most effective or
industrial). Line management and hierarchy seem still to have the floor.

But what does a hierarchical structure in school tell the pupils? It tells them that
in an age of cultural pluralism there is one person who is given the final say on
matters of value, rather than these matters being discussed. It tells them that in
terms of knowledge, even the expert must defer to the non-expert if this non-expert
happens to have been granted a title of 'head'. It tells them that in the end their
voice counts for nothing, nor does that of their teachers. They may be asked for
their opinion, but it does not have to be accepted, as neither does the teachers'. In
a democratic society, in *the* institution where democracy has a real chance of existence, it does not exist. They can draw two conclusions. Either the institution is
irrational, for who could possibly invent such ridiculous structures? If this is their
conclusion, then alienation is the answer. Or this seeming irrationality is the cloak
for something more sinister, and the Marxist theory may have something to it.

Whichever of the two answers they choose, the situation cannot be a healthy one.
Within current approaches to management in the schools is a dangerously explosive
mixture which can satisfy only those who are not concerned about the education of
the majority of children or about the job satisfaction and professional development
of their teachers. Where the prevailing philosophy is one of treating people as means
to ends, whether pupils or teachers, the inevitable result is alienation and conflict.
But if the preceding analysis is correct it does not even serve the needs of industry.
Short-term benefit is lost in long-term loss of quality. The good of society is defined
in terms of more than its present GNP, and healthy future GNP is guaranteed only
by the acceptance of the professionalism of schools and teachers and a rich and
complex view of education. Educational management must concern itself with ends
– educational ends, teachers and pupils. Perhaps it is time for education to begin
exporting some of these ideas to industrial theory. Educational institutions – and
society in general – would be much more humane places.

What then might be the positive suggestions coming out of such a critique? There
would seem to be essentially four.

Firstly, and most crucially, there must be a change in attitude and perception by
those officials in LEAs and the DES towards teachers and pupils. Undoubtedly,
parts of the nature of their job necessitate a perspective which sees teachers as means

to ends. In such things as manpower planning, the placement of teachers in teaching vacancies and the construction of an education service to fit the future needs of society, viewing teachers as means rather than as ends is to some extent inevitable. This perspective, however, should cease to be the overriding one as soon as the teacher is in place. Instead of treating teachers as inferior members of a hierarchy and children as products to be processed, an attitude of fellow professionalism with teachers – engaging in the same pursuit as officials, but with different aspects in different locations – can filter down to teachers in terms of respect and co-operation rather than as bureaucratic manipulative indifference. If it cannot, because the DES or the LEAs are unable through sheer force of habit to adopt another perspective, this can only point to the management training of teachers being made the responsibility of some other body. The need for a professional body from within the teaching profession itself may then find support.

Secondly, heads and deputy heads on management courses must be urged, initially at least, to treat their staff as fellow professionals whose judgement is to be respected and trusted instead of as resources to be allocated most effectively. It is the difference between treating human beings as persons and as things. Human beings, not surprisingly, enjoy and respond much better to the former. This perspective is crucial, because from a philosophy or ideology of practice stems the practices themselves. Change the ideology and you change the practice.

Thirdly, the onus must not be placed solely upon those at the top of the hierarchy in educational management. One must also place a responsibility on those at the bottom – the teachers. Democratic participation may be given from above, but to survive it must be employed and practised by those below. Teachers, then, must come to see that this participation in the running of the school is not a free gift which they can pick up or put down depending on what else they have to do. It demands time and commitment which may be tedious, irksome and at times threatening. Democracy in schools must be seen by staff as a duty rather than just as a right. It must be seen as an essential part of the education of the child, and can be no more a matter of choice than is education in reading.

Finally, there must be a re-opening of the debate, a redefinition of the ground, about the purposes of education. The initiative at the moment appears to be with the non-educationalist definer of education, who uses terms which pay scant regard to the insights and pleas of those actually in the profession. Instead of the – by now – accepted wisdom of education as the process of producing employable manpower, attention must be directed past this to other questions. What is economic wealth for? What is the desired end state for society? Where does education fit into this overall design? Questions like these can suggest that descriptions of the functions of education have become stuck on the consideration of means, and have lost sight of ultimate ends. In terms of educational management, a greater consideration of ends will issue in a new vision of relationships within the school. If it does not, impoverishment of education – and ultimately of society – will be the consequence.

Chapter 14

Civic Responsibility, Morality and the School

At the Conservative Party Conference on 12 October 1988, Mr P. Gallie, the member for Cunninghame North, bemoaned the present lawless state of Britain (reported in the *Guardian*, 13 October 1988). He pointed out in a speech that day that in 1950 14 out of every 1,000 crimes were classed as violent compared with 282 out of every 1,000 in 1988. Similarly, he noted that in the 20 years after the war, the average number of murders per year in Britain was 140, whereas in the last 20 years it had been on average 700 per year. The need for more police and stiffer penalties for offenders was clear.

It will be apparent by now that the present writer does not hold the same opinion. The argument above suggests a link between antisocial behaviour and heavy punishment which is simply assumed, rather than argued for. However, it is still an argument to be noted, if only for the fact that much of the debate surrounding issues of law and order and civic responsibility, frequently does not reach a higher level of inquiry.

There are notable exceptions to this rule. Speaking at the same Conference on the same day, Douglas Hurd, the Home Secretary at that time, was aware of these facts, but his answer to them was rather more wide-reaching and rather less knee-jerk in reaction. He argued that a fundamental change in attitude was needed by society as a whole if present difficulties were to be overcome. As he said:

> The challenge of the 1990s is to rekindle our strong tradition of citizenship. The game of dodging responsibility, of passing the parcel of blame from one group to another simply has to stop.
> (Quoted in the *Guardian*, 13 October 1988)

He continued by saying that it was the duty of parents to teach their children that they had responsibilities as well as rights; schools had to put self-discipline and respect for others at the heart of the curriculum; and broadcasters should consider the effect their programmes had, particularly on the young (*ibid.*).

His vision, then, was one which argued the need for a number of agencies to play their part in the generation of responsible citizenship – the family, the school, the media. This need for civic responsibility had been directly related to schools by Douglas Hurd when he had spoken on the BBC television programme *Panorama* of 9 October of that year:

> Somewhere during those hours and hours when children are at school, when they decide whether the tree is going to grow straight or crooked, somebody should be trying to

influence them that other people do have rights, that the law is there for a purpose, that the police are there to protect people.
(Quoted in the *Daily Mail*, 10 October 1988)

The advocacy of the development of civic responsibility in the youth of a country generally brings (and is intended to bring) a warm glow to the law-abiding citizen's heart. It is similarly tempting to see the engendering of such civic responsibility as little more than a problem of inculcation, rather than as a complex and demanding task which cannot be dealt with by simplistic solutions. Douglas Hurd went some way along this path by suggesting that different agencies might all help in the furtherance of such a task. But it could be argued that rather more needs to be done than was suggested in these speeches. There must be, for example, extremely careful consideration of what are the factors needed to produce a responsible citizen and, moreover, a similarly careful consideration of what means should be used to achieve this end. A little reflection on the first will show that this is no simple task, which means that the second is probably going to be equally complex.

There is a very real danger here that the unthinking may swallow the notion of civic responsibility whole, voting into power those who claim that they will promote it and then finding that the means suggested for its achievement are not at all what they would have desired had they given the matter some initial consideration. Equally likely, simplistic solutions may be suggested and then left to other agencies (schools, families, probation officers, the media, etc.) to implement. When such measures fail to cure the ills they were designed for, the blame is then conveniently passed to the practitioners, rather than to those who designed the 'medicine' in the first place.

Thus very different means may be proposed for achieving 'civic responsibility'. These different means derive in part from different possible meanings of 'civic responsibility'. So what, then, is meant by the term? It appears to consist of a number of different elements, most notable amongst them being:

(a)   a pride in one's society and its institutions, which will result in a desire to uphold the laws and norms of that society
(b)   a belief that one has a duty to help in the upholding of these laws and norms
(c)   an understanding that people must work together if they are to exist in a society worth living in
(d)   a suggestion that if society has an increased crime rate, greater violence, etc., then *all* of its members are to blame for this state of affairs, as they are all contributors to this society.

A number of things need to be said about this account.

Firstly, this is clearly what sociologists call a 'functionalist' argument of how society works, for it sees society as essentially made up of a collection of people who may be very different in many respects but who are all fundamentally aiming for much the same kind of community, and who only really differ in the places they inhabit and the functions they perform in keeping that society running. On such a perspective, schools are created as kinds of half-way houses between the family and society for the child.

Perhaps the most famous proponent of such a view was the late nineteenth-century French sociologist Emile Durkheim. In his book *Moral Education*, Durkheim (1961) saw the school as vital because it enabled the child to understand that rules are more than a product of the family situation. Rules are the necessary creation of any form of social unit, and the school gives the child a valuable distancing from personal relationships, thus allowing the child to grasp their abstract conception, a thing impossible within the family because of the way in which rules are associated with personalities. But also, and conversely, Durkheim sees the school as vital to the health of society because it is small enough for children to feel a part, and not merely alienated, isolated individuals in the crowd as they would were they to move out of the family straight into the maelstrom of society. As Durkheim said (1961: 233–5):

> If . . . with the exception of the family, there is no collective life in which we participate, if in all the forms of human activity we are in the habit of acting like lone wolves, then our social temperament has only rare opportunities to strengthen and develop itself. . . . It is precisely at this point that the role of the school can be considerable.

Modern calls, then, for the school to play its part in the personal, social and moral development of the child in order for the child to develop civic responsibility were anticipated by Durkheim almost 100 years ago. The clarion call for civic responsibility is nothing new.

However, even though the school is called upon by Durkheim to play its part in this engendering of civic responsibility, it cannot be called upon to shoulder all or even most of the burden. The school is but one institution within society, and if one wishes to change the attitudes of those within that society then the other institutions must play their part as well. Durkheim (1961) argued that the cure for indiscipline and deviancy in school – and hence the furtherance of civic responsibility – was a combination of at least three things. These were: an obedience by all to the same moral rules; an increased attachment to social groups; and an increased understanding of the rules. In like manner, precisely these three ingredients are needed for the combating of indiscipline and deviancy in society at large. Crucially, none of these should be seen in isolation from one another or thought of as being viable without the others. Thus a simple increased understanding of the rules will not promote greater civic responsibility on its own for it needs to be backed up by the other two conditions, which means that *all* within society should obey – and benefit equally from – its rules, and all must feel a greater attachment to that society before civic pride and responsibility can be engendered. The consequences of holding a thorough-going functionalist position are clear: if one wants all members of society to act responsibly, then society must first act responsibly towards all members. Schools will be ineffective in such a task if the society in which they are located is perceived as unjust by all or a section of those members.

Now this functionalist position is clearly in stark contrast to a 'conflict' account of society. Such a view argues that instead of society being reasonably harmonious, interlocking and interdependent, society is instead characterized by discord and struggle. It is moreover necessarily so, because of the different degrees of power held by groups within that society. One group will inevitably achieve dominance within that society – whether it be tribal chiefs, feudal barons or the owners of industry – and will then do all in its power to hold on to that position. (See the introduction to Karabel and Halsey, 1977 for a description of these differing accounts.)

In such a model of society, schools have a very different role to play from that of the functionalist account. In the conflict model, schools are created by the dominant group to ensure its – the dominant group's – continued domination. Clearly the most famous exponent of such a position is Karl Marx. (Marx wrote little specifically on education, but see Marx, 1964 or Engels, 1981. Modern statements are given by Bowles and Gintis, 1976, Harris, 1979 and Matthews, 1980.) From such a perspective, if pupils are badly behaved in school this is not because there is something wrong with the child, or because not all are acquiescing to the rules and morals which undergird that society, but rather because they are rebelling against unjust dominance strategies by teachers who, consciously or unconsciously, are furthering the interests of the dominant class by attempting to socialize children into behaviours which will make them more responsive and compliant to what the dominant class requires. Some of this has already been described in Chapter 1, with the imposition in the nineteenth century of a ruler and ruled code of social morality. Toffler (1970: 354–5) described the translation of such a code for the working classes into actual classroom strategies when he said:

> Mass education was the ingenious machine constructed by industrialism to produce the kind of adults it needed . . . the solution was an educational system that, in its very structure, stimulated this new world . . . the most criticised features of education today – the regimentation, lack of individualisation, the rigid systems of seating, grouping, grading and marking, the authoritarian role of the teacher – are precisely those that made mass public education so effective an instrument of adaptation for its time and place . . . the child did not simply learn facts that he could use later on: he lived, as well as learned, a way of life modelled after the one he would lead in the future.

There is plenty of evidence to suggest that such strategies have been carried into the twentieth century. At the level of practice, many classes still bear the scars of rigid rows of seating, of an obsession with timetables, with a profound belief in the infallibility of the teacher. At the level of educational assumptions, if one looks at the approach which tends to 'blame the victim', one finds it was common both here and the USA in educational policies in the 1960s and 1970s, and may now be returning with the notion of civic responsibility. For example, in examining working-class children's scholastic achievement, explanation has taken the form of a genetic deprivation in intelligence, alluded to by people like Jensen (1969), or a sociocultural deprivation due to home background or language code, described by Bernstein (1973), or a combination of these. The approach is well illustrated by the assumptions underlying the Headstart programme in America, and the EPA scheme in England. As Grace (1978) pointed out, such an approach tends to locate the problem of underachievement with the recipients of education and hence to blame them, whilst taking for granted the efficacy and blamelessness of the educational institutions, its practitioners and the society they represent. Such educational assumptions are then translated back into the practice of the classroom.

For example, Keddie (1971) in England and Cicourel and Kitsuse (1977) in the USA illustrate how the judgement of individual pupils by teachers and educational bureaucrats can be as much a function of the pupils' dress, behaviour, attitude and educational stream as it is of their actual performance. Keddie, for instance, showed that a reply by a child in a higher grade at school tended to be judged as relevant and meaningful by the teacher, whilst precisely the same reply would be judged as the displaying of poor comprehension if given by a child from a lower form. Similarly Rist (1977), utilizing a labelling theory approach and the phenomenon of the self-fulfilling prophecy developed by Rosenthal and Jacobson (1968), showed that a teacher's judgement would be internalized by the child who would come to accept the teacher's assessment.

The question to ask surely is: are such practices a function of the replication of power relationships within a capitalist society or simply a description of patterns of interaction between individuals? The latter description simply will not do as it stands, as it fails to explain why the teacher labels and assesses in this manner in the first place. If, in Keddie's example, the teacher treats children's replies on the basis of their differing social class, the problem is not answered by simply warning teachers to be aware of this possibility in their interactions. The question to be asked is: why did it happen in the first place? Why did the teacher treat children differently because of their social class? This fits the Marxist account quite neatly, in that it suggests that teachers are socializing children into different roles in society, precisely because of their differing social origins.

Having said this, it could still be argued that the Marxist hypothesis fits the situation now much less well than it did in the past. Hurn (1978), for example, has argued that schools are now confronted by the problem of having to transform an institution bearing the heavy marks of its original aims in a past historical epoch into one more in keeping with a modern liberal democracy. On this account, talk should not be so much about conspiratorial capitalist machinations, nor even the inexorable trans- mission of power status values, but more of simple educational inertia. This is much like the analysis which Silberman (1973: 11) gave when he argued that, when considering teachers:

> it simply never occurs to more than a handful to ask *why* they are doing what they are doing – to think seriously or deeply about the purposes or consequences of education.

In a word, Silberman (p. 10) called their general attitude one of 'mindlessness'.

If this is the case, then the kind of remedies argued by conflict theorists need not be accepted. If pupils *are* rebelling against such unjust dominance patterns, and these patterns are the results primarily of educational inertia, then there is no need to accept that the cure must be a change in the pattern of economic relationships within society. This is simply because such dominance patterns may not exist in the form seen in the nineteenth century, and therefore such radical changes are inappropriate. Even if there are still vestiges of such dominance patterns in school disciplinary procedures and organizational processes, these can be changed.

This could be argued, but it is not conclusive. Teachers may be transmitting messages from the past which they would change if they thought about them, but society as a whole may still be acting according to conflict theory. This would suggest that the kind of 'black box' account so often adopted by conflict theorists is unnecessary. This account simply assumes that schools must transmit what 'the ruling class' requires. There are two things wrong with this.

Firstly, a 'ruling class' may not be as obvious or monolithic as the Marxist point of view suggests. Within a conflict model, there may be power groups in society which each hold a portion of the overall control, without any one having total control. Schools, then, need not be simply transmission stations, for there may be no one simple message to transmit.

Secondly, even if some single group were in control, schools and teachers might hinder the transmission of such a message and instead try and send their own. Where lip-service, at the very least, is paid to the notion of a liberal democracy by all members of western societies including those in power, the teacher may feel capable of transmitting such messages with impunity.

But even if there is freedom for schools and teachers to transmit messages which run counter to the standard Marxist thesis, this still does not address the fundamental question of whether the kinds of injustices described by Marxist theory still exist within society. There may still be considerable room for change in society which is undoubtedly beyond the abilities of schools to deal with, and the remediation of which would enable schools to perform their job in a better fashion. Indeed, if injustice does exist in society, then it would appear to be incumbent upon society, whatever model of society one adopts, for that society to deal with it, and thereby make the nurturing of civic responsibility a more attainable ideal for educational institutions.

In this respect, it is salutory to note that the overwhelming conclusion from the evidence of social mobility studies – Blau and Duncan (1967) and Jencks (1972) in America, Boudon (1977) in France and Halsey *et al.* (1980) and Goldthorpe *et al.* (1987) in England – all point inexorably in the same direction: educational reforms in these countries have significantly failed to alter the rates of mobility to any significant extent over the last 50 years. Educational opportunities may have increased, but the extra places created in the system have been disproportionately occupied by the higher status levels.

The evidence does *not* necessarily point to the fact that schools are irrelevant in the creation of a better and fairer society. Evidence from both the secondary level by Rutter (1979) and the primary level by Mortimore *et al.* (1988) strongly suggests that the school which one goes to can make a large difference to one's cognitive and social attainments. But the school is only one – even if a major – institution within society. It would be foolish to expect that it could achieve really major effects without corresponding changes in the functions of other influential institutions, such as taxation, housing, health care and social security. Education can certainly play a major part but cannot shoulder the burden on its own.

Where does this leave the school? It is obviously in no position to effect social reforms, so does it have any part to play in promotion of civic responsibility? Before coming to a conclusion about this, some preliminary points need to be made.

Firstly and perhaps most importantly, one must draw a distinction between two forms of civic responsibility rather like the contrast between patriotism and jingoism. One can love one's country, one can die for one's country, but that does not mean to say that one must not criticize one's country. Love of something must not blind one to its faults. It is all too easy to wrap oneself in the flag and ignore the fact that the other side might on occasions be right.

Similarly, civic responsibility may suggest a pride in one's society and a belief in one's duty to uphold its laws and norms, but it does not suggest that one does this uncritically. An uncritical acceptance of the laws and mores of one's society would be an essentially stagnant attitude, and would prevent the implementation of changes needed to make society a fairer and more just place to live in. Only the person who believed that society was already perfect in every respect could argue for an uncritical implementation of civic responsibility. Where elements of social reconstruction are necessary, an approach to the subject of civic responsibility is needed which, as this book has suggested throughout, involves tolerance, flexibility, critical analysis and care.

This would obviously be a very different approach from that which saw such fostering of civic responsibility as unproblematic. Such a view would assume that one somehow *started* by inculcating civic responsibility, in order that the other things – lower crime rates, less violence, less vandalism – would follow. It would suggest that there are similarly unproblematic methods of producing this civic responsibility. As questioning and criticism would not be necessary, such methods would involve habit formation of an essentially non-rational kind. On this account, 'the good' is known, and it is merely a matter of pointing people in the right direction by the most efficient means.

Similarly, with such an approach, pupils' willing and thinking agreement to such pointing is seen as neither methodologically nor ethically necessary. It is not methodologically necessary because there are well-proven techniques which can inculcate these attitudes – the use of punishment or reward (essentially behaviourist conditioning), the modelling of such behaviours and exhortation. Likewise, it is not seen as ethically necessary because if one believes that 'civic responsibility' is a 'good thing', then there can be no argument over the methods used to achieve it. However, the argument of this book so far would suggest that neither of these points of view is acceptable.

Firstly, whilst non-rational techniques can be effective, they are generally ineffective where there is cognitive dissonance – where what is being suggested as right and proper clashes with other profoundly held perceptions and beliefs. For example, where it is being suggested that one should have pride in one's society and responsibility towards it, this may well clash with beliefs held by unemployed youngsters in depressed regions of the country. They might well argue that they can see little to feel proud about, and that their society does not appear to care about them. In other words, there has to be an ethos corresponding to the message being propounded before it is likely to have any effect.

Secondly, even if such conditions did not pertain and hence such non-rational techniques were methodologically possible, they could never be ethically acceptable. For a start, such techniques show the same level of respect for those receiving them as for the subjects on which they were originally tested – lower-order animals. Whilst it may be accepted that animals could never appreciate a reasoned argument, and therefore such techniques are essential for their well-being, this argument cannot be put for human beings – no matter how little they may initially appear to react to such persuasion. As has been noted above, society must provide a just and fair ethos if such reasoned argument is to take root. Merely to tell or to condition people to be responsible citizens is not enough. If there is to be genuine pride in society, genuine commitment to its institutions, laws, norms and ideals, then youngsters must feel that such civic features apply to all, and most notably to them. This, I suggest, puts the onus squarely back on those who devise such institutions and laws, and who most obviously benefit from them. If these people are serious about wishing to engender a sense of civic responsibility then they, holding the reins of power, must see that *all* within society benefit from that society. This is rather more than those in power merely exhibiting civic responsibility themselves (and thereby suggesting that this is what everybody should do), for it is relatively easy to exhibit such responsibility when the institutions, norms and laws favour oneself. As Rawls (1971) has suggested, society must aim at a social structure which starts off from a consideration of the conditions of those least well off within it. If such a perspective is not taken, then it should come as no surprise to anyone that those at the bottom of the heap do not respond to appeals to their civic responsibility.

So what part can the school play? If it is accepted that 'civic responsibility' is a blanket term which must be looked at more closely before attempts at achieving it are embarked on, and if it is accepted that it is not something which can or should be imparted in a non-rational manner, then what kinds of practices should schools be involved in? On the foregoing analysis, there must be a number of aspects to be dealt with in developing strategies which suggest a thoughtful, caring approach. If this is accepted, then it would seem that the four focuses of concern described throughout this book should be at the centre of an approach to this problem. It will be remembered that the four focuses of concern suggested have been:

(a) the promotion of rationality
(b) the heightening of the child's empathy
(c) the fostering of the child's self-esteem
(d) the furthering of co-operation.

Each of these has different but related functions to play in the development of a sense of civic responsibility.

The promotion of rationality has both positive and critical dimensions; it must be used for the appreciation of society's strengths and virtues, but also for the analysis of society's problems and of other people's difficulties within that society. Similarly, it must be used not only to suggest the benefits, duties and responsibilities stemming from the adherence to just laws and norms, but also possible criticisms of them, the development of alternative means of achieving ends and the planning, structuring and implementation of new solutions to old problems. Thus it *may* be used to analyse and criticize existing attitudes to, for example, women or ethnic minorities, but it must be used to suggest ways of changing such attitudes as well. Rationality must be used for empowerment as well as for understanding. The development of true civic responsibility will engender action as well as thought, and this action may entail the furtherance or the change of the existing status quo.

The fostering of the child's self-esteem leads directly from this. Empowerment leads directly to feelings of worth and value. Whilst disenfranchised and disempowered, one naturally feels ignored, undervalued and alienated. There is now quite a body of psychological literature which suggests that the fostering of self-esteem leads to feelings of altruism towards others, simply because one feels good about oneself. (See, for example, Staub and Sherk, 1970, Staub, 1971, Mischel and Mischel, 1976 or Rosenhan *et al.*, 1976.) Civic responsibility will come about, at least in part, through initial feelings of self-worth.

The heightening of children's empathy in both a cognitive and an emotional sense will provide them with a hitherto neglected understanding of others within society who may have different outlooks from themselves, but who still hurt and feel as they do. It may lead to more respect for the environment, a better attitude towards the elderly through an appreciation of their needs and the better treatment of minorities through the heightened understanding of how it feels to be a minority. The work of Hoffman (1976, 1982) described in Chapter 7 provides strong theoretical support for this position.

The furthering of co-operation in many ways incorporates the other three focuses of concern. Empathy towards others' different needs is required if really appropriate help is to be given to them. The act of co-operation improves children's self-esteem by showing that they are important agents in others' learning and personal development. Clear thinking is needed in assessing, structuring and implementing ways of facilitating this co-operation. In itself, co-operation promotes a positive attitude to others, an essential if civic responsibility is to make any sense. A society based on individual competition which sends a clear message to its youth that success in life is to be measured by the bettering of others clearly runs counter to the basic assumptions of civic responsibility.

These four factors, then, provide the kind of groundwork which is needed for an increase in civic responsibility. They also form, not surprisingly, the groundwork for the promotion of a truly moral attitude to others in school, for school is essentially a preparation for participation in society. The relationship between civic responsibility, morality, school and society is essentially reciprocal. One may have immoral schools and therefore an immoral society, just as one may have an immoral society and hence immoral schools. Or one may have moral schools producing a moral society, and moral society producing moral schools. The promotion of civic responsibility is part of the remit of the school, but the school should not be seen as the only concerned body. Schools have an immensely important part to play, but the development of civic responsibility is not the domain of one institution; it is the domain of all. Perhaps those instituting policies would do well to remember this. As Durkheim noted 100 years ago, the promotion of any social attitude is only completely successful where *all* participants accept their responsibility. The morality of the school, then, is a part of a larger picture, and draws much of its life from that larger canvas.

Appendix 1

Moral Dilemmas on Computer

INTRODUCTION

The initial impetus to develop a moral dilemmas exercise using computers came from two related observations. The first was that discussions of dilemmas can be very productive and very stimulating, but they can also be tedious and uninteresting. A discussion may produce exciting and insightful debate, or it can go very flat. There are a number of reasons for this. The children may not find the dilemma particularly interesting in itself; the teacher may not be very inspired or inspiring; it may be attempted on Friday afternoon, when thoughts of home are uppermost. However, a major reason for relative failure could be a lack of structure in the lesson. Thus a teacher might begin an exercise extremely well but find the whole thing tailing off because discussion ended up a blind alley, or he or she may simply not know how to take the exercise any further than the initial discussion. Introducing structure, therefore, is seen as a way of giving the teacher a format within which to work without unduly cramping creativity.

This leads directly into the second observation. Without structure, an enormous burden is placed upon the teacher. Whether the teacher adopts the position of a 'neutral chairperson' or takes a more actively participant role, at some stage in the proceedings he or she will almost certainly have to intervene. This may be because the discussion has failed to consider counter arguments to those most consistently suggested. Or it may be because the debate has become side-tracked and whole areas of debate and concern have been neglected. Whatever the cause, if the teacher has to intervene, he or she must know how to do so and with what sort of arguments. It was thought to be asking an awful lot of any teacher's memory and flexibility to expect him or her to have all possible arguments to hand, and to be able to apply the correct one to a particular stage of thinking. If the teacher's load could be made a little easier, it was felt, subsequent discussion might be much more productive.

RATIONALE

The moral dilemma taken was a variation of one created by the American developmental psychologist Lawrence Kohlberg; the 'Heinz' dilemma (see Chapter 3). As it stood, it was not felt appropriate for English children, firstly because 'Heinz' brought unproductive and confusing images of baked beans, and secondly because the 'chemist' in the story had connotations of street corner dispensers of aspirins, not scientific researchers. The 'Heinz' dilemma therefore became the 'Jim' dilemma:

> A woman is dying because she is suffering from a very dangerous disease. So far there has been no medicine which can cure the disease. But now a scientist invents a drug which can cure the disease. The scientist wants a great deal of money for the drug. The sick woman's husband, Jim, tries to raise the money for the drug, but can't find enough to pay the scientist. What should he do?

A little thought shows that there are a limited number of replies to this question, which might be described as:

(a) continue trying to raise the money
(b) ask the scientist to sell the drug at a lower price, but otherwise do nothing
(c) if neither of these works, steal the drug.

However, whilst there are a limited number of replies to the question, each reply may be made for different reasons. Kohlberg believed that these could and should be described on a developmental scale, so that one started off at a lowest level of reasoning and worked upwards to more sophisticated levels. Simply stated, if a child believed that Jim should just continue trying to raise the money, the lowest level reason for this might be something like 'because if I do anything else, I will be punished and sent to jail'. Kohlberg's suggestion is that one should present children with a counter argument at the next highest level of reasoning so as to stimulate them to develop a more comprehensive viewpoint. There has been much argument about whether people's thought does develop in the manner Kohlberg describes, or whether these levels exist at all, but the description of the types of argument used at different levels does provide a solid checklist from which to create counter arguments to those produced by the children. And whilst it was felt that a rigid adherence to such levels is unnecessary, they did provide a guide for matching appropriate arguments. In fact, on occasion, two or three counter arguments were supplied to one reply by the child. These arguments might be just below the stage, at the same stage, and one above the present stage used by the child – simply because even if the theory is neat in theory and application, my experience with children suggests that their thinking does not match this neatness.

This, then, was the basis for the computer program. The computer was programmed to pick up the pupils' underlying reasons for their replies, and then to deliver back to them a contrary reason or an unpleasant consequence of the decision at the same or a slightly higher level of reasoning, 'higher' being determined by Kohlberg's stages.

How did the computer pick out these reasons? This was performed by means of there being certain key words associated with each level of reasoning which were programmed into the computer's memory. When the children typed in their decision, the computer identified the key words and returned the 'appropriate' answer. But how did the children know to use the key words? Because each group leader was given a list of these key words, and asked to incorporate them into the group's answer without distorting the reason itself. Where a group failed to use a key word in its decision, the computer was programmed to throw up a request to the children that they see the teacher, who would then help them to rephrase the decision.

An example of this can be taken from Jim's position. Reasons for Jim deciding to do nothing more than asking the scientist to sell the drug at a lower price might be:

(a) I'll be punished if I do more.
(b) I'll be sent to jail.
(c) I'll lose my job.
(d) People will think I'm rotten if I don't do something.
(e) It's against the law to do more.
(f) It would be wrong to steal the drug.
(g) We can't just break the law when we want to.
(h) What would happen if everyone else stole as well?

Key words for these reasons might be (a) 'punished', (b) 'jail', (c) 'lose job', (d) 'rotten', (e) 'against the law', (f) 'wrong', (g) 'break the law', (h) 'everyone else'.

When the reasons are typed into the computer, counter arguments and consequences are thrown back to the children. These might be:

for (a), (b) and (c)

your wife will almost certainly die
people will probably think you are rotten
how would you feel if you were her?

for (d):

people will probably still think you're rotten because your wife will almost certainly die.

for (e) and (f):

your wife will almost certainly die
people will probably think you're rotten
it's more wrong to let her die than to steal.

for (g) and (h):

your wife will almost certainly die
you'll feel more guilty at doing nothing
it's more wrong to let her die than to steal.

To recapitulate then, a dilemma was chosen, possible responses to it were listed, the reasons for such replies detailed, and the counter-replies and consequences to these reasons programmed onto a computer. The next problem, then, is to structure a lesson.

LESSON STRUCTURE

The lesson is split into two distinct phases; the dilemma discussion itself and the judge's option. As we shall see, they present two independent though closely linked exercises.

The dilemma discussion

(a) The dilemma is read to the class as a whole. Then the class is split into three different groups representing Jim, Jim's wife and the scientist. This assigning to groups is generally performed as a game, with children given the name of one of three farmyard animals written on small cards. Their task is to find other members of their group using only the noises of their animal.
(b) Once the groups are seated and settled, they are each given one of the characters in the dilemma. They are told that each of these characters has, at the start of the dilemma, an initial 'set' opinion. These are:

> *Jim*:   I'll ask the scientist to lower the price of the drug, but I'll do nothing else.
> *Wife*:   Steal the drug! I'm dying!
> *Scientist*: I'll not sell cheaply. I'm going to make money.

These roles are discussed by each group in private, and strategies and possible answers to other groups' challenges are discussed. Group leaders are asked to focus specifically on the following questions:

'Why would Jim/wife/scientist say this?'
'What might the others say to them if they said this?'
'How would Jim/wife/scientist reply?'

(c) Once the groups have had time to discuss such questions, they all meet and the character's stances are discussed. The teacher in charge chairs the discussion, ensuring approximately equal time for each group's contribution.
(d) At the end of the class discussion, each character/group withdraws and is given a list of choices for further action on a piece of card. They may now change their opinion. They discuss these options in the withdrawal groups, eventually decide upon one of them and then phrase the reasoning for this choice, using the key words provided to the group leader.
(e) The group moves to the computer. The computer asks them who they are, what their opinion is, and they are invited to write their reasons for their choice on the computer screen. As described earlier, the key words call up the counter arguments/consequences to their choice, which they write down and take back for discussion.
(f) The group now discusses all arguments, counter arguments and consequences, and decides upon the adoption of one position.

(g) The groups all meet again, and each character's position is announced to the other groups/characters, and the reasons for its adoption given.

(h) A general discussion now takes place as to who should change their role position so that a solution to the dilemma can be arrived at.

(i) If agreement is reached, the discussion ends with an out-of-role discussion of characters, their motives and the principles involved.

(j) If there is no agreement, three options are possible:

  (i)   each group re-examines its choice and reasons for that choice, possibly changes them and tries the new choice and reasons on the computer

 (ii) players change role, and see if a different perspective alters their outlook

(iii) roles are discarded and a general discussion ensues as to why agreement was not possible

(iv) the judge's option is played.

The judge's option

If the scientist refuses to sell the drug more cheaply, and Jim decides to steal the drug, then the judge's option is automatically brought into play. However, it can be played regardless of the discussion outcome as a separate exercise in weighing punishments and intentions.

All the class play in this section. The computer is the judge, but the children are the jury – they recommend the correct balance, and they discuss the appropriateness of the sentence which the judge metes out. The option proceeds in the following manner.

(a) The following statement is read out to the class:

> 'The judge has to sentence a man for stealing a drug to save his wife's life. The normal sentence is five years in jail. What does he do?'

(b) In their original withdrawal groups, the children discuss the balance of reasons which is presented to them on individual sheets. They are given four separate balances:

  (i)   Jim stole, and this must be punished.
       Jim is a thief.
       Jim should get the usual jail sentence.

 (ii) Jim stole, and this must be punished.
       But Jim stole for a 'good' reason.
       So we must take the 'good' intention into account when punishing a 'bad' action.
       So Jim must go to jail, but not for as long as normal.

(iii) Jim was doing a 'good' thing in saving his wife's life.
       However, we must show that stealing is generally a bad thing.
       So we must warn him and others against stealing, without punishing them.

(iv) Jim was doing a 'good' thing in saving his wife's life.
       It was really all the scientist's fault that Jim was forced into the position of having to steal.
       So Jim is not really to blame at all.

(c) Once a balance of reasons is agreed upon, the group moves over to the computer, keys in a balance, and the computer (which is already programmed with the appropriate response) delivers the sentence. These are:

balance (i) = 5 years in jail
balance (ii) = 1–2 years in jail
balance (iii) = a 'suspended' sentence
balance (iv) = Jim is not guilty and is set free.

THE COMPUTER DILEMMA IN THE PRIMARY SCHOOL

The original 'Heinz' dilemma was designed with secondary children in mind. A computer dilemma for them presents few problems. But can it be used with primary age children? Initial reactions might not be too optimistic. Reasons for this might include:

(a)   the situation is beyond the children's normal experience
(b)   there are too many factors within the situation for them to be able to evaluate it completely
(c)   primary children do not fully understand the notion of intentionality
(d)   some of the concepts may simply be too complex.

Classes of 7 to 9-year-olds were used to test these assumptions. At no time did the children behave or reason in a manner which suggested that the subject under discussion, because it was not within their own personal experience, was beyond their capabilities to comprehend and discuss. After all, how many adults have actually been in a Jim-type dilemma?

Further, considerable creativity was displayed by the children within the discussion sessions, showing that the structure provided did not constrain them. Several of the children felt that the dilemma as presented did not cover all the options available. For example, two children (both 8 years of age) independently suggested that Jim could have offered to pay by instalments, a notion understood by the rest of the class. It was argued that as Jim had already raised quite a bit of money, the scientist wouldn't be out of pocket for very long. It is interesting to note that in discussions with adults on this dilemma, the same desire to stretch the confines of the story is also displayed. Neither group accepts the dilemma as it stands, but believes that there are options for Jim which the scenario does not cover.

Finally, reasoning was *not* confined to Kohlberg's lower stages, as his theory would have predicted. There was a fairly even spread between the following reasons for taking a course of action if one happened to be Jim:

(a)   I won't steal, because I'll be sent to jail (level 1)
(b)   He has to steal, it's not right to let somebody die (level 3?)
(c)   It's wrong to steal (level 4)
(d)   Jim should steal the drug, because life's more important than money (level 5?)

Whatever the levels, the lessons displayed a range of reasoning and argument which would not have been predicted on the Kohlbergian model.

CONCLUSIONS

It is possible to draw the following conclusions. Firstly, dilemma-type situations produce creative and intelligent responses from children as young as 7 years of age. Secondly, Kohlbergian developmental sequences may help in the construction of such programs without one having to adopt the full-blown Kohlbergian theory. Lastly, putting such dilemmas onto a computer program can give structure and facilitate discussion without necessarily constricting debate.

Appendix 2

The Jigsaw Lesson

This appendix will be divided into five major sections: what the jigsaw technique is; the difference between the present approach and traditional approaches; a description of the technique used, with the inclusion of a sample lesson; problems encountered and dealt with in arriving at the technique; and final conclusions.

DESCRIPTION OF THE TECHNIQUE

The jigsaw technique focuses upon the idea of dividing a class into groups of four, five or six. The groups all have the same amount of information to comprehend, but all members of the group are given one part of the total exclusively to themselves. Their job, once they have learnt their part, is to teach it to the other members of the group. As each member has a piece vital for the comprehension of the overall 'jigsaw', the members must co-operate in order to understand the whole. At the end of the group session, a test is given to the entire class to test their understanding.

The research findings are quite impressive. Aronson *et al.* (1978) reported that children in the jigsaw classrooms performed as well or better than in 'normal' classrooms, with white children performing about equally well and black and Chicano children performing significantly better.

However, whilst academic results are important, the jigsaw classroom produces significant gains in other areas as well. Students in jigsaw classrooms increased their liking for their groupmates without decreasing their liking for other people in the classroom. Students started to like school (or dislike it less) than students in 'normal' school. Self-esteem increased in much the same way. And finally, children co-operated much more and saw others as learning resources much more often than they did in 'normal' classrooms.

Two major reviews of the technique, comparing it with other techniques of co-operative learning, are provided by Sharan (1980) and Slavin (1980).

DIFFERENCE BETWEEN THE PRESENT TECHNIQUE AND MORE TRADITIONAL APPROACHES

The technique was designed with secondary students in mind. As it stands, it is not appropriate for the primary classroom. Adjustments are needed if the strategy is to be used with younger pupils. It would be a shame if it were restricted to the older pupil, as it could be argued that increases in co-operation, self-esteem and school liking would have even more beneficial effects if begun in the early years. This appendix, then, describes a modification of the technique for the primary school.

DESCRIPTION OF THE TECHNIQUE USED

There are essentially five phases to the jigsaw lesson as practised in the primary school:

Division into main groups, and handing out of cards

At the start of the day, the register is checked to see who is present and who absent, and the class is divided on paper into groups of four, each group having at least one good reader. A pleasant way of dividing the class into fours follows.

Each group is given a colour, shape, number or letter. Each child's name is then written on a piece of paper and the group symbol added to the paper. The pieces of paper are given to the children, and the children are asked to keep the group symbol secret. When all pieces of paper are handed out, the children are asked to find the other members of their group, but without showing other members of the group their paper or talking to them. After some initial hesitation, children start pointing to colours on the wall, or the clothes they are wearing, or start drawing shapes, letters or numbers in the air. In a very little time, the groups are formed in an enjoyable way.

Once the groups are formed, each member is handed his or her own card and allowed to examine it for a short time. No attempt to teach others is asked for at this time.

Withdrawal into counterpart groups and practising of cards

Once the children know the other members of their group, and have their individual cards, they are then moved into what are called 'counterpart' groups. These may best be illustrated if one imagines a class of 20:

Group	A	B	C	D	E
Member	1	1	1	1	1
	2	2	2	2	2
	3	3	3	3	3
	4	4	4	4	4

The formation of counterpart groups means that all the 1s withdraw to practise and rehearse their parts together, all the 2s do the same, and so on. As all the 1s have the same material, better readers can help poorer readers. The groups should be so organized before the start of the lesson that there is also at least one good reader in the counterpart groups as well. The good reader, or a child voted by the other members of the counterpart group as reader, then reads the card to the group, and the focusing questions are then read, discussed and answered.

Re-formation of main groups and practice in twos

Once it is felt that each child is happy with his or her card, children move back into the original jigsaw groups and people with cards 1 and 2 work together on their cards, as do 3 and 4.

Collaboration of all four members in groups to achieve the overall 'jigsaw'

Once this has been worked through, the group as a whole gets together and each child reads his or her card to the group and asks the focusing questions. Where very poor readers are involved, either the teacher or a good reader from the group helps them.

Testing of information gained

On completion of all four cards, the test is given. Once finished, each child is allowed to mark his or her own papers, and then sheets are handed in.

Sample set of cards and questions – *Baboushka*

Baboushka Card 1

The story of Baboushka comes from Russia. Baboushka was a housewife who kept the cleanest house in the whole village. In fact, that is all she was interested in. When a new star appeared in the sky, she wasn't interested. She just kept cleaning. But then there was a knock at the door.

1. Where does the story of Baboushka come from?
2. What did Baboushka like doing most?
3. What appeared in the sky?

Baboushka Card 2

Baboushka opened the door. There were three kings outside! They wanted to stay at Baboushka's house until night-time, when they would follow the star again. They said that the star would lead them to a baby called Jesus who would be king of Earth and Heaven. Baboushka made them a lovely meal, and they stayed until night-time.

1. Who was at the door?
2. What did they want?
3. Where would the star lead them?

Baboushka Card 3

When night came, the kings were ready to follow the star. They asked Baboushka if she would come with them. They said she could take the baby some food or a toy as a present. But Baboushka said she would have to clean first, and she would follow later on. So she cleaned and cleaned and cleaned . . . until she fell asleep. When she woke up, it was morning.

1. What could Baboushka give as a present?
2. What did she say she had to do first?
3. When did she wake up?

Baboushka Card 4

Because it was morning, Baboushka could not see the star, and so she could not follow the kings. She went from place to place asking people if the kings had been there. Yes, they had, but now they had gone. At each place she stopped, she left some of her presents for little children. The Russian people say that Baboushka is still looking, and it is *her* who leaves presents for children at Christmas.

1. Why could Baboushka not see the star?
2. What did Baboushka do?
3. Which people say that Baboushka leaves presents at Christmas?

Baboushka – Questions

Q. Who is Baboushka?
    (a) a dog   (b) a woman   (c) a man
(Q is the warm-up question the teacher does with the class before they answer the questions seriously.)
1. Which country does the story come from?
    (a) France   (b) England   (c) Russia
2. What did Baboushka like to do?
    (a) clean   (b) play   (c) talk
3. Who were at Baboushka's door?
    (a) three women   (b) three kings   (c) three children
4. Where would the star take them?
    (a) to Jesus   (b) to treasure   (c) home
5. What did they ask Baboushka to do?
    (a) let them stay until night   (b) let them sleep there   (c) show them the way
6. When did the kings leave?
    (a) an hour later   (b) a day later   (c) when night came
7. Why could Baboushka not go with them?
    (a) she had to clean   (b) she didn't have a present   (c) she didn't want to go
8. Why couldn't Baboushka follow the kings?
    (a) they hadn't left a map   (b) someone came to visit   (c) the star had left the sky
9. Who do the Russians say it is who leaves presents at Christmas?
    (a) Father Christmas   (b) Baboushka   (c) St Nicholas

PROBLEMS ENCOUNTERED AND DEALT WITH IN ARRIVING AT THE TECHNIQUE

Four problems will be considered in this section:

(a) poor readers
(b) deciding on appropriate material
(c) to test or not to test
(d) problems of organization.

The problem of poor readers

There are a variety of techniques which can be used to remediate this situation.

(a) One can give the slower reader easier material than other readers in their group.

(b)   Material can be prerecorded on cassettes, and then used in conjunction with written material. A major practical problem with this solution concerns the number of cassettes available to the class teacher – it is more than likely that each group will want one, and if they do not get one each, this could cause resentment between groups.
(c)   Better readers can be assigned to coach and work directly with poorer readers.
(d)   The technique of 'counterpart' grouping already mentioned can be used.
(e)   The technique of intergroup training, also previously mentioned, may be used. Practice has led to the belief that four is the optimum size for a jigsaw group at the primary age range. Any more in the group than this and there is too much material for the children to master. Using four in the group also means that once the counterpart group has been used, members 1 and 2 can get together to practise their parts on each other, as can members 3 and 4, before all members of the jigsaw group get together to form the whole 'jigsaw'.
(f)   Focusing questions are also a useful device. The amount of material on the child's card obviously varies with the child and his or her ability, but primary children find it helpful to have two or three focusing questions placed at the bottom of the card. Take, for example, card 2 of *The Boy Who Cried Wolf*:

The boy decided to play a trick on the other people of his village so that he would not be bored. He ran into the village and told everyone that a wolf was killing the sheep.

1.   Why did the boy decide to play a trick?
2.   Where did he run to?
3.   What did he say was attacking the sheep?

What kind of material works best?

(a)   Continuous story versus separate topics on a theme. Continuous story works rather better, though separate topics are within workable limits. The greater effectiveness of continuous story seems to be due to the fact that there is more incentive for the child to learn another card if that other card was necessary for complete understanding of one story. Separate topic learning does not provide this incentive.
(b)   Independent versus conceptually interwoven material. It is most important when preparing workcards that conceptual interweaving is avoided – that the person with card 3 does not need to know the material from any other card to understand his or her own. The cards must stand in their own right for initial comprehension, but at the same time add up to a complete story when all cards are joined together.
(c)   Conceptually novel versus conceptually familiar material. The jigsaw technique places considerable demands on the child at this young age, and material which demands of the child that they come to grips with novel concepts will probably be asking too much. The best material, therefore, appears to be narrative, historical or social studies topics which do not demand of the child a skill to be learnt over and above that of the material itself.

To test or not to test

This is possibly the most controversial aspect of the jigsaw technique carried over from the secondary level into the primary level. It is an integral part of the secondary technique, and is perhaps better suited to curriculum demands which have exams at the end of the course. However, where the function of the lesson is to co-operate, it may seem counter to the efforts of the technique to introduce a possibly competitive element – a test.

It could be argued, of course, that this test is not actually one which publicly differentiates between pupils – there is no need for the teacher to tell the class what scores particular children achieved. Further, the test can have some benefits. It is a really firm form of academic feedback. It does provide a secondary source of motivation for learning the other people's cards. It does provide a focus for the end of the session. And lastly, provided that the test is handled in the correct way, it can add fun and variety to the classroom which the children undoubtedly enjoy.

In the end, though, this has to be a matter for the individual teacher to decide upon. If a test is used, then one of 8 to 9 questions, on a multiple-choice basis, gives the poorer readers the least difficulty. A practice question at the beginning also helps the children to become used to the format.

Problems of organization

The technique involves some quick organization by the teacher at the beginning of the day. Each group must have at least one good reader, and the teacher must be aware of possible personality conflicts within the groups. Moreover, the technique needs groups of four or five – what if there are 22 in the class? Or if there are normally 24, but two are away on the day of the exercise? Experience indicates that the best way to organize the class is to do so at the start of the day and not before, so the actual number present is known. If it is, for instance, 22, then five groups of four can be organized, with the two remaining children being poor readers who can be assigned to one other person in the group who is a good reader, so that this good reader can coach the poorer one.

FINAL CONCLUSIONS

There are major benefits in developing and teaching these lessons.

(a)   The increased focus on co-operative behaviour between children in the classroom allows for the practice of such behaviour, and because of the positive feedback from such co-operative behaviour, improves the chances of its repetition.

(b)   The almost total absence of 'chalk and talk' by the teacher allows the children to feel much more active and important in the learning process, and gives the teacher a chance to take a more guiding and advisory role.

(c)   All readers, both good and poor, are given real reason and motivation for attempting to comprehend materials.

(d)   There is undoubtedly – and, in some cases, unexpectedly – a high retention rate of materials used. The enjoyment of the children in this experience transfers to the learning of the topics and stories chosen.

(e)   It adds an interesting and entertaining variety into the teaching situation for both pupils and teachers.

Appendix 3

The Subjigtive Lesson

In Appendix 2, the 'jigsaw' technique was described. Its principal aim is to foster co-operation between children in learning activities by dividing the class into groups of four or five, and getting each child in the group to learn a piece of the total lesson and teach it to the others in their group, until the pieces taught make up the total 'jigsaw' of the lesson. The 'subjigtive' lesson pursues this theme again, at the level of primary school children, but also highlights the important feature of the subjectivity of judgements as well. Hence the combination of 'jigsaw' and 'subjective' into 'subjigtive'.

The subjigtive lesson, then, aims to do several things. Principally its main objectives are:

(a) to improve co-operation between children, and
(b) to get children to see that their own point of view can be very limited, and that to get a more objective point of view they have to consult others and pool their information.

But it does several other things as well:

(c) it aids children in the understanding of moral rules through situations where they actively construct these rules and thus come to see both their necessity and their limitations
(d) it aims to improve the child's self-concept by stressing that each member of the group has an essential part to play in the solving of the problem, regardless of their academic ability
(d) it highlights and practises language usage in focused discussion
(e) it gives children practice in the use of cloze procedures in a meaningful situation.

HOW DOES IT WORK?

The groups are composed of three children each. The actual membership of these groups is not normally decided until the day of the lesson, as one can never be sure who is going to be present. Having said that, organization only takes about 10 minutes. Some lessons are with mixed-sex groups, some single-sex (see examples below). The lesson proceeds in six phases.

(1) Strip Distribution

Each child receives a strip of paper with his or her character's name on, underlined in a particular colour. If there are 18 children in the class that day, then the six groups will be assigned a different colour each. The members of the six groups will then be able, at phase 3, to find the other members of their group quickly and easily.

The strips from one lesson were:

Sue: I swapped my doll with Tina, but I'm going to get into trouble with my mum. I
            want my doll back.
Tina: I really like this doll of Sue's. I don't want to swap it back.
Teacher: I know that Sue's doll was a birthday present from her Nana last week. Her mum's
            going to be hopping mad if she swaps it.

All the children have a quick look at their strips individually before they move into the second
phase.

(2)   Withdrawal Groups

The children move into 'withdrawal' groups of the main characters involved – in other words,
all the 'Sues' get together, all the 'Tinas' and all the 'teachers'. In these groups they then read
and discuss their particular character parts until even the least able members feel confident
that they can tell the 'situation' groups of their particular character's stance.

(3)   Situation Groups

Having practised their parts, the children now move into groups of three – the 'situation'
groups, where all three characters combine to form the total situation. As noted above, each
group has already been assigned a colour underlining their character's name on their strip of
paper. A bit of fun can be added to the proceedings by asking the children to find their other
colour group members *silently*. Once in the groups, the children take it in turns to read out
their part, prefacing this with 'I am Sue', or 'I am Tina', etc. Once all three parts have been
read out, the children discuss together what the overall story could be. Having decided upon
the story, they are ready for the fourth phase.

(4)   Cloze Procedures

The teacher hands out a cloze passage describing the actual situation. The children's job is to
fit the words at the bottom of the piece into the appropriate places. The cloze passage on Sue,
Tina and the teacher looked like this:

Sue was given a - - - - for a birthday present, but she swapped it with - - - -. Now Sue wants
it back. Her - - - will be very - - - - - if she finds out.
Words: angry Mum Tina doll

The children are encouraged to co-operate, and to discuss why they might arrive at different
answers. Undoubtedly the risk of simple copying exists, but experience with children has led
to the conclusion that this is the exception rather than the rule.

(5)   Group Discussion

Once this passage has been marked by the teacher, the group is directed to a general question
at the bottom of the sheet. On the example so far given, it was:

What should the teacher do? Why?

The children are asked to try to come to a group decision, one on which all three can agree.
This in effect asks the children to compare their solutions, to discuss any differences and arrive
at what seems the best consensus. They are, however, advised that if no such group consensus

is possible, then they are not to worry, but to write down their individual solutions and why they could not agree.

(6) Class Discussion

In the final phase, the class is brought together and different views are compared. It is important to lay down certain ground rules for the children at the start, otherwise discussion tends to degenerate into one child talking over another and others rapidly losing interest. If the ground rules of 'hands up if you want to speak' and 'teacher decides the order of speakers' are obeyed then the discussion tends to be much more productive and far more interesting for the children, if judged in terms of numbers wanting to contribute, length of discussion session and lack of disaffected behaviour.

Obviously, such discussions are open-ended occasions and one can never quite predict how they will go. Having said this, it is useful to get an initial reaction from as many children as possible to the general question asked of the groups before exploring in depth any of the answers provided. This allows for initial participation by most of the class, and prevents the focus becoming too quickly centred on one particular group and one particular aspect.

It is also useful to jot down certain leader questions which can be interjected into the discussion if it starts to lag. With the discussion of the situation described above, these might be:

(a) Why do people swap things?
(b) Why will Sue's mum be upset?
(c) Will Sue's Nana be as upset as Sue's mum? Why?
(d) Is Tina to blame for the situation? Why or why not?

On coming to the question of what the teacher should do, a variety of responses might be given. These might include:

(a) make them give the dolls back
(b) tell the mums and let them sort it out
(c) stop children from swapping in school.

One suggestion the present writer threw in – that the teacher might allow the children to swap things at school, but there should be a 'cooling off' period of one day during which time either party could swap back – was emphatically rejected by many children, on the grounds that a toy might be damaged by one child who would then try to swap it back, or it could be a battery-operated toy whose batteries would then be run down. Any alterations to the 'cooling off' rules to overcome such difficulties, it was felt, would be messy and difficult to operate. The class in question came to the consensus decision that the only sensible rule to have in school was simply to ban swapping – it caused too many difficulties. The children were genuinely surprised when it was pointed out that this was precisely the rule that the school had in force at that time. The children had done what Piaget said all along they should do – they had constructed the rule for themselves and thus realized why it was there in the first place.

The process, however, does not stop there. In another story, Harry's dad had a rule that Harry did what his dad said, or Harry got sent to bed. But on this occasion, Harry arrived at the shops too late because he stopped to help an old lady cross the road. What should his dad do?

Most children came to see that the circumstances of the situation and Harry's intentions made a substantial difference to the application or non-application of the rule. When in the class discussion the question was put of what Dad should do in a situation where Harry didn't reach the shops in time because he stopped to play football with a friend, most of the children rather quickly came to an opposite conclusion!

Some children may take the matter further by introducing the perspective of Dad's intentions. Was he too lazy to go himself? Was Harry too young to be going to the shops on his own in a world where nasty things happen to little children alone on the streets? This naturally leads on to the question of the rights and responsibilities of parents and children, and the reasons why children obey adults in the first place.

FURTHER MATERIALS

Subjigtive 2

Lisa: My dad said that I had to stand up for myself. Lynn knocked me down in the playground and now I'm going to knock Lynn down.

Lynn: Lisa called me a name and that's why I knocked her down.

Toni: Children must let the teacher sort out an argument. They must not take the law into their own hands.

Situation

- - - - knocked Lisa down in the - - - - - - - - - - because Lisa called her a - - - -. Lisa is going to hit Lynn now. Toni thinks that they should let the - - - - - - - sort it all out.

Words: name   teacher   Lynn   playground

Question: What should happen next? Why?

Subjigtive 3

Jo: Mr Smith is moving house, and my big sister Sue says that he'll miss his flowers. I'll help him by pulling them all out so he can take them with him.

Me Smith: That little girl is destroying my garden! She's pulling out all my best flowers!

Sue: Mr Smith is very proud of his flowers. But I don't know how he will take them with him when he leaves.

Situation

Sue tells - - that Mr Smith really loves his - - - - - - -, and that he is moving. Jo tries to help him by - - - - - - - - - the flowers. She doesn't realize that pulling them up will - - - - them. Mr Smith sees her and gets very - - - - -.

Words: flowers   kill   Jo   pulling up   angry

Question: What should Mr Smith do? Why?

Subjigtive 4

Dad: When I tell my son Harry to get to the shops before they close, he should or he'll get sent to bed.

Harry: I had to help that old lady across the street or she would have got run down. It's just bad luck that I was too late for the shops.

Old lady: I'll get run over if someone doesn't help me cross the busy road.

Situation

Dad has sent - - - - - to the - - - - - for him. But on the way, Harry stops to help an - - - - - - - cross the road. When he gets to the shops, they are - - - - - -.

Words: closed old lady Harry shops

Question: What should dad do to Harry? Why?

Subjigtive 5

Tom: My dad said that I had to stand up for myself. Lee knocked me down in the playground, and now I'm going to knock him down.

Lee: I wasn't looking where I was going when I knocked Tom down, I didn't mean it.

Teacher: Children must let the teacher sort out an argument. They must not take the law into their own hands.

Situation

Lee has knocked - - - down by accident. Tom is very - - - - - and thinks that Lee did it on purpose. The - - - - - - - is trying to stop a - - - - - and sort it out herself.

Words: angry teacher Tom fight

Question: What should happen next? Why?

Subjigtive 6

Susie: I saw Anne stealing at school from Jo's pocket. Anne is my best friend. Jo is not.

Anne: Jo has got some sweets. I can't afford them. I like sweets, and she won't share them. I'll take some.

Jo: My mum gave me some sweets. I'm not going to share them. I don't have to.

Situation

Jo has some - - - - - - but doesn't want to share them. - - - - can't afford any and steals some from Jo's - - - - - -. Susie, who is Anne's best - - - - - -, sees Anne taking the sweets.

Words: Anne   pocket   friend   sweets

Question: What should Susie do now? Why?

Subjigtive 7

Sam: My dog is starving, but I've no money. I'll have to steal some dog food.

Shopkeeper: The only way to stop people from stealing is to call the police and prosecute them. If I don't, they'll put me out of business.

Dave: I know Sam is stealing for his dog because he's got no money, but the shopkeeper is not very well off either.

Situation

Dave sees - - - stealing - - - food. He knows that Sam is stealing because he hasn't any - - - - -, and the dog is - - - - - - - -, but the shopkeeper isn't rich either. If he tells, the shopkeeper will almost certainly call the - - - - - -.

Words: starving   police   dog   Sam   money

Question 1:   What should Dave do? Why?
Question 2:   If Dave tells the shopkeeper, what should the shopkeeper do? Why?

Appendix 4

The Pooling Technique

The impetus for this technique is not new, and many teachers and lecturers will have used it in the past. It is the NASA exercise 'Lunar Landing' (see Table A.1). In its original form it was used by NASA as an exercise comparing individual and group decision making. Essentially the exercise centres around the plight of a space crew forced to crash land on the moon 200 miles from the mother ship. With no possibility of help reaching them, they have to decide what equipment to take with them. They are given a list of fifteen items and asked, initially, to prioritize these items on their own. There are three parts to the exercise:

(a) an individual worksheet
(b) a group worksheet
(c) a comparison between individual and group scores.

Table A.1 *'Lunar Landing' exercise*

Individual Instructions:
You are a member of a space crew originally scheduled to rendezvous with a mother ship on the lighted side of the moon. Due to mechanical difficulties, however, your ship was forced to land at a spot some 200 miles from the rendezvous point. During landing, much of the equipment aboard was damaged, and, since survival depends on reaching the mother ship, the most critical items available must be chosen for the 200-mile trip. Below are listed the fifteen items left intact and undamaged after landing. Your task is to rank order them in terms of their importance to your crew in allowing them to reach the rendezvous point. Place the number 1 by the most important item, the number 2 by the second most important, and so on, through number 15, the least important.

Once this is completed, you move into the group situation.

Group Instructions:
Your group is to employ the method of group consensus in reaching its decision. This means that the prediction for each of the fifteen survival items *must* be agreed upon by each group member before it becomes a part of the group decision. Consensus is difficult to reach. Therefore, not every ranking will meet with everyone's complete approval. Try, as a group, to make each ranking one with which *all* group members can at least partially agree.

INDIVIDUAL WORKSHEET	GROUP WORKSHEET
_____ Box of matches	_____ Box of matches
_____ Food concentrate	_____ Food concentrate
_____ 50 feet of nylon rope	_____ 50 feet of nylon rope
_____ Parachute silk	_____ Parachute silk
_____ Portable heating unit	_____ Portable heating unit
_____ Two .45 calibre pistols	_____ Two .45 calibre pistols
_____ One case dehydrated milk	_____ One case dehydrated milk
_____ Two 100-lb tanks of oxygen	_____ Two 100-lb tanks of oxygen
_____ Stellar map (of the moon's constellation)	_____ Stellar map (of the moon's constellation)
_____ Life raft	_____ Life raft

_____ Magnetic compass	_____ Magnetic compass
_____ 5 gallons of water	_____ 5 gallons of water
_____ Signal flares	_____ Signal flares
_____ First-aid kit containing injection needles	_____ First-aid kit containing injection needles
_____ Solar-powered FM receiver-transmitter	_____ Solar-powered FM receiver-transmitter

Once both sheets are completed, they are provided with an answer sheet (Table A.2), on which NASA scientists provide the correct ordering, and the reasons for this ordering. It is then a simple mathematical exercise to work out which method – individual or group – is the nearest to the answer sheet. Experience shows that the group method is almost invariably more accurate.

Table A.2 *Answer and scoring sheets*

Correct Number		Rationale
__15__	Box of matches	No oxygen
__4__	Food concentrate	Can live for some time without food
__6__	50 feet of nylon rope	For travel over rough terrain
__8__	Parachute silk	Carrying
__13__	Portable heating unit	Lighted side of moon is hot
__11__	Two .45 calibre pistols	Some use for propulsion
__12__	One case dehydrated milk	Needs water to work
__1__	Two 100-lb. tanks of oxygen	No air on moon
__3__	Stellar map	Needed for navigation
__9__	Life raft	Some value for shelter or carrying
__14__	Magnetic compass	Moon's magnetic field is different from earth's
__2__	5 gallons of water	You can't live long without this
__10__	Signal flares	No oxygen
__7__	First-aid kit containing injection needles	First-aid kit might be needed but needles are useless
__5__	Solar-powered FM receiver-transmitter	Communication

Scoring
(1) Score the net difference between your answer and the correct answer. For example, if the answer is 9, and the correct answer is 12, the net difference is 3 (the same applies if the answer is 12, and the correct answer is 9). 3 becomes the score for that particular item.
(2) Total these scores for an individual score
(3) Next, total all individual scores and divide by the number of participants to arrive at an average individual score.
(4) Score the net difference between the group worksheet answers and the correct answers.
(5) Total these scores for a group score.
(6) Compare the average individual score with the group score.

Ratings

0–20	= Excellent
20–30	= Good
30–40	= Average
40–50	= Fair
Over 50	= Poor

So far, then, one has an interesting exercise on the advantages of co-operation. There are, however, other insights and issues to be derived from the exercise.

Firstly, it becomes apparent very quickly that co-operation and consensus on group choices inevitably involve some negotiation and possible conflict between members. This is an important aspect of instructions and de-briefing after the exercise. It is not always an easy exercise to perform, particularly if one feels very strongly about a choice and finds oneself in a minority of one over its priority! The process of co-operation and consensus is not all sweetness and light – there is a price to be paid, and it is well for members to be aware of this and allow for it.

Secondly, co-operation takes time. If both individual and group exercises are performed properly, invariably the group exercise will probably take twice as long as the individual exercise. This has clear implications for a teacher with limited lesson time, or a head pressured to arrive fairly quickly at a solution. It is undoubtedly quicker to do things other ways, to do them individually. Co-operative ventures may be more exact but the price may be that, in certain circumstances, the decision is not reached quickly enough. This, again, is something one should be aware of.

Thirdly, it is doubtful if even the NASA scientists can be described as being 'objectively correct' in their listing of the items. For instance, two of the items on the list are

– one case of dehydrated milk, and
– a portable heating unit.

These are given priorities 12 and 13 respectively, yet one can well imagine other scientists disagreeing with this and reversing the order. As even the most cursory glance at the history of science shows, judgement is still permeated by subjectivity.

Thus, whilst the NASA answer sheet gives security to the participants, the security of expert advice, it would be wrong to term the answer sheet 'right'. It is almost certainly much more accurate than most people would arrive at, but it still has a certain subjective element to it.

Further, it is hardly the case that when faced with problems in real life, we are able to call on experts to solve them. We must use our own best resources, and the help of friends, to solve our difficulties. We may believe that several minds are generally better than one when coming to a decision, but there are no cast-iron criteria guaranteeing success.

Now this is an insight which, it was believed, could and should be turned into a worthwhile educational lesson. In so doing, we not only show that co-operation is a 'good' thing, but also introduce pupils to the difficulties, the mystery and the excitement of lack of certainty in life.

How is this to be done? A similar exercise to the 'Lunar Landing' exercise may be run, but this time performed without an experts' answer sheet at the end. Look at Table A.3, the 'Desert Island' exercise. This exercise can be run in just the same way as 'Lunar Landing', with

(a) an individual worksheet
(b) a group worksheet, and then
(c) a comparison of individual and group attempts, but this time without the 'objective' list.

Table A.3 *'Desert Island' exercise worksheet*

Your ship has hit a rock and is slowly sinking. You swim to a desert island close by and see that there are birds, fruit trees and a fresh water stream. You have time to swim back to the ship and rescue some things before it sinks. Which things will you take with you? Put a 1 next to the most important item, 2 next to the second most important one, and so on all the way down to 12. Remember:

– You have time for only one trip

– You could be on the island a long time

– You've only had time for a quick look on the island

– It is warm all year, but rains a lot.

ITEMS

☐ telephone   ☐ umbrella

☐ boxes of matches   ☐ jars of coffee

☐ gun and bullets   ☐ inflatable raft
☐ tanks of water   ☐ portable radio
☐ first aid kit   ☐ extra clothes
☐ axe   ☐ candles

Questions like the following may be asked:

- why did you change your individual score?
- why do you think the group score is better?
- how can the group score seem better when you have nothing to compare the two scores with?

Such questions lead down intriguing and exciting paths, not only into the advantages of co-operation, but also into the mysteries of the possibility of levels of objectivity and subjectivity.

CREATIVE POOLING

The 'pooling' exercise can be taken a step further by simply providing no list of items to help judgement at all. Instead, the pupils are asked to devise their own lists. Table A.4 gives an example of one such exercise. This really throws open the possibilities for creative thought, and 'brainstorming' techniques would be very useful in such a situation.

Table A.4 *'Over the Ice' exercise*

Your ship has hit an iceberg but you can just make it to land. Now you must make your way across 200 miles of snow-covered land to the nearest help. What will you take with you? Put a 1 next to the most important item, 2 next to the second most important item, and so on all the way down to 12. Remember:

- There are mountains, and deep cracks in the ground

- There will be very bad snow storms

- It will always be very, very cold.

It should be noted that 'pooling', and especially 'creative pooling', lend themselves admirably to cross-curricular collaboration between teachers, because it cannot be expected that children will have the knowledge necessary either to prioritize items adequately, or to invent a list from scratch. Topics like weather conditions and their effects, the body's performance capabilities and its needs, the properties of air, water, heat and cold, can all be dealt with beforehand as necessary background to making an informed decision. In this way pooling, like dilemma situations, becomes the applied focus at the end of a learning sequence. It gives meaning, application and practice in the use of varied areas of knowledge.

Appendix 5

Co-operative Squares

Co-operative squares is not a new technique. It is normally provided in the form below, with five identical squares cut into pieces like so:

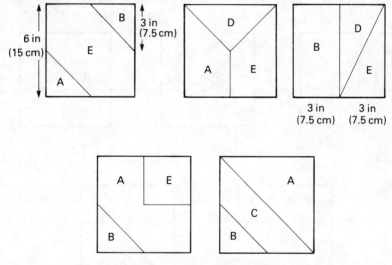

Figure A.1 'Pooling' exercise

The pieces of these squares are then irregularly placed in five envelopes,

4 pieces in envelope A
4 pieces in envelope B
1 piece in envelope C
2 pieces in envelope D, and
4 pieces in envelope E.

Five people are given the envelopes and asked to each make a square so that all squares are the same size. The crucial rule, however, is that *no person may ask for another piece*, either by word, look or gesture. The only way in which squares can be completed is by members of the group seeing other people's needs and then helping them by giving one of their own pieces.

This invariably causes confusion at first, in some groups more than others and in some individuals more than others, as it dawns on people that they must dispense with the assumption that taking and making their own is the way to overall success in the task, and that perceiving others' needs and giving are more appropriate.

A debriefing session afterwards is always necessary, when questions like the following may be asked:

(a)   How did you feel when you started/as the game progressed?
(b)   How did the holder of envelope C feel?
(c)   How did you feel when you saw that someone was holding on to a piece they did not need, while you did?
(d)   Could you perform the task quicker next time? Why?

The exercise proves to be fascinating to watch and illuminating to participate in. It asks for a whole new style of thinking – co-operative thinking. However, as it stands, it will probably be too hard for some children, particularly primary school children. This is not because the notion of co-operativeness is a concept which only develops later – far from it. There is reason to believe that co-operativeness is a notion drummed out of children as they get older. What is difficult is the fact that the forming of actual squares with similar coloured card is a fairly difficult geometrical problem. How, then, can one simplify the squares without interfering with the basic nature of the task?

There seem to be two major ways of doing this. One is to reduce the complexity of the pieces used to make up the squares. The other is to introduce meaning and pattern into the squares to make the assembling of them that much easier.

Thus, firstly, one may simplify the way in which the squares are cut. Designs might then be:

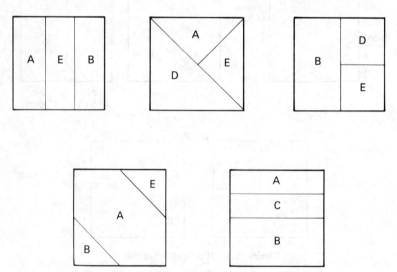

Figure A.2   Revised co-operative squares

Secondly, meaning and pattern may be introduced in at least three different ways of varying difficulty. All involve keeping the same irregularly cut squares, but with something added. If we call the original exercise (squares made from the same coloured card) design A, then design B consists of the same size squares, each square now having the same identical picture, like so:

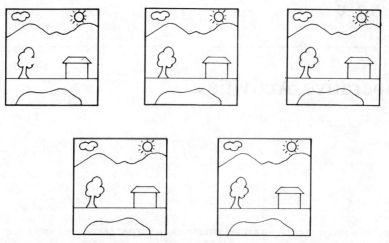

Figure A.3 Co-operative squares – design B

This provides a pattern to the squares which aids completion rather more than just blank card.

Design C, slightly less difficult again, consists of five different pictures, and one could even subdivide these into C1 – black and white pictures and C2 – coloured pictures. This helps not only through the use of pattern recognition, but also through *different* pattern recognition.

Design D, the simplest, consists of the five squares again, but this time each is made from a different coloured card.

Experience has shown that children of 5 and 6 years of age can perform well on design D and then move on to design C, and some even master design B. Difficulty appears to lie as much with actually *making* the square as anything else. This is why the combination of pattern recognition and simplification of square pieces produces the best results.

Appendix 6

Co-operative Activities

Games are like society: they impose rules, structures and expectations upon those participating. We are shaped by them, and so in turn we shape others.

Below are four sets of activities – choosing, PE games, games for the fun of it and setting co-operative goals – which are a radical departure from the normal competitive perspective.

CHOOSING

(a) Partner choosing – choose someone of the same height as you are; born in the same month, day or year; wearing a colour that you are wearing.

(b) Team choosing – the teacher picks two children, A and B, who then pick two more, C and D. C and D then choose E and F, and so on. In this way, each team member will have the opportunity to choose someone – but teachers must make sure that the last person is not the same each game, by choosing the last as A and B next time.

PE GAMES

(a) Lap ball – all the players sit on the floor in a circle with their legs extended in front of them so that everybody's feet are in the centre. The players' hands support their bodies by being placed behind the bodies on the floor. Heels are not to be lifted and hands must stay behind the back, although they can move. The object of the game is to keep the ball off the ground, while passing it quickly from lap to lap. If it gets stuck around the ankles, the group must think up some way of getting it moving again. The fun increases when two balls are being passed simultaneously in different directions. The co-operative challenge of the game is evident when two players are working together to keep the ball from falling between them to the floor.

(b) Collective blanketball – using a beach ball and blanket, two teams throw the ball over a volleyball net. Each throw and catch together counts as one point. The game continues until the ball is dropped, at which point the two teams see how many points they have collectively accumulated and then try to better this score.

(c) Bump and scoot – this is similar to game (b). It involves two teams of about 7 players, with a volleyball net and a beach ball. Whenever a player hits a beach ball over the net, he or she must scoot under to join the other side. Can both sides exchange without the ball being dropped?

(d) Transfer scorer – when a player scores a goal or a point in any team game, that player then switches to the other side. No one from the other team is exchanged.

(e) Reverse score – when a side scores in a team game, the points go to the other team.

(f)   All play – every member of the team must touch the ball before a point is scored or a shot taken.

(g)   All score – for a team to win, everyone on a side must score.

(h)   Stuck in the mud – one or two players are chosen as catchers in a safe area. When they tig one of the other players, that player must stand still until another player frees him or her by crawling through his or her legs. The game ends when every player is stuck in the mud, or the teacher judges the chasers have chased enough!

(i)   Co-operative jumping rope – two players turn a rope. The other players line up to jump. The first player jumps once, runs out and takes one end of the rope. The player who had that end before goes to the end of the line. Meanwhile the second player has to jump twice, run out and take the rope from the other player who has been turning it, relieving that player to go to the end of the line. The third player jumps three times and runs out, the next player four times, and so on – each player taking alternate ends of the turning rope. If a 'miss' occurs, the next player begins over again, jumping once, the next twice, and so on.

(j)   Centre throw – players form a circle with one player standing in the centre. The centre player throws the ball to any player in the circle and immediately runs to any other. That player then runs to the centre to receive the ball thrown by the player last receiving it. The game continues until all have been the centre player.

(k)   Three deep – players form a double circle, each player of the inner circle having someone standing immediately behind him or her. One player stands in the centre of the circle. The centre player throws a ball to someone in the inner ring. Immediately after releasing the ball, the centre player runs and stands behind the outer-player partner of the one to whom they have thrown the ball. The player who receives the ball – now one of a three-deep set – must then run to the centre and throw the ball to another inner player, run to the back of that set, and so the game continues.

(l)   Chain tig – one player acts as chaser, and on catching another joins hands with them. Then a third is caught, and they form a chain of three. When the fourth is caught, they split into teams of two and co-operate in chasing others. Alternatively, one huge chain can be formed until everyone is a member of the chain.

(m)   Partner pull up – partners sit facing each other, and pull each other up. Then they sit back to back, and pull each other up again.

GAMES FOR THE FUN OF IT

(a)   Musical laps – there are several versions based on musical chairs. In one, the chairs are taken away as usual but when the music stops everyone has to sit on a chair, a cushion or someone's lap until at last there is one chair and everyone is sitting on the lap of the person on it. It is best to have a rule that they sit with legs outstretched if it would be too heavy or uncomfortable for some children.

(b)   Animal partners – each pupil has a slip of paper with the name of an animal. There are two for each animal, and either by miming or making the noise of the animal the pupils find their counterparts.

(c)   Catch the snake's tail – four, five or six children in a row clasp the waist of the one in front of them. The chaser tries to catch hold of the snake's tail and the snake tries to escape; if the chaser succeeds he or she becomes the tail and the head becomes the chaser.

(d)   Laughing logs – six or more players lie next to one another on their tummies on the floor. One player lies on his or her tummy across the upper part of their back. All logs roll in one direction, giving the person on top a ride. When they reach the side of the room, the rider becomes the first log and the last one becomes the rider.

(e)   Blind man's buff – in a *safe* restricted area, as people get tagged they are also blindfolded and work together in pairs, then threes, and so on until the last one is caught.

(f)   Are you the ghost? – everyone wanders around, eyes closed, in a safe area. One is the ghost, but no one knows who, so the pupils wander round asking people softly 'are you the ghost?' If they say 'no, I'm not the ghost', they go on to ask someone else. If the ghost is asked, he or she doesn't reply. Pupils join hands with him or her and carry on until there is just one big ghost.

(g)   Giant sack – all the children get into one giant sack and attempt to move the sack from one point to another by co-ordinated action.

(h)   I love you honey but I just can't smile – participants sit in a circle and one begins by saying to the person to the right or left: 'do you love me honey?' That person responds: 'yes, I love you honey, but I just can't smile.' The first person then attempts to make the second person smile. This continues around the circle until the first person is asked 'do you love me honey?' and is made to smile.

(i)   Singing syllable – all pupils sit in a circle and one goes out of the room. The rest of the group picks one word with three or more syllables, for example, 'November'. The syllables are counted off so that each group has a syllable. Then a simple tune is chosen such as 'Row, row, row your boat . . .'. Each player sings his or her syllable to the tune of the song. Then the person who volunteered to go out of the room returns and tries to put the different syllables together and identify the word.

(j)   One-word story – in a circle, each person in turn says one word which will add to the story that is developing. For example 'I . . . saw . . . a . . . monster . . . in . . . the . . . lemon . . . soup . . .' and so on.

(k)   Water-cup pass – everyone stands in a circle with a paper cup in their teeth. One person's cup is filled with water. That person begins by pouring water into the next person's cup without using his or her hands, and so on around the circle. This is a good game for a hot summer day.

(l)   Pass the mask – this is a good game for young children. The group of children sit in a circle and the first child makes a funny face. The next child (to the left or right) makes the same face and then makes one of his or her own to the next child who then repeats it and then makes a new face. Thus everyone in the circle has to imitate and invent a funny face.

SETTING CO-OPERATIVE GOALS

(a)   Discuss with children how they would like others to behave towards them.

(b)   Display desirable goals for all to see.

(c)   Take slides and pictures of children being co-operative and display them.

(d)   Practise co-operative activities by tackling tasks together (for example, paddle a canoe together, put up a tent, hold back a flood).

(e)   Provide children with social toys rather than isolate toys (a swing for two, a seesaw, a giant ball, a huge sack).

(f)   Take videos of co-operative activities, point out the co-operation and discuss the problems.

Appendix 7

Exercises for Improving Self-concept and Self-esteem

Because many of the following exercises involve self-concept and self-esteem they can be extremely helpful and uplifting to an individual if handled sensitively, or very upsetting if handled badly. This in turn depends upon the relationship between the teacher and the class and the relationships between the students themselves. The utilization of the exercises will therefore depend upon the teacher's judgement of these factors.

CLARIFYING SELF-CONCEPT

Pupils are asked to record a personal description, including not only overt physical or mental attributes but issues such as what they like, what they think they are good at, what they would like to be, what they think they cannot do very well, what they would like to do very well. Once this is completed, the pupils are divided into small groups and the teacher and pupils supply deepening questions about these personal descriptions, either in respect of clarification or in terms of validity, evaluation, causation, etc. Thus one can move in at least three directions with this exercise.

(a) By using others' perceptions one can contrast each personal description with a description of the individual supplied by the teacher and other members of the class. Why are there discrepancies?

(b) By adding new dimensions. Using others' perceptions as described in (a), what specifically is added by others that the individual omitted and why? What is added by the individual which others failed to see?

(c) By discovering influences and sources. Using the personal descriptions, one can list the salient features of each description and attempt as a group to determine the origins of these features and what has influenced them the most.

GETTING TO KNOW THE CHILDREN'S NAMES

All the children sit in one large circle. One child begins by saying his or her name and what he or she likes. Thus one might begin with 'my name is Rosie and I like horses'. The next says something like 'my name is Sam and I like television, and her name is Rosie and she likes horses.' The next says 'my name is Sue and I like reading, and his name is Sam and he likes television, and her name is Rosie and she likes horses.' This continues until someone forgets. Then the process begins again with the person who forgot. With very young children, an initial game using just the names of the children can be used as a warm-up to the main game.

GETTING TO KNOW EACH OTHER

The children divide off into twos, picking out a person who they do not know very well in the class. Each child is then given two minutes to tell their partner who they are and some personal details about themselves. At the end of the four minutes the two move around the room to meet two more. They sit down as a foursome, and one person tells the other two about his or her partner.

THE SECRET BIOGRAPHY GAME

Children are given cards and asked to write some facts about themselves – what they like, what they do, what they are proud of. They should not include names or obvious physical characteristics. Teachers should include their own description. All cards are handed in and shuffled and the teacher reads out each one in turn. Can the class guess whose card is whose? Discussion can lead on to how little we may know about people, how easy it is to misunderstand and how each can look at a situation from a different perspective.

THE BRAGGING GAME

Use groups of four, five or six. Each member of the group must boast about something they have done which is true (fantasizing is not allowed). The only rule for staying in the game is that as listeners, other members of the group must never put down someone else's boast – they have to support the boast by encouraging words.

Have suggestions for this game prepared beforehand for members of class with very low self-esteem. Bragging might include:

(a)   I helped my little brother/sister to school
(b)   I help mum with the washing up
(c)   I scored a goal at football
(d)   I can juggle three balls at once
(e)   I can paint nice pictures
(f)   I helped an old lady across the road.

A PERSONAL COAT OF ARMS

Explain what a family coat of arms is. Have large sheets with coats of arms ready drawn. Each is to have four sections on it, and in each section children are to draw:

(a)   the most important event in their lives
(b)   their greatest success or achievement
(c)   what they think they are good at
(d)   their greatest ambition.

Now on a card underneath, ask children to write the three words they would most like other people to say about them (have suggestions ready like kind, friendly, helpful, funny, useful, speedy, clever, happy, generous, quiet). Once completed, these should provide endless discussion topics.

A SELF COLLAGE

Have magazines available, and ask the children to produce a collage which suggests themselves, their thoughts about themselves and their wishes. (Have an example of such a collage of yourself ready as an illustration.) Once completed, ask them *not* to sign it. Show the completed collages to the class, and ask the class to guess whose collage is whose and explain why they think so. Obviously, children sitting next to or near to each other in class will already know the identity of some collages' inventors. Ask them not to guess until others have had a go.

In groups of four children then have a turn at describing to the others why they chose the pictures they did.

Now place names on the collages and display.

'I LIKE' SILHOUETTES

Prior discussion will be needed for this lesson to find something nice to say about everybody in the class. Stress that finding something about everybody is an essential part of the exercise. Ask the children to imagine how it would feel to be the one with nothing nice said about them.

Now divide children into twos. One lies down while the other draws round them on a large sheet (unless they are too young or their co-ordination is too shaky, in which case the teacher can do this part beforehand).

Children (or teacher) cut out their own silhouettes and begin to draw and colour in self-portraits, using mirrors. As they do so, the teacher asks each child to think of one sentence beginning 'I like . . . because . . .'. The completed sentences are pasted on the chest of the silhouette drawing and displayed. Thus each child ends up with $(n-1)$ compliments about themselves to read.

IALAC (I AM LOVABLE AND CAPABLE)

Take a large sheet with the letters IALAC on them and tell the children what they mean. Now read the following or a similar story to the children, ripping off part of the paper until only a small part of the paper remains.

> Tommy is in bed having a nice dream. His IALAC is this big. Suddenly a hand shakes him. 'Get up you lazy thing', someone shouts, 'you'll be late for breakfast.' (rip)
> He goes to the bathroom, but the door is locked. His sister is in. She tells him to get lost. She's busy. (rip)
> He goes to get his socks on, and there's a hole in one. His mum says she's too busy to bother with that. He'll just have to wear them until she gets round to it. (rip)
> When he gets to the breakfast table, the cornflakes are all eaten up. (rip) 'You should be quicker, then you'd get some' he's told. (rip)
> He sets off for school, gets ten yards down the road and his mum calls him back. 'You've forgotten your packed lunch, you dozy clot' she shouts. (rip) 'You'd forget your head if it wasn't fastened on.' (rip)
> On his way to school, some big boys pinch his baseball hat and they won't give it back. (rip) They throw it in a puddle. (rip) Because of this he gets to school late and everyone's already in assembly. (rip)
> During the first lesson, he is reading out loud to the class and makes a mistake on a word. All the others laugh at him. (rip)
> In football, he is the last to be chosen for sides. (rip)
> On the way home, he is chased by the same boys (rip) and falls in some mud, (rip) so when he gets home he is sent to bed early for coming home dirty. (rip)
> When he goes to sleep, his IALAC is this big.

Exercises

In groups of four, on large sheets of paper, pupils write down the ways in which Tommy's IALAC gets torn up. They then write down the ways in which their own IALAC gets torn up.

Now in the same groups, and on paper again, they write down some of the ways in which they sometimes do the same to others. (Teachers take the lead by admitting to a couple of things.)

Finally, in the same groups, on the paper, they write down some ways in which they can help people enlarge their IALAC signs. Display these for all the class to see, and discuss them.

NICKNAMES

Every child invents a nickname he or she would like to be called by. These are to be told to the class which has been told beforehand that there is to be no poking fun at people's wishes.

Now in groups of four, on large sheets of paper, brainstorm words or names which make the children feel bad.

Now the same thing is done for those words or names that make them feel good.

Now all members of the class are asked to draw a picture of themselves living out their invented nickname. Mount and display these.

STORIES FOR YOUNGER CHILDREN BY OLDER CHILDREN

Older children use their reading books to find words to make stories to read to younger children in the school. These stories are not to be those in the reading books, but ones which they have invented themselves. The children are taken on a prearranged walk to a younger class, and the older children read their stories to the younger.

MAGIC GLASSES

In a large space such as the school hall, put children in twos and tell them that one of them is wearing magic glasses. These glasses make them see the world in one way only – happy, sad, aggressive, etc. The teacher puts on his or her own imaginary pair, and acts out a couple of different moods.

Now the children act out 'sad', 'angry', 'nobody loves me', 'suspicious', 'show-off', etc. when their partners ask them a straightforward question like the way into town. Each child has a go at the role.

Discussion

In fours, and on sheets, the children write down some reasons why people seem to be like that all the time.

In the same situation, they write what they can do if they feel like that. Again, what can they do to help others who feel like this?

Each group displays their ideas to the class as a whole and they all discuss them.

THE ANIMAL SCHOOL

Read this story out to the class. Do the children identify with any of the animals in the story? If so, what can be done about the situation?

Once upon a time, the animals decided they must do something to cope with all the problems of a new kind of world, so they organized a school.

They adopted an activity curriculum, consisting of running, climbing, swimming and flying. To make it easier to administer the curriculum, all the animals took all the subjects.

The duck was excellent in swimming, in fact better than his instructor; but he only just scraped through in flying, and was very poor in running. Since he was slow at running, he had to stay after school and also drop swimming in order to practise running. This was kept up until his webbed feet were badly worn, and he was only average at swimming. But average was acceptable in school, so nobody worried about that except the duck.

The hare started at the top of the class at running, but her performances soon began to tail off because of having to do so much extra work to keep up to the average at swimming.

The squirrel was excellent at climbing until he developed frustration in the flying class where his teacher made him start from the ground up instead of from the tree top down. This tired him out so much that he was soon getting poor grades at both running and climbing.

The eagle was a problem child and was disciplined severely. In the climbing class she beat all the others to the top of the tree, but insisted on using her own way to get there.

The rabbits stayed out of school and refused to come because the administration would not add digging and burrowing to the curriculum. They appenticed their children to a badger and later started a successful private school.

References/Bibliography

Adelstein, D. (1972) 'The philosophy of education – or the wisdom and wit of R. S. Peters' in Pateman, T. (ed.) *Counter-Course – A Handbook of Course Criticism.* Harmondsworth, Middx: Penguin.

Aronson, E., Blaney, N., Stephen, C., Sikes, J. and Snapp, M. (1978) *The Jigsaw Classroom.* Beverley Hills, CA: Sage Publications.

Axelrod, R. (1984) *The Evolution of Cooperation,* New York: Basic Books.

Bacon, W. (1986) 'Headteachers and school governors' in Bush, T., Glatter, R., Goodey, J. and Riches, C. (eds) *Approaches to School Management.* London: Harper & Row.

Bandura, A. (1977) *Social-Learning Theory.* Englewood Cliffs, NJ: Prentice-Hall.

Barton, J., Becher, T., Canning, T., Eraut, E. and Knight, J. (1986) 'Accountability and education' in Bush, T., Glatter, R., Goodey, J. and Riches, C. (eds) *Approaches to School Management.* London: Harper & Row.

Belbin, R. M. (1981) *Management Teams – Why they Succeed or Fail.* London: Heinemann.

Bell, L. (1988) *Management Skills in the Primary School.* London: Routledge.

Bergling, K. (1981) *The Validity of Kohlberg's Theory.* Stockholm: Almqvist and Wiksell International.

Bernbaum, G. (1976) 'The role of the head' in Peters, R. S. (ed.) *The Role of the Head.* London: Routledge & Kegan Paul.

Bernstein, B. (1973) *Class, Codes, and Control.* London: Routledge & Kegan Paul.

Blau, P. and Duncan, O. (1967) *The American Occupational Structure.* New York: Wiley.

Borke, H. (1971) Interpersonal perception of young children – egocentricism or empathy?, *Developmental Psychology* **15**(2).

Bottery, M. P. (1987) The Jigsaw Lesson: cooperative learning and the primary classroom, *Values* **2**(2). Exeter: Moral and Religious Education Press.

Boudon, R. (1977) 'Education and social mobility: a structural model' in Karabel, J. and Halsey, A. (eds) *Power and Ideology in Education.* Oxford: Oxford University Press.

Bowles, S. and Gintis, H. (1976) *Schooling in Capitalist America.* London: Routledge & Kegan Paul.

Brent, A. (1978) *Philosophical Foundations of the Curriculum.* London: Allen & Unwin.

Bruner, J. S. (1977) *The Process of Education.* Cambridge, MA: Harvard University Press.

Buber, M. (1958) *I and Thou.* New York: Charles Scribner's Sons.

Callahan, R. (1962) *Education and the Cult of Efficiency.* Chicago: University of Chicago Press.

Campbell, C. A. (1957) *On Selfhood and Godhood.* London: Allen & Unwin.

Campbell, R. J. (1985) *Developing the Primary School Curriculum.* Eastbourne: Holt.

Carr, E. H. (1982) *What is History?.* Harmondsworth, Middx: Pelican.

Cicourel, A. and Kitsuse, J. (1977) 'The school as a mechanism of social differentiation' in Karabel, J. and Halsey, A. (eds) *Power and Ideology in Education.* Oxford: Oxford University Press.

Coleridge, D. (1862) *The Teachers of the People.* London: Rivingtons.

Collins, H. M. and Pinch, T. J. (1979) 'The construction of the paranormal: nothing unscientific is happening' in R. Wallis (ed.) *The Social Construction of Rejected Knowledge*. Keele, Staffs: University of Keele Press.

Commonwealth Immigrants Advisory Council (1964) *Second Report*. London: HMSO.

Cooper, D. E. (1987) 'Multicultural education'. Paper given at the SVRC Conference at the University of Hull.

Cox, C. B. and Boyson, R. (eds) (1975) *Black Paper 1975*. London: J. M. Dent.

Cupitt, D. (1984) *The Sea of Faith*. London: BBC Publications.

Dawkins, R. (1976) *The Selfish Gene*. Oxford: Oxford University Press.

Day, C., Johnston, D. and Whitaker, P. (1985) *Managing Primary Schools*. London: Harper & Row.

DES (1977) *A New Partnership in our Schools* (The Taylor Report). London: HMSO.

DES (1981) *The School Curriculum*. London: HMSO.

DES (1985) *Better Schools*. London: HMSO.

Desmond, A. (1980) *The Ape's Reflection*. London: Quartet Books.

Dewey, J. (1921) *Democracy and Education*. New York: Macmillan.

Docking, J. (1980) *Control and Discipline in Schools* (1st edn). London: Harper & Row.

Docking, J. (1987) *Control and Discipline in Schools* (2nd edn). London: Harper & Row.

Donaldson, J. (1978) *Children's Minds*. London: Fontana.

Downey, M. and Kelly, A. V. (1978) *Moral Education: Theory and Practice*. London: Harper & Row.

Downey, M. and Kelly, A. V. (1986) *Theory and Practice of Education* (3rd edn). London: Harper & Row.

Duckworth, E. (1979) Either we're too early and they can't learn it, or we're too late and they know it already: the dilemma of applying Piaget, *Harvard Educational Review* **49**(3).

Durkheim, E. (1961) *Moral Education*. New York: Glencoe Press.

Egan, K. (1983) *Education and Psychology: Plato, Piaget, and Scientific Psychology*. London: Methuen.

Eisenberg, N. (ed.) (1982) *The Development of Prosocial Motivation*. New York: Academic Press.

Eisner, E. (1985) *The Art of Educational Evaluation*. Lewes, Sussex: Falmer.

Engelman, S. E. (1971) 'Does the Piagetian approach imply instruction' in Green, D. R., Ford, M. P. and Flamer, G. P. (eds) *Measurement and Piaget*. New York: McGraw-Hill.

Engels, F. (1981) 'Herr Eugen Dühring's revolution in science' in Marx, K. and Engels, F. *Basic Writings on Politics and Philosophy* (ed. Feur, L. S.). London: Fontana.

Everard, K. B. and Morris, G. (1985) *Effective School Management*. London: Harper & Row.

Feyerabend, P. (1970) 'Consolation for the specialist' in Lakatos, I. and Musgrave, A. (eds) *Criticism and the Growth of Knowledge*. Cambridge, UK: Cambridge University Press.

Feyerabend, P. (1979) *Against Method*. London: Verso.

Foorman, B., Leiber, J. and Fernie, D. (1984) Mountains and molehills: egocentrism in recent research, *Oxford Review of Education* **10**(3).

Freire, P. (1972) *Pedagogy of the Oppressed*. Harmondsworth, Middx: Penguin.

Ginsberg, M. (1968) 'On the diversity of morals' in *Essays in Sociology and Social Philosophy*. Harmondsworth, Middx: Peregrine/Penguin.

Goldthorpe, J. H. (1987) *Social Mobility and Class Structure in Modern Britain* (2nd edn). Oxford: Clarendon Press.

Goodall, J. (1971) *In the Shadow of Man*. London: Collins.

Grace, G. R. (1978) *Teachers, Ideology and Control*. London: Routledge & Kegan Paul.

Graves, N. B. and Graves, T. D. (1982) 'The cultural context of prosocial development' in Bridgeman, D. (ed.) *The Nature of Prosocial Development*. New York: Academic Press.

Greco, P. (1959) 'L'apprentissage dans une situation à structure opératoire concrète: les inversions successières de l'ordre linéaire par des rotations de 180' in *Apprentissage et Connaissance*. Paris: Presses Universitaires de France.

Gregory, R. L. (1972) *Eye and Brain*. London: Weidenfeld & Nicolson.

Grusec, J. (1982) 'The socialization of altruism' in Eisenberg, N. (ed.) *The Development of Prosocial Motivation*. New York: Academic Press.

Halsey, A., Heath, H. and Ridge, J. (1980) *Origins and Destinations*. Oxford: Clarendon Press.

Handy, C. (1976) *Understanding Organisations*. Harmondsworth, Middx: Penguin.

Handy, C. (1978) *Gods of Management*. London: Souvenir Press.

Hargreaves, D. (1967) *Social Relations in a Secondary School*. London: Routledge & Kegan Paul.

Harris, K. (1979) *Education and Knowledge*. London: Routledge & Kegan Paul.

Heidegger, M. (1962) *Being and Time*. London: SCM Press.

Hersh, R. H., Paolitto, D. P. and Reimer, J. (1979) *Promoting Moral Growth*. New York: Longman.

Hirst, P. (1974) *Knowledge and the Curriculum*. London: Routledge & Kegan Paul.

Hjelle, L. A. and Ziegler, D. J. (1981) *Personality Theories – Basic Assumptions, Research and Applications*. New York: McGraw-Hill.

Hoffman, M. L. (1976) 'Empathy, role-taking, guilt, and development of altruistic motives' in Lickona, T. (ed.) *Moral Development and Behaviour*. New York: Holt, Rinehart & Winston.

Hoffman, M. L. (1982) 'Development of prosocial motivation: empathy and guilt' in Eisenberg, N. (ed.) *The Development of Prosocial Motivation*. New York: Academic Press.

Holt, M. (1987) *Judgement, Planning and Educational Change*. London: Harper & Row.

Hoyle, E. (1975) 'The creativity of the school in Britain' in Harris, A., Lawn, M. and Prescott, W. (eds) *Curriculum Innovation*. London: Croom Helm.

Hughes, M. (1975) *Egocentrism in Pre-school Children*. Unpublished doctoral dissertation, Edinburgh University.

Huntsman, R. (1984) Children's concepts of fair sharing, *Journal of Moral Education* 13(1).

Hurn, C. J. (1978) *The Limits and Possibilities of Schooling*. Boston, MA: Allyn & Bacon.

Hymns Ancient and Modern (1924). London: Clowes.

Israely, Y. (1985) The moral development of mentally retarded children: review of the literature, *Journal of Moral Education* 14(1).

Jackson, P. W. (1968) *Life in Classrooms*. New York: Holt, Rinehart & Winston.

Jencks, C. (1972) *Inequality – A Reassessment of the Effects of Family and Schooling in America*. London: Allen Lane.

Jensen, A. (1969) How much can we boost IQ and scholastic achievement?, *Harvard Educational Review* 39(1).

Johnson, D. B. (1982) Altruistic behaviour and the development of the self in infants, *Merrill-Palmer Quarterly* 28(3).

Jonathan, R. (1983) The Manpower Services model of education, *Cambridge Journal of Education* 13(2).

Kamenka, E. (1969) *Marxism and Ethics*. London: Macmillan.

Kamii, C. and Derman, L. (1971) 'Comments on Engelman's paper' in Green, D. R., Ford, M. P. and Flamer, G. P. (eds) *Measurement and Piaget*. New York: McGraw-Hill.

Karabel, J. and Halsey, A. (1977) *Power and Ideology in Education*. Oxford: Oxford University Press.

Keddie, N. (1971) 'Classroom knowledge' in Young, M. F. D. (ed.) *Knowledge and Control*. London: Macmillan.

Kliebard, H. M. (1968) Curricular objectives and evaluation: a reassessment, *The High School Journal*.

Kohlberg, L. (1970) 'Education for justice: a modern statement of the Platonic view' in Sizer, N. F. and Sizer, T. R. (eds) *Moral Education*. Cambridge, MA: Harvard University Press.

Kohlberg, L. (1971) 'From Is to Ought: how to commit the naturalistic fallacy and get away with it' in Mischel, T. (ed.) *Cognitive Development and Epistemology*. New York: Academic Press.

Kohlberg, L. (1981a) *The Philosophy of Moral Development*. San Francisco: Harper & Row.

Kohlberg, L. (1981b) 'Indoctrination versus relativity in value education' in *The Philosophy of Moral Development*. San Francisco: Harper & Row.

Kohlberg, L. (1981c) 'Justice as reversibility' in *The Philosophy of Moral Development*. San Francisco: Harper & Row.

Kohlberg, L. with Power, C. (1981) 'Moral development, religious thinking, and the question of the seventh stage' in *The Philosophy of Moral Development*. San Francisco: Harper & Row.

Kohlberg, L., Levine, C. and Hewer, A. (1983) *Moral Stages: A Current Formulation and Response to Critics*. Basel: Karger Press.

Kuhn, T. S. (1970) *The Structure of Scientific Revolutions*. Chicago: Chicago University Press.

Lakatos, I. (1970) 'Falsification and the methodology of scientific research programmes' in Lakatos, I. and Musgrave, A. (eds) *Criticism and the Growth of Knowledge*. Cambridge, UK: Cambridge University Press.

Lakatos, I. and Musgrave, A. (eds) (1970) *Criticism and the Growth of Knowledge*. Cambridge, UK: Cambridge University Press.

Lawton, D. (1980) *The Politics of the School Curriculum*. London: Routledge & Kegan Paul.

Lawton, D. (1983) *Curriculum Studies and Educational Planning*. London: Hodder and Stoughton.

Leuba, J. H. (1912) *A Psychological Study of Religion*. New York: Macmillan.

Lewis, C. S. (1947) *The Abolition of Man*. London: Centenary Press.

Lickona, T. (1976) 'Research on Piaget's theory of moral development' in Lickona, T. (ed.) *Moral Development and Behaviour*. New York: Holt, Rinehart & Winston.

Linaza, J. (1984) Piaget's marbles: the study of children's games and their knowledge of rules, *Oxford Review of Education* **10**(3).

Lockwood, A. L. (1975) A critical view of values clarification, *Teachers College Record* **77**. New York: Columbia University.

MacDonald, B. (1987) 'Evaluation and the control of education' in Murphy, R. and Torrance, H. (eds) *Evaluating Education: Issues and Methods*. London: Harper & Row.

MacDonald, G. (1976) 'The politics of educational publishing' in Whitty, G. and Young, M. (eds) *Explorations in the Politics of School Knowledge*. Driffield, N. Yorks: Nafferton.

McGregor, D. (1960) *The Human Side of Enterprise*. New York: McGraw-Hill.

McPhail, P., Ungoed-Thomas, J. R. and Chapman, H. (1972) *Moral Education in the Secondary School*. London: Longman.

MacQuarrie, J. (1972) *Existentialism*. London: Hutchinson.

Marsden, W. E. (1977) 'Education and social geography of nineteenth century towns and cities' in Reeder, I. (ed.) *Urban Education in the Nineteenth Century*. London: Taylor and Francis.

Marx, K. (1959) *Capital*. Moscow: Foreign Languages Publishing House.

Marx, K. (1964) *The German Ideology*. Moscow: Progress Publishers.

Matthews, M. R. (1980) *The Marxist Theory of Schooling*. Brighton: Harvester.

Meighan, R. (1981) *A Sociology of Educating*. Eastbourne: Holt, Rinehart & Winston.

Midgley, M. (1983) *Animals and Why They Matter*. Harmondsworth, Middx: Penguin.

Milgram, S. (1974) *Obedience to Authority*. London: Tavistock.

Mischel, W. and Mischel, H. N. (1976) 'A cognitive social learning approach to morality and self-regulation' in Lickona, T. (ed.) *Moral Development and Behaviour*. New York: Holt, Rinehart & Winston.

Mortimore, P., Sammons, P., Stoll, L., Lewis, D. and Ecob, R. (1988) *School Matters: the Junior Years*. Wells, Somerset: Open Books.

Mueller, E. (1972) Maintenance of verbal exchanges between young children, *Child Development* **43**.

Murphy, L. B. (1937) *Social Behaviour and Child Personality*. New York: Columbia University Press.

Musgrave, P. W. (1978) *The Moral Curriculum: a Sociological Analysis*. London: Methuen.

Nias, J. (1986) 'Leadership styles and job satisfaction in primary schools' in Bush, T., Glatter, R., Goodey, J. and Riches, C. (eds) *Approaches to School Management*. London: Harper & Row.

Nietzsche, F. (1977) 'The gay science' in *A Nietzsche Reader*. Harmondsworth, Middx: Penguin.

O'Hear, A. (1987) 'A GCSE philosophy of education'. Paper given at the SVRC Conference on Education and Values at the University of Hull.

Orlick, T. (1978) *Winning through Cooperation*. Washington, DC: Acropolis Books.

Passmore, J. (1980) *Man's Responsibility for Nature*. London: Duckworth.

Passow, A. H. (1984) 'Tackling the Reform Reports of the 1980s' in *ERIC Clearing House on Urban Education*. New York: Teachers College, Columbia University.

Paton, H. J. (1978) *The Moral Law*. Milton Keynes: Open University Press.

Peters, T. and Waterman, R. (1982) *In Search of Excellence: Lessons from America's Best Run Companies*. New York: Harper & Row.

Piaget, J. (1932) *The Moral Judgement of the Child*. London: Routledge & Kegan Paul.

Piaget, J. and Inhelder, B. (1956) *The Child's Conception of Space*. London: Routledge & Kegan Paul.

Piele, P. K. (1979) 'Neither corporal punishment nor due process due' in Hyman, I. A. and Wise, J. H. (eds) *Corporal Punishment in American Education*. Philadelphia: Temple University Press.

Plato (1941) *The Republic*. Oxford: Oxford University Press.

Plowden Report (1967) *Children and their Primary Schools*, Central Advisory Council for Education. London: HMSO.

Polanyi, M. (1958) *Personal Knowledge*. London: Routledge & Kegan Paul.

Popper, K. (1945) *The Open Society and Its Enemies* (2 vols). London: Routledge & Kegan Paul.

Popper, K. (1963) *Conjectures and Refutations*. London: Routledge & Kegan Paul.

Popper, K. (1970) 'Normal science and its dangers' in Lakatos, I. and Musgrave, A. (eds) *Criticism and the Growth of Knowledge*. Cambridge, UK: Cambridge University Press.

Popper, K. (1972) *Objective Knowledge*. Oxford: Clarendon Press.

Popper, K. (1974a) 'The centre of the dispute: the problem of demarcation' in Schilp, P. (ed.) *The Philosophy of Karl Popper*. La Salle, IL: Open Court.

Popper, K. (1974b) 'My solution of Hume's problem of induction' in Schilp, P. (ed.) *The Philosophy of Karl Popper*. La Salle, IL: Open Court.

Popper, K. (1982) *The Logic of Scientific Discovery*. London: Hutchinson.

Pring, R. (1972) Knowledge out of control, *Education for Teaching* (Autumn). London.

Pring, R. (1976) *Knowledge and Schooling*. Wells, Somerset: Open Books.

Raths, L., Harmin, M. and Simon, S. (1966) *Values and Teaching: Working with Values in the Classroom*. Columbus, OH: Charles E. Merrill.

Rawls, J. (1971) *A Theory of Justice*. Cambridge, MA: Harvard University Press.

Rist, R. C. (1977) 'On understanding the processes of schooling: the contribution of labelling theory' in Karabel, J. and Halsey, A. (eds) *Power and Ideology in Education*. Oxford: Oxford University Press.

Robinson, J. A. T. (1963) *Honest to God*. London: SCM Press.

Robinson, J. A. T. (1964) *Christian Morals Today*. London: SCM Press.

Rosenhan, D. L., Moore, B. S. and Underwood, B. (1976) 'The social psychology of moral behaviour' in Lickona, T. (ed.) *Moral Development and Behaviour*. New York: Holt, Rinehart & Winston.

Rosenthal, R. and Jacobsen, L. (1968) *Pygmalion in the Classroom*. New York: Holt, Rinehart & Winston.

Rousseau, J. (1950) 'Discourse on the Origin of Inequality' in *The Social Contract and Discourses*. New York: E. P. Dutton.

Rubin, Z. (1980) *Children's Friendships*. Wells, Somerset: Open Books.

Rutter, M. (1979) *15,000 Hours*. Wells, Somerset: Open Books.

Sadler, M. E. (ed.) (1908) *Moral Instruction and Training in Schools*. London: Longmans Green.

Sagi, A. and Hoffman, M. L. (1976) Empathic distress in newborns, *Developmental Psychology* **12**.

Sartre, J. P. (1952) *Existentialism and Humanism* (ed. Mairet, P.). London: Methuen.

Schweitzer, A. (1949) *Civilization and Ethics*. London: Allen & Unwin.

Scott, N. Jr (1978) *Mirrors of Man in Existentialism*. New York: Collins.

Scriven, M. (1967) 'The methodology of evaluation' in Stake, R. E. (ed.) *Perspectives of Curriculum Evaluation*. Chicago: American Educational Research Association/Rand-McNally.

Severy, L. J. and Davis, K. E. (1971) Helping behaviour among normal and retarded children, *Child Development* **42**.

Sharan, S. (1980) Cooperative learning in small groups: recent methods and effects on achievement, attitudes, and ethnic relations, *Review of Educational Research* **50**(2).

Shatz, M. and Gelman, R. (1973) The development of communication skills: modifications in the speech of young children as a function of listener, *Monographs of the Society for Research in Child Development* **38** (5, serial no. 152),

Silberman, C. (1973) *Crisis in the Classroom*. New York: Random House.

Simner, M. L. (1972) Newborn's response to the cry of another infant, *Developmental Psychology* **5**,

Singer, P. (1976a) *Animal Liberation*. London: Jonathan Cape.

Singer, P. (1976b) 'All animals are equal' in Regan, T. and Singer, P. (eds) *Animal Rights and Human Obligations*. Englewood Cliffs, NJ: Prentice-Hall.

Singer, P. (1979) *Practical Ethics*. Cambridge, UK: Cambridge University Press.

Singer, P. (1981) *The Expanding Circle*. Oxford: Clarendon Press.

Skilbeck, M. (1976) 'Ideologies and Values'. Unit 3 of Course E203: *Curriculum Design and Development*. Milton Keynes: Open University Press.

Slavin, R. (1980) Cooperative learning, *Review of Educational Research* **50**(2).

Staub, E. (1971) A child in distress: the influence of nurturance and modeling on children's attempts to help, *Developmental Psychology* **5**.

Staub, E. and Sherk, L. (1970) Need for approval, children's sharing behaviour, and reciprocity in sharing, *Child Development* **41**.

Stenhouse, L. (1978) *An Introduction to Curriculum Research and Development*. London: Heinemann.

Stevenson, L. (1984) *Seven Theories of Human Nature*. Oxford: Clarendon Press.

Steward, J. (1979) Modes of moral thought, *The Journal of Moral Education* **8**(2).

Stradling, R., Noctor, M. and Baines, B. (1984) *Teaching Controversial Issues*. London: Edward Arnold.

Toffler, A. (1970) *Future Shock*. London: Bodley Head.

Trivers, R. L. (1971) The evolution of reciprocal altruism, *Quarterly Review of Biology* **46**.

Turnbull, C. (1976) *The Forest People*. London: Picador.

Wardle, D. (1976) *English Popular Education, 1780–1975*. Cambridge, UK: Cambridge University Press.

Wellington, J. J. (ed.) (1986) *Controversial Issues in the Curriculum*. Oxford: Basil Blackwell.

White, P. (1984) 'School management: a case for workplace democracy?' in *Education PLC?* Bedford Way Papers **20**. London: University of London, Institute of Education.

Williams, N. and Williams, S. (1969) *The Moral Development of Children*. London: Macmillan.

Wilson, J., Williams, N. and Sugarman, B. (1967) *Introduction to Moral Education*. Harmondsworth, Middx: Penguin.

Wise, J. H. (1979) 'The carrot not the stick' in Hyman, I. A. and Wise, J. H. (eds) *Corporal Punishment in the Classroom*. Philadelphia: Temple University Press.

Wood, D. (1988) *How Children Think and Learn*. Oxford: Basil Blackwell.

Woodhouse, D. (1986) A view from the Bronx, *Values* **1**(1). Exeter: Religious and Moral Education Press.

Wright, D. (1972) The punishment of children: a review of experimental studies, *Journal of Moral Education* **1**(3).

Zahn-Waxler, C. and Radke-Yarrow, M. (1982) 'The development of altruism: alternative research strategies' in Eisenberg, N. (ed.) *The Development of Prosocial Behaviour*. New York: Academic Press.

Index